THIS SIDE OF FREEDOM
Life After Clemency

By Anthony Papa

For information go to: www.15tolife.com

Book and Cover design by Anthony Papa
(Papa at the Whitney Museum of American Art) Photo credit: HELP USA
Layout by Penoaks Publishing, http://penoaks.com

ISBN-13: 978-1530731640
Second Edition: October 2016

Dedicated to my son Anthony K. Leuzzi Papa

CONTENTS

ACKNOWLEDGEMENTS

There are many people and organizations to whom I owe thanks to for helping me in my work - far too many to list. Special thanks to my book agent, Noah Lukeman, for giving me the push to write this important book. Tony Newman, my pal who is a media wizard over at DPA, along with Sharda Sekaran and Ethan Nadelmann and the DPA staff with whom I have worked for the last 10 years. I must give thanks to my pal celebrity chef Pasquale Marino who passed on along with my writing teacher Fielding Dawson. Also, a special thanks to Dr. J. Juechter and her team at Bronx Community College for their editing and creating a study guide for this book.

For more information about my art and activism go to my website www.15tolife.com

The Drug Policy Alliance (DPA) www.drugpolicy.org is the nation's leading organization promoting drug policies grounded in science, compassion, health and human rights. DPA and advocates around the world support policy in which people are no longer punished for what they put into their own bodies. Punishment must only be for crimes committed against others, and in which the fears, prejudices and punitive prohibitions of today are no more. Our mission is to advance those policies and attitudes that best reduce the harms of both drug use and drug prohibition, and to promote the sovereignty of individuals over their minds and bodies.

INTRODUCTION

With more states looking for an economic solution to solve their budgetary problems there are now more prisoners being released early from their sentences. The question I pose is what will we do for felons once they get out? How will they survive as ex-offenders once they return to the real world? Politicians are calling for ways to let individuals out of prison faster because of the economics of doing so. Surprisingly, almost 70 percent of them return to prison within three years. Why are the recidivism rates so high?

HBO's John Oliver answers that question and exposes how America sets up these prisoners to fail, by imposing terrific legal barriers in receiving employment, housing and education. I was one of those lucky enough not to return to prison after being released. I had served 12 years of a 15-to-Life sentence for a first-time, non-violent drug offense. I was sentenced under the mandatory minimum provisions of the Rockefeller Drug Laws, which were the precursor of the federal drug laws, which lock up hundreds of thousands of individuals for minor non-violent drug crimes. This sadly, has led to the mass incarceration of Americans.

My story begins in 1985. Twenty-five years old, I had never committed a crime in my life. That winter, living in the Bronx with a wife and child, broke and desperate, I was duped into delivering an envelope containing four-and-a-half ounces of cocaine for the sum of five hundred dollars. I was set up and walked directly into a police sting operation.

Given the draconian Rockefeller laws, in the strictest state in the nation, as a first-time nonviolent drug offender I was walloped with two 15-to-life sentences for one isolated drug sale in Westchester County, New York. Since it was my first time, the judge gave me a break and sentenced me to only one 15-years-to-life term in prison. I did my time at Sing Sing, one of America's most dangerous maximum-security prisons. While there, I acquired several college degrees from CUNY and a Master's degree from the New York Theological Seminary and, as well, discovered my talent as an artist. I fought for many years behind bars to regain my lost freedom. After twelve years of living in a six-by-nine-foot cell, I finally accomplished my goal.

In 1994, as I was still serving time, my famous painting, 15-to-Life self- portrait was exhibited at the Whitney Museum of American Art, which eventually led to my release from prison. New York Governor George Pataki granted me executive clemency in 1997. The chronicles of this period of time are in my critically acclaimed book *15 To Life*: How I Painted My Way to Freedom.

In many ways, though, this is where my story begins. Immediately upon my release from Sing Sing, I set out to shed my prison identity. I rejected the standard handouts offered to all NYS prisoners leaving the system: some cheap clothing, a forty-dollar check, and a one-way train ticket home. Astonishingly, for prisoners without family or friends this limited assistance is their only financial support when trying to establish a fresh start upon release. I traveled back to the South Bronx, where I was reunited with my mother Lucy and other family members. Overwhelming joy and happiness dominated my first few days' home, but once these initial emotions began to fade, I realized the freedom I fought so long and hard to win was not what I imagined it to be. The way of life I once knew was gone, along with my friends and most of my support base. I discovered I was alone in a new world that had drastically changed without me.

I tried to reunite with my daughter, Stephanie, whom I left at the age of 7. She was 19 years old when I was released . Sadly, she found me to be a complete stranger. I also struggled with the most mundane tasks. I was released under the guidelines of parole and for the next five years, I lived in dread of violating its conditions. A simple walk in the neighborhood, or a train ride, was elevated to a state of panic because of the fear I might violate parole and return to prison.

I searched for a solution to my problems and realized that when my cell door was shut behind me, I did not leave behind those twelve years of hard time. When those prison doors close behind you and you leave its confines, you are not free. You are still doing time—just doing it on the other side of the bars. I soon found out that prison life was deeply rooted into my present existence; a decade of life in an environment where survival mechanisms and behaviors were hardwired into daily existence had changed me profoundly. In prison, one essentially lives one's life on the head of a needle, with the constant sense that death hovered at all times.

Being hard-wired for survival was a good thing. In the free world, though, it was another matter, especially when these mechanisms would surface suddenly and without warning. The tools that were once lifesaving had become a tremendous burden as I tried to get my life back together. I had survived the prison experience and made my way to freedom by creative self-expression, painting, but I was soon to learn that freedom had its costs.

No longer guided by the paternal benefits of institutionalized dependency, I found roadblocks at every level of my existence. For many, including myself, carrying the stigma of being an ex-offender is often debilitating. From being denied employment and housing, to not knowing how to establish healthy relationships, life became exceedingly difficult. In addition, maintaining that freedom, I soon found, was no easy task while wrestling with the haunting memories of my past imprisonment. I always felt as if I were one-step away from returning to prison.

Finally, I landed a job as a paralegal for a large corporate law firm in New York City, and then as a communications specialist for the Drug Policy Alliance (the largest group in the United States advocating against the war on drugs), and I soon found myself in the center of a media storm. The Rockefeller drug laws were on the verge of changing, and given my unique case, I became its spokesperson. I became a sought-after advocate around the nation for drug-law reform and criminal justice issues. My syndicated blog on the *Huffington Post* and stinging editorial pieces about the war on drugs appeared in news sources across the country. After many years of fighting, I helped lead my organization to dismantle the draconian Rockefeller Drug Laws. In April of 2009, historic reform of the Rockefeller Drug Laws was achieved, and I was in the middle of it all.

Along the way, I was profiled on Walter Cronkite's "Great Books" series, a television documentary about Victor Hugo's novel *Les Miserables*, narrated by Uma Thurman. Through my drug conviction, the producer of the piece asserted that I became the modern version of Hugo's epic character, Jean Valjean - a good man condemned to hard labor for a petty theft of a loaf of bread. When Valjean is released from prison, he must carry a yellow passport that identifies himself as a former felon. While I don't have to carry a yellow passport like Valjean, I felt the sting of being branded with the label of "ex-felon."

Like Valjean, in "This Side of Freedom: Life After Clemency", I go through heart-wrenching trials and tribulations as I seek to regain my lost roles as a father, husband and productive citizen, all while fighting to end the draconian drug laws that irrationally imprisoned me and many others. This book will tell a riveting, compelling story, with an arc as dramatic as my prison life.

'This Side of Freedom' is a much-needed book that will help those formerly incarcerated and their families know what to expect, to know that they are not alone in what they are experiencing. It will offer a positive role model, in as much as I am a former incarcerated individual, one of the minority, of those who never returned to prison.

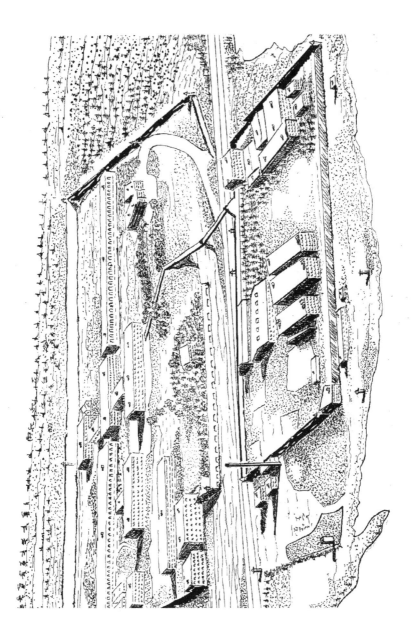

CHAPTER ONE

Out of the Frying Pan and into the Fire

Big Don was the ultimate gangster who practically had his hand in every criminal activity inside of Sing Sing, from drug dealing to extortion. As I was on my way out the door in 1997 and headed toward freedom for the first time in 12 years, he caught up to me while I waited for a van to bring me to the front gate. "Hey, man, I heard you're leaving us," he said, not sounding particularly happy for me. He wanted me to do him a favor and needed my phone number.

I did not know what to do as I knew Big Don knew everyone on the outside, and if I declined, it could have been a very short-lived freedom. I hesitated. "Sure thing," I finally said, giving him a fake number. "You sure it's good?" he asked. "If not, your ass will be grass." "Sure," I replied. "You think I would kid you?" This is one of the ways I survived 12 hard years in prison: by learning how to con a con.

As we drove away, I waved to Big Don and bid farewell to the housing unit I had lived in for the past 2 years. Tappan was Sing Sing's medium-security compound, downhill from its maximum part. It was bitter sweet to live there because the compound was located on the banks of the Hudson River, which hosted a glorious view of majestic mountains. In the summer months, I use to sit out in the recreation yard and sketch the sail boats that floated by. However, the drawings always contained a repetitive motif of my art—the reality of my life--slabs of barbed wire and miles of fence that separated me from my freedom.

Now finally my dream of regaining my freedom had arrived. The driver of the van escorted me up to Sing Sing's State shop, located in its maximum-security area where I spent 10 years. I was then transferred to Tappan. The shop was a place where prisoners transferred in and out of the prison. It was there I was about to make my astounding transformation from prisoner #85-A-2837 back to my civilian identity— Anthony Papa, father, painter, human being.

I knew even then that this would be no easy feat because for the past 12 years I had been under the care and supervision of Sing Sing. My daily existence was defined by rules and regulations. The rules and regulations were enforced by annoying methods of control like the constant ringing of bells that signaled the time for you to sleep, when to get up, when you went to the yard and when you went to eat. Corrections officers barked orders at you every day, and made sure you felt like you were not in control of your life and were doing hard time. The prison had filled many voids and became my paternal replacement, leaving me dependent on its institutional ways. I did not realize at the time how completely they controlled my existence.

When I arrived at the state shop, I changed from my green prison uniform into clothing that I ordered through a mail catalogue company. Looking in the mirror, I saw that I looked like a rebel. All the clothing I bought from my black silver tipped cowboy boots to my black fedora hat was considered contraband by the administration. This was because the color black was not allowed and the choices of clothing that a prisoner was allowed to possess were limited.

I wanted to make a bold statement to the administration that I was now free and I could wear anything I wanted to. I walked passed a holding cage and in it, I saw many men who were new jacks; prisoners that had just entered the system. Looking at their scared faces, I recalled my first days at Sing Sing, where some of the most horrible incidents I experienced had occurred.

This was the most dangerous period of imprisonment because of all the predators who roamed the cell blocks looked for fresh meat and were ready to abuse newly arrived prisoners. They were convicts who were doing extraordinary amounts of time, did not care about anything, and had become lost to a dysfunctional system of living. With no morals or any value for life itself, these prisoners would kill you for a pack of cigarettes without blinking an eye. I recalled the time a well-known prison rapist, Primo, sat naked on my bed and masturbated. Primo tried me out, but he got a rude awakening when I found the courage to stand up to him.

Although I was not a violent person, I literally was forced to protect myself, which was manifested in a vicious fight with him; I stopped his attempt to rape me. I cracked his head open with a sweat sock full of double AA batteries. After that, I never had a problem with Primo again. This was the way of life in Sing Sing, you fought either when someone tried you out. If you did not fight, you would become a victim. Once you wore the label of being a victim, other predators would stand in line to victimize you.

When the count finally cleared and movement was allowed, I was escorted to the Watch Commander's office where we secured the paperwork that I needed in order to exit the prison. I waited a very long time for the escort van, to bring me to Post 18, where I would be released. After waiting, what seemed to be an eternity, the gates opened. I stepped out onto the street a free man. I should have been the happiest person alive, but I wasn't. My optimism and excitement was tempered by cautiousness. This was because in my many years at Sing Sing I saw others leave the prison only to return a few months later on a parole violation.

The days leading up to my release from Sing Sing prison were full of anticipation. My mind, riddled with doubt to be honest, I was really scared. My main concern was the same one it seemed everyone who had done a long stretch in prison had as they approached their release date, would I be able to survive life on the outside? The question haunted me.

I had lost everything I owned when I entered prison. Now I was re-entering the world with only the clothing on my back and a few hundred bucks in my pocket. I knew I had to shed the institutional dependency of the prison so I rejected the typical handout they gave to all prisoners. Upon release, a one-way train or bus ticket to their destination of choice, and a check for forty dollars was the policy. For most prisoners that offering is all they had to start their new life. The rejection of the handout signified to me the start of my independence. Despite all my apprehensions, I tried my best to convince myself that I could rebuild my life and become a productive tax-paying citizen.

I felt as though my first few steps out of the prison were akin to the first walk on the moon by astronaut Neil Armstrong. I felt born again, and all my senses suddenly became alive just by the thought of being free! Waiting to greet me beyond the prison gates was my good friend Linda. She waited outside the prison for several hours waiting for my release. "What happened to you?" she asked as I walked up to her. I explained that I had waited for hours as the prison administration slowly processed my paperwork. The delay even had me worried that they were not going to let me go. Whether planned or not, the final incident, on my last day waiting at the gate, reminded me how the prison controlled every aspect my life.

"The nightmare is over," Linda said, as she warmly reached out to embrace me. Linda was a writer for a local paper who had written several stories about me and was very sympathetic to my quest to regain my lost freedom. Through her visits to the prison to interview me, we became friends. This was despite the prison administration's policy that frowned upon civilians who entered the prison in any sort of professional capacity, from getting personally involved with prisoners.

When I first met Linda, she had come to Sing Sing as a reporter. From her questions, it seemed to me like she thought she had an easy story to tell. As she got to know me and researched the laws that were used to sentence me to a mandatory 15-years-to-life sentence, her easy story became a much tougher one to tell. Learning about what had happened to me and how I was dealing with it took her through a hundred different avenues, leaving her both frustrated and filled with conflicting emotions. She saw me as a first time, nonviolent offender who had fallen through the cracks of New York's draconian Rockefeller Drug Laws, but more importantly, she saw me as her friend.

Linda surprised me with a steak lunch she planned at a local restaurant not far from the prison. As we walked across Main Street in the village of Ossining, I got the first lesson of my new life on the outside when a car came close to hitting me as I crossed the street. The driver honked his horn and the blaring sound caused me to freeze in my tracks. I had my first epiphany, as I stood silent and frozen in the middle of the road; I realized that I had actually forgotten how to cross a street. Still trapped in the moment, I did not know whether to laugh or cry. I felt a little like an infant, new to the world, taking my first steps all over again. I turned to Linda and said, "I haven't had much practice lately." "Come on. You would hate to get arrested for jay-walking and violate your parole," Linda said jokingly, extending her hand. We looked at each other and shared a brief laugh as she helped me cross safely to the other side of the road.

Twenty minutes later, I was sitting at a table in a nice restaurant enjoying the first fruits of my newly found freedom, however, those fruits quickly turned sour when I found myself staring strangely at the table setting. Just a typical table setting that included drinking glasses and flatware. These items would not have been startling to the average dinner patron. As someone who just got out of a maximum-security prison, they were overwhelming for me to look at. In prison, these everyday eating utensils and objects of the free world were considered contraband.

From the water glasses to the flatware on that restaurant table, in those objects I saw the representation of years of my oppression. In prison, it was against the rules to possess any glass or metal because those materials could, conceivably be used to create weapons. If you were found with any of these contraband objects, you would automatically be thrown into solitary confinement – a prison within a prison. Through punishment, the administration controlled and formulated everyone's resulting mentality. I remembered when they found a small glass jar in my cell that I stored paint in. I had borrowed it from the hobby shop. I was given a misbehavior report and thrown into solitary, after that I never dared to possess a glass jar again.

I realized in that moment at that table that I had dragged along all the baggage of imprisonment with me into the free world. I was truly now in shock just from sitting down at a table in an ordinary restaurant for a simple meal! How would I possibly be able to deal with the rest of freedom?

"Tony, what's the matter with you?" Linda inquired, seeing something was troubling me. "I don't know. I feel like I'm bugging out," I said explaining what was going on with me. She had a look of puzzlement on her face, but asked me if I wanted to leave.

aught up to Dominic and almost killed him.

As I calmed myself down on the train that day, I observed several other passengers being bumped twice as hard as I was. They did not react at all, making me realize that bumping passengers was a way of life in a New York City subway train. It was at that point I discovered a commonality I believe is shared by everyone who does hard time. We former prisoners drag along into the free world all of the defense mechanisms we developed to survive the prison experience. In prison, you essentially live with the constant sense that your life could end at any moment.

So, you cultivate instinctual survival tools that become instrumental in mastering and transcending the negativity. "No," I said, "I have to adjust to the real world and put my past behind at some point." I cautiously picked up a glass of water and held it for a while. I was strangely in awe of its beauty as the water, it seemed, danced along the rim. It was a surreal experience feeling glass for the first time in so many years.

I slowly began adjusting to the presence of the entire table and took a deep breath as I picked up the knife to cut my steak. The texture of the metal felt so strange. I had forgotten what metal tableware felt like pressed against my fingertips. I never imagined that picking up a ketchup bottle could be a Zen-like experience. Under these conditions it was. It was not just the glass and flatware. It was the whole experience.

Typically, meals in prison were not about socializing at all. You had about 15 minutes for the entire process. This included entering the mess hall, picking up your plastic utensils, going to the counter and filling your plastic tray with food. Then you sat down on uncomfortable benches while being watched over by many corrections officers.

No doubt, the whole atmosphere was created, in part, to make you feel so uncomfortable that you would not want to linger there for any extended period. This caused prisoners to be on edge, which resulted in daily fights that sometimes broke out into full-on riots.

Once you finished your meal, you were supposed to exit the mess hall making sure the plastic forks and spoons were collected, after displaying them to a corrections officer. This was because even the plastic utensils could be fashioned into weapons if smuggled out into the general prison population.

Even in the face of these rules, we tried to make the best of it, especially on holidays. I remember one Thanksgiving Day when a group of us hatched plans to put together a special dinner. Everyone in the group volunteered to have a family member bring up an item. "Old Man Chino" was going to cook the five-course meal we were planning.

A hot plate to cook on was fashioned by a prison electrician who stole the materials needed from old discarded stoves. Other cooking ingredients, including veggies, were smuggled out from the kitchen. Our plan fell through when the twenty-pound turkey was denied entry into the prison because the officials said it could be stuffed with drugs and weapons. We wound up cancelling the meal and ate a disappointing, mediocre holiday meal in the prison mess hall. It was nothing like the meal that I was eating now at the restaurant.

After finishing the steak dinner, we went to Linda's house in Ossining, not far from the prison, to pick up some property of mine she had been storing while I was in prison. We loaded a few boxes and several paintings in the back of her pickup truck. I got my first taste of modern technology while sitting in my seat when the automatic seat belt almost took off my head. Linda and I laughed hysterically. We then drove down to the South Bronx to my mother Lucy's apartment, where I had lived until the age of 21. Now at the age of 42, I returned to live there once again.

When we got to my mom's apartment building late in the afternoon everything about being free again hit me. I had been free for four hours and realized my old life looked and felt completely alien to me. The sidewalks looked narrow and everything around me seemed cluttered and distorted. My clothing suddenly felt too tight and my vision did not seem to jive with the objects I was looking at.

The only things that looked normal were things associated with prison, like the bars on the building windows, the gates that surrounded the building and the wired fence in the parking lot across the street. It would take a long while for me to fully adjust to some very basic things in the free world. Linda and I embraced and I thanked her for all the help she had given me before she drove away to go to work.

My mother's neighbor, Bee, was waiting on the front stoop of the apartment building. She called for my mom in front of the house as I picked up my boxes of my belongings and entered the building. Lucy quickly stuck her head out of the second floor window and screamed with joy. As I climbed the stairs, I could not believe my eyes when I saw that the hallway walls were decorated with balloons and "welcome home" signs. After twelve long years I was finally reunited with my mother Lucy and other family members.

When I finally made my way across the threshold of her apartment, we hugged each other tightly relishing the moment we had waited years to experience. Bright ribbons adorned gift boxes that contained clothing and essentials that I would need to start my life over again. Lucy even prepared all of my favorite dishes and stocked the refrigerator with my favorite foods. I became overwhelmed with joy and happiness; every emotion I had was intensified. In fact, when I first came home, everything I experienced touched my soul in a mystical way. The simplest act was like a religious journey filled with wonder and sometimes now I wish I could go back and once again live in the purity of those feelings

Lucy had remained in the same rent-controlled apartment for more than 30 years. My sister, Angela, wanted her to move down to Florida but she refused, saying she wanted to wait for me to return to her. She was the typical Italian mamma who had unconditional love for her only son. Soon after my arrival, my mother's phone was ringing off the wall with media requests.

The governor's office had distributed a press release alerting the media of my clemency. My sister Angela gave me her cell phone to respond to some calls but I didn't even know how to operate it! She had to help me make calls. Later on when I went to turn on the TV, even the use of the remote became a challenge for me. It seemed that modern technology had advanced while I stayed stuck in the past. The first day of my freedom was full of events that welcomed me to the beginning of a new life. As I fell asleep on the couch in the brightly colored living room of my mother's apartment, I realized I had a lot to learn.

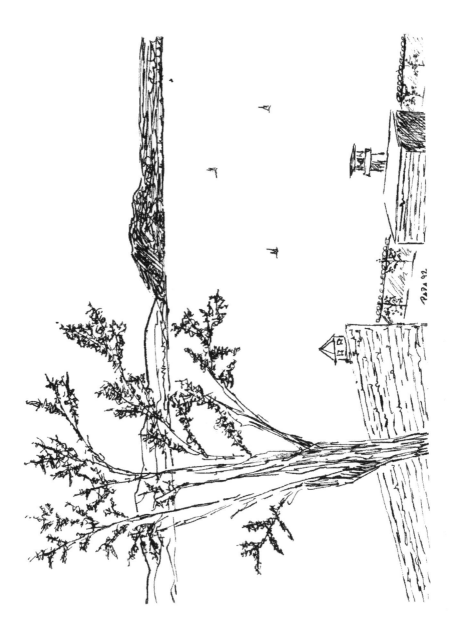

CHAPTER TWO

Adjusting to Life in the Real World was Hard

My mom did her best to make me happy but living arrangements were tight. Johnny, a 23-year-old former neighbor was already living there. He was a childhood friend whose parents had died. My mother took him in because he had nowhere else to live. Her bedroom was sandwiched between Johnny's room and the living room. With no doors to separate us, I had very limited privacy. This situation reminded me of being back in prison where privacy eluded me most of the time because of nosey prisoners and surveillance by the guards. I guess the lack of privacy was also part of my punishment.

After a few days, I got the urge to paint. I wanted to reenact the routine I had done for many years while back in prison. In Sing Sing, this routine resulted in the creation of hundreds of paintings and helped me survive the prison experience. At the foot of my bed facing the window I set up the small portable wooden easel I brought home with me from prison. On it, I placed an 18-by-24-inch canvas. At my side was a shoebox full of paints and some brushes. I sat and stared at the blank canvas for hours. Nothing came to me. Something was wrong; I could not paint. In prison, I had painted hundreds of pieces of art.

Now I found myself stuck. I walked into the living room to look for some magazines. When I painted in prison, I sometimes got ideas from the images I found in them. I looked at the magazine rack next to the television. My eyes glanced below where, on a stand under the television, proudly displayed was a broken yellow ceramic clown and propped up with a roll of green thread.

The clown tilted over to the left because it was missing a piece of his left arm and one leg. It would be considered junk to the average person. To my mother it was sentimental trophy of the love shared between us. I had given her that clown many years ago and my mother had kept it despite it being ready for the trashcan. The four-room apartment was full of paintings, drawings and ceramics that I had sent her from prison over the years. Hanging on the walls were copies I had done of masterworks by Renoir, Picasso and Michelangelo. Other paintings were my originals, bright and lively watercolors of beach scenes and majestic mountains. Lucy claimed that it was the best art collection in South Bronx, often showing the art to her neighbors.

I do not know if it was because of her art collection or not, but eventually she installed three locks on her apartment door. This included a heavy police lock that had a four-foot metal bar buried into the floor that wedged into a metal socket. It looked as though it could stop a tank from knocking down the door.

The answer for all this protection could have also been that the neighborhood had deteriorated almost to the point of no return. It was flooded with the ingredients that destroy inner-city neighborhoods. Crime and poverty paralyzed those that lived there. The same disenfranchised and marginalized people that I had lived with in prison were everywhere. My mother and many of the people who lived in the building were elderly, clinging tightly to their purses when venturing out of their homes to go shopping.

In a way, I shared a similar fear with them. Every time I left the apartment, I thought for sure that I would somehow violate the conditions of my parole. Violating parole was very easy to do. Any negative police contact would trigger a violation. My fear came from everyday simple acts that I associated with my past life in exile. This reality came to me one day when I was riding a crowded train and a passenger bumped me from behind.

I knew back in prison a simple bump could lead to a brutal confrontation. I automatically went into a defensive mode. I gripped the overhead handrail tightly, as my heartbeat elevated and my adrenaline started to pump into my veins. I bit my lip and tried to calm myself down. I thought about the time Raymond the porter bumped crazy Dominick.

One day I walked past a cell and saw someone hiding in the corner. A voice called out my name "Tony come here" It was Dominick, a big Italian guy who I worked out with; he was doing time for murder. I walked toward the cell when it swung open. "In here", he said. I walked in the cell and Dominick uncovered the hood he had over his head. "Did anyone follow you?" he asked. "No" I said. Dominick's eyes were open wide. He looked like he was high on something. He was wearing a heavy army jacket stuffed with thick library books to block a potential stabbing. "Good", he replied. I want you to do me a favor. I just had a beef with, Raymond, the porter. The dirty bastard bumped me in the slop sink.

He caught an attitude with me and pulled out a razor blade. "Nobody pulls out on me", he angrily said. "I ran to my cell and got my piece. I cornered him in near the slop sink and stuck him two times. He cried like a bitch and begged me to stop. I know his boys are looking for me now. All the Latinos in the block are going to back him."

"This is war," he said, so mad that spit was flying from his mouth. It's us against them he muttered as he reached in his jacket. He pulled out a shank, a makeshift knife made out of metal, and tried to hand it to me. "This is yours," he said. I looked at it, but did not make a move to accept it. My reaction was cautious. Dominick looked like he had flipped out. I did not want anything to do with this. I had nothing to do with his problem and was one move closer from getting involved with a dangerous situation.

This was the way of life in Sing Sing. You became involved with other people's problems because there was nowhere you could go to isolate yourself from others. I did not take the weapon from Dominic. I told him that I had to use the phone and had to leave. Dominic just stared at me as I walked away. It was a mad man's look. One that was associated with someone that didn't care about life. He was lost in the system and wanted to take on anyone who disrespected him. He also knew he was in for a big fight because Raymond was a Latino. This meant that Dominic did not only stab him, theoretically, he had stabbed Raymond's entire Latino crew. Eventually they imminent danger--of the surrounding environment. Now I realized that the same tools that could surface both at will and without warning would become a serious burden to me in the free world. I needed to learn how to put them in check before they became my downfall. I was to serve five years under parole supervision. Even though I was technically free, I could go back inside at any time at the whim of my parole officer.

A simple confrontation could result in a violation of my parole. I had one foot in the free world and the other still stuck in the cycle of incarceration. I really hated that feeling and to offset it, I kept myself busy by speaking about my imprisonment at different venues such as colleges and churches.

One such speaking engagement turned my world upside down. I was contacted by a writer named Anthony Davis who asked me to speak to the students he taught in a creative writing class at Spofford Juvenile Center located in the South Bronx. Spofford was the focus of criticism and controversy for many years. For a variety of reasons, it became known as a place that exacerbated the problems of juvenile delinquents. Despite this, Davis thought that people that cared could make a difference in these kids' lives.

I left my mother's apartment early in the morning and met Davis. We walked to the facility, which was about 15 minutes away. To my surprise, Spofford was just down the road from where I used to work at a radio installation shop on Bruckner Blvd. The area was pretty run down and all the buildings looked about the same until we got close to Spofford. From about a half a block away I zeroed in on an object that almost made my heart stop beating. It was a row of coiled barbed wire sticking out from the top of a fence. It just hung in the air, swaying back and forth, calling me to its attention.

As we got closer, I saw that heavy fences were topped with rows of sharp razor wire surrounded the building. The windows of the building were covered with steel gates and painted in battleship gray. It was surely an institution and it reminded me of a miniature Sing Sing. What blew my mind was it even had a mini-wall that looked like a small version of the wall that surrounded the maximum-security prison I lived in.

Its entrance had enforced double doors that looked like they were bullet proof. We walked through the doors and I saw a glass booth that contained two guards that controlled entry in and out of the institution. Davis called for someone to escort us in. A beefy looking sergeant came out and asked if he could search me. I reacted quickly and without even thinking, I automatically spread my legs and threw my arms against the metal detector booth. I had automatically assumed a search position. The move raised eyebrows and telegraphed the fact that I was an ex-con. The guard chuckled, and said all he wanted me to do was walk through the booth, not give him a song and a dance. I looked at Davis and we both laughed.

The escort took us in the building. He unlocked several doors using a large metal key about seven inches in length. To my surprise, the doors contained the similar lock mechanisms as the cell doors in Sing Sing prison. In a few minutes, we entered the heart of the institution and took an elevator to the fourth floor where we walked through several more locked doors. We passed what was considered to be a library.

I glanced around the room and was amazed that it looked like it had been through an institutional shakedown. In Sing Sing these shakedowns were conducted on a regular basis, which often resulted in finding knives and drugs hidden in books. Davis told me that the room had been in that condition for a while and the administration was trying to get it together. The hallways were totally empty and resembled a ghost town. It was surely a setting that taught young kids to be ready for a life in prison.

We entered the director's office. Her name was Ms. Washington and she told me she had read many articles about me in the newspapers and her kids would enjoy my talk. We talked for a while. I met some of her staff and I arranged for a projector to show some slides of my artwork to the kids. About 40 minutes later, we were led to the auditorium. I was not prepared for what I was about to see. There sitting in the audience were about 50 boys and girls, aged 10 to 15 years old, dressed in their prison uniforms.

In front of me sat a young looking Latino boy who looked about 8 years old. He wore braces and was maybe 4 feet tall. I found out later he was 12 years old and was doing time for murder. I tried to keep my composure, even though I was in a state of shock. When I went to the facility, I had prepared to talk about stress management. The same talk I had given visiting several community colleges. Now I knew I could not talk about this subject to these kids because they would not understand. I found out that most of them had grade one to grade three reading levels, almost the same level of adult prisoners in the system I was in. I opened up my talk by showing them a 16x20 photo of myself in my prison cell and told them, this was the place that I had lived for the past twelve years. The little kid in the front row was amazed and asked if I did twelve straight years? I said yes and then he dropped a bomb on me, "Did you ever get raped in there?" All the kids in the room grew quiet in anticipation of my answer, sitting on the edge of their seats. I told them that someone had tried but they didn't succeed. They continued to ask me many questions about my life in prison. I guess they were interested because many of them would eventually go to prison when they became old enough. For some of them cycling in and out of jails would become a way of life. It was, sadly, a routine implanted deep within their souls at an early age.

While giving them a slideshow of my art I could not help but think I was standing in front of the future residents of maximum prisons like the one I spent 12 years in. Looking at them, I saw faces on kids, nothing more. Faces on kids in prison didn't tell a story like faces on adults in prison. Back in Sing Sing, you could look at imprisoned men and their faces told vivid tales. These kids looked so innocent, so needful for love and understanding. I prayed that I had made some sort of connection that would prevent just one of them walking the road I had taken.

I left Spofford a different person. The experience had secured my need to confront my demons head on and to make a difference not only in my life, but the life of others. It was a good feeling to be free. After a month, however, when the initial response to my newly found freedom had faded, I realized that the freedom I fought so hard to obtain was not what I thought it would be.

CHAPTER THREE

Mending Broken Relationships

During my imprisonment I had tried to commit suicide, been stuck with a knife, and was beaten with a pipe, but nothing hurt me more than my separation from my daughter. I had not seen her in over seven years, now I was free and I wanted desperately to reestablish out relationship. Stephanie was now nineteen years old and it hurt me deeply that we were complete strangers to each other. I felt I had abandoned her when I went to prison even though the circumstances were beyond my control. The Westchester District Attorney had offered me a plea bargain of three years to life and I rejected the offer because I did not want to leave her. Instead, I went to trial to fight for my freedom. I lost and paid dearly for going to trial and received a mandatory 15 years to life sentence.

Stephanie visited me often in the beginning of my incarceration. I remember her first visit to Sing Sing prison as clear as a bell. At seven years old, she had smuggled a photo of herself with Santa Claus in the fold of her sweater. As time went by, she learned about the reality of our situation. No child should have to experience the horrible conditions she had to go through; such as body searches, long waiting lines and abusive correction officers. Little by little, her beautiful child-like demeanor disappeared, replaced with a sadness and depression generally seen in a much older person. By the time she was 12, she had become psychologically damaged and so traumatized by the prison experience that she could no longer visit me.

I had kept all the letters and drawings she ever sent to me while I was in prison in an old shoebox. It was one of my most prized possessions and I carried that box with me through my years of incarceration. Stephanie didn't know it, but her letters to me were worth their weight in gold and saved my life. Her childlike innocence gave me the will to live when I wanted to die. Every time I felt I couldn't go on I would pull out a letter to pick me up. One in particular I loved to read, especially when I was depressed. The letter was illustrated with three snowmen with reindeer. It read:

Dear Daddy:

I love you very very very very much and miss you very very very very much. Answer all the questions. Do you love me? Do you miss me? Do you love mommy and miss her too? Love forever and always Marry Christmas.

I love you, Stephanie.

When I was granted clemency, I called her on the phone to tell her that I was coming home. We both cried and made plans to get together as soon as I was released and forge a father-daughter relationship. I was very excited, but also very nervous. I wanted to see my daughter very badly. I felt like a failure as a father because I could not provide for her and give her even a minimal portrayal of what a father and daughter relationship was all about, as I perceived it; one of the most painful experiences I went through. I was powerless to do anything about it while I was in prison. Now it would be different or so I thought.

When I was released I managed to fumble our relationship from the beginning. Instead of contacting her the day I was released, Stephanie found out I was granted clemency from the governor by reading it in the NY Daily News. This was something that bothered her tremendously and it hurt our relationship. She yelled at me and asked why I did not call her as soon as I came out. To tell the truth when I came home I was not prepared for freedom. It was a cultural shock. I realized this cultural shock is one of the main reasons for the high rate of recidivism that exists.

Was this cultural shock one of the primary reasons that two thirds of those released from prison would return to prison within 3 years? Worst of all for me in my newly found freedom was the hurtful fact that I had forgotten how to be a father to my daughter. When you go to prison, you need to shed the identity you had in the free world. You do this to cope with life inside. I had to forget the roles I played as a father and a husband. Call it a safety mechanism or whatever you want but one thing is for sure is that the tools you use in prison to survive are totally detrimental to your being once you are part of society again. No matter how hard I tried to remember how to be a father to her, I could not do it. To make matters worse she did not have the patience to deal with developing our relationship.

I was trying to balance getting my life together while re-establishing relationships. It was not an easy task for me. For most prisoners returning to society this was one of the most difficult tasks. Prisons break up families and destroy relationships. There was no denying this but I needed to try to salvage some sort of relationship with Stephanie.

I called my ex-wife Marylou and tried to arrange a visit to see my daughter. I had not seen her in 7 years and we had drifted apart. We were divorced after 3 years of my incarceration. She could not deal with the situation and had struggled with her life in trying to raise our daughter Stephanie while I was in prison. For me the only way I could survive imprisonment was to forget about the world outside. For Marylou, it was to forget about me being inside. Both of us survived this way. For many it was a typical reaction to the situation.

Marylou agreed to meet me in front of my mom's house. In the back of my mind, I wondered if there was a romantic spark left in our relationship. I had not seen her in years and thought about the possibility of getting together with her for the sake of my relationship with my daughter. My mother Lucy walked into the bedroom and told me she was in front of the house. Lucy was angry with me for wanting to meet her. I could not blame her. Marylou had not only cut off my daughter from me, she also prevented my mother from seeing her granddaughter. My mother was old school and could hold a grudge forever - taking it to the grave with her. I explained to her that I needed to see her in order to see Stephanie.

When I got into her car, I gave her a kiss on her cheek and we embraced. As I held her in my arms, I knew instantly that our relationship was over for sure. I felt nothing. The years that I spent in prison had distanced us to the point that it destroyed whatever love I had for her. I told Marylou I wanted to see our daughter Stephanie. She told me she would be home soon and agreed to bring me to our old apartment where they still lived. We lived in a three-room basement apartment in the Tremont section of the Bronx. As soon as I walked through the kitchen door, it brought back memories of when we were a loving family. The same kitchen table was there along with the glass display cabinet that held photos of our daughter.

We went into the living room where I sat on the couch distancing myself far from Marylou. We tried to make small talk and engaged in a conversation. I was polite and kept my answers short and sweet. I avoided any conversation that would try to make excuses why our relationship was over. I knew the reason why. The prison experience does not end at the wall that imprisons individuals. It goes beyond it and reaches those family members outside of it. Marylou and my daughter Stephanie had become so deeply traumatized by the experience that they could not deal with it. We were all damaged from my imprisonment and the consequences, both directly and indirectly.

As Marylou spoke, my eyes honed in on a corner of the room where an array of dog toys sat in a doggy bed. Probably everything a dog could dream of wanting to own. My daughter's boyfriend had given the pet boxer to her for a birthday gift many years ago. Then the strangest thought invaded mind. The dog became an essential part of their family. In a way the dog took my place and was living better than I had lived in prison. The thought became magnified in my mind. It bounced back and forth in my mind making me crazy. It made me remember our relationship as it had been and how it dissolved into nothing over the years. Now here I was 12 years later returning to the apartment I had lived in feeling like a complete stranger to the woman I once loved. On top of that, I was comparing my life with their dog. I could not believe it, prison really fucked up my mind. It was a tragic moment of realization, which made me tremendously sad. I told her I needed to go and told her to tell Stephanie I would be in touch soon.

On the train home, I reflected on the situation. I realized the reason I felt so bad about leaving Stephanie was that I had experienced abandonment by my father when I was a baby. Roberto was an abusive alcoholic that made my mother's life a living hell. My mom told me that when I was 6 months old, my father, in a drunken stupor held me by one foot and hung me out of the third floor window of their South Bronx apartment. He screamed and cursed in his native Latin tongue and threatened my mother that he would drop me to my death.

My mom soon divorced him. The next time I had contact with him was on my eighteenth birthday. I walked out the same front doorway of the south Bronx apartment I now lived with my mother Lucy. As I was about to enter my car a man crossed the street and approached me. He looked like he was homeless. The first thing I noticed was a two-inch-long cut caked with dry blood on his left hand. I tried to ignore him when he put out his wounded hand, palm facing me, and placed his fingertips on my chest. "Do you know who I am?" he said. I looked very deeply into his eyes and something from within knew the answer. I replied, "Yeah, you're my father." We embraced.

He spoke to me in Spanish. He was surprised when I told him I did not speak the language. He shook his head in disbelief. I asked him why he had left me. He stood silent as he put his head down and he slumped in shame. Roberto looked at me. His eyes swelled with tears and he embraced me. I arched my back up high towards the sky and my arms dropped pressing my sides purposely so they would not touch him. We stood there in the middle of the south Bronx Street for what seemed to become an eternity. I thought of all the years I wanted to have a father, but did not. My childhood memories were void of his existence. It made me feel inferior as a child growing up not knowing him. I asked the question again. "Why did you leave me?" He looked at me with deep silence. He could not answer. I gently put my hand on his shoulder and purposely avoided looking at him as I walked away. He understood. I never saw him again.

Now I was experiencing this hurtful memory once again through my daughter Stephanie. Only this time the roles were reversed and I knew the hurt my daughter had felt firsthand. I needed to resolve the personal issues that prevented me from seeing my daughter.

My biggest obstacle was trying to develop a way to explain to her what happened to the relationship I had with her mother and why the love we had once shared disappeared. My relationship with Marylou was doomed from its start. Her parents were immigrants from Italy and were very strict in raising her. We lived in the South Bronx a small pocket of blocks that were occupied by mostly Italian immigrants that had lived there for years. Racism was prevalent and was the rule of thumb for many. The neighborhood whites were constantly fighting in the Alfred E. Newman Vocational School yard with blacks from the nearby Melrose projects. It was 1973 when I met Marylou when I was washing my 1969 Ford Torino in front of Our Lady of Pity Church.

I lay upside down, my head under my dashboard when I heard a voice call out, "Hey, turkey what you doing?" I jerked my head out to see the voice belonged to a young pretty girl. I had seen her in the neighborhood before but she was only a kid. Now, at age 17, she looked all grown up. This was the start of our love affair. It was not a normal relationship. We had to hide our relationship because of her parents. Typically, we met in the back of Teresa's grocery store on the corner of 151st street and Morris Ave.

Between the aisles that separated the dry goods from the dairy products Marylou and I exchanged kisses. Sometimes we would get bold and embrace each other behind the vestibule stairs in the hallway of her building. Whenever we met, it had to be in secret in fear of her parents finding out. Then one day our fear became a reality. Marylou's parents found out through neighborhood gossipers that she was seeing me. These were people that had nothing better to do with their lives but gossip. Some of them were racists, raised in the 1960's.

Racism had followed me through my life growing up; I felt the sting of racism over the years. It was sad that this situation mirrored my mother's relationship with my father. He was from Puerto Rico and married my mother Lucy who was of Italian descent. Her family did not approve of my mother mixing blood. Bottom line was that he was a 'spic'. Now the baton of racism was being passed on to me. I had inherited the ingredients, which made my mother's life miserable. The neighborhood had its share of people who hated other people because of the color of their skin. I remember clear as a bell when I was a teenager marching in an Italian Day parade and Joey my best friend's cousin yelled out "Hey, you're a spic. You don't belong in the parade." When I heard those words I ran off into the crowd and wanted to bury my head deep into the ground because I was ashamed of whom I was.

In order to solve the problem, Marylou's parents decided to send her to Italy in the summer of 1976. I was head over heels in love and devastated when I found out she was gone. To make matters worse I was helpless to do anything about it. I went into a deep depression and wanted to die. I was lovesick and could not eat nor sleep. Weeks had passed by when I finally received a phone call from Marylou. I was happy beyond belief to hear her voice. "I need to tell you something," she said. "Ok, Baby tell me". "Tony, I am pregnant", she whispered. I was in shock. At that moment, I felt as though my life had instantly changed.

I was just a 22-year-old kid living at home who was going to college. I thought now I was going to be a father. I held my composure and told her "Oh, Baby, that's great!", but inside I was scared as hell. I didn't have a pot to piss in. "When are you coming home?" I asked. She told me at the end of the summer. For the next two months, I was anxious. I told a few close friends and my stepfather Tony whom I worked for part-time in his auto radio shop. He asked me if I was going to abort the child. When he told me that would be the best thing to do, I panicked. I did not know what to do. I knew that our life together was tough now and imagined it would be even harder with a child. We were only two kids who barely knew how to take care of ourselves, let alone a baby. What was I to do?

Two months later Marylou came back from Italy. I saw her. She looked so beautiful! We were so happy to be in love with each other that nothing else really mattered. Sadly, our love and happiness was cut short when her parents found out that she was still seeing me. They decided to move from their south Bronx neighborhood. They bought a house in the Morris Park section of the east Bronx.

It was like a game of checkers. Her parents would make a move then I would respond and try to counter their move. This time I decided that I needed to be close to her so I made what was to be the biggest decision in my young life. I decided to move out of my mother's apartment. I was lucky to have found out about a residence-nursing program that was available to nursing students at Bronx Community College. For fifty dollars a month, I could get a room there. I was going to enroll in that college and switch curriculums from my studies in Electrical Technology, but I found out I did not have to.

Registering in the program at Jacobi Hospital was lax. All the proof they wanted was a student identification card. The nurse's residence soon became full of students that were less than desirable. Among those that moved in were mentally ill Veterans and drug dealers with fake student identification cards. Nonetheless, it was a solution to my problem.

My mother was heartbroken when I moved out of her apartment. But she knew I wanted to be closer to Marylou. Soon Marylou was visiting me at the hospital and everything was going fine. I was going to college and working part-time installing radios and alarms at my stepfather's auto radio shop. The time flew by fast until one day I was suddenly awoken early in the morning when someone began beating my door with what I thought were fists. It was Marylou. She began to scream, "Tony open the door." I jumped out of bed, ran and opened the door to find Marylou standing in a puddle of water. "Oh my God what happened?" I asked.

Marylou grabbed her belly with her two hands and told me that her water broke. I stood there looking puzzled. I was so naive I did not know what she was talking about. "Your water what", I said squinting my eyes and looking at the water. "I'm going into labor," she said. Then I got it and suddenly I freaked out and didn't know what to do. She told me she didn't want to have the baby at the hospital I lived in. It was also too close to her home and she didn't want her parents to find out.

She had hidden her pregnancy from them saying her extra-added weight was due to her getting fat. She didn't really look pregnant except for the bulge in her belly. But I could not imagine how she felt hiding her pregnancy from her parents. Looking back in hindsight, I could not believe her mother did not know she was pregnant. "OK, I'm getting Mike to drive us to another hospital", I said.

The residence had 48 apartments split-up in two wings of 24. Mike lived at the end of the right wing. He dealt drugs, mainly angel dust. In fact, many of the residents who lived there were not students. The word got out that many people who lived there did not belong there. More than a few started dealing drugs out of their apartments. This led to crazy parties that sometimes lasted for days. I remembered I missed a week of school and work from partying. I started out in Wayne's room who was dealing speed and woke up three days later passed out in the shared bathroom.

I got Mike and we ran downstairs to his van. Marylou was contracting and screaming in pain. Mike looked at Marylou lying in the back of the van, turned to me, and said 'We'll never make it to another hospital I nodded in agreement. We drove 100 yards to Jacobi's emergency room entrance. I yelled for a hospital attendant who quickly grabbed a rolling stretcher. I waited in an area where other expecting fathers were sharing stories of past births and handing out cigars. Instead of enjoying the moment, I only sulked thinking of what the future would hold. Here we were two young kids that didn't even go out on a single date who were having a baby. On top of that, her family hated me.

I couldn't believe that I was going to be a father. About an hour later, a nurse called out my name. I nervously stood up and walked towards her. She put out her hand to congratulate me and said "Mr. Papa, congratulations you are the proud father of a healthy baby girl". A smile came to my face and a breathed a sigh of relief when I found out that both my daughter and Marylou were fine. I went inside to the maternity ward where I looked through the plate glass to see my daughter Stephanie for the first time. I never saw a prettier vision and felt I was struck helpless by looking into her eyes. She was so beautiful I forgot all of my worries.

Soon after Stephanie's birth word quickly got to Marylou's family and they did the unthinkable. They sent word that they had officially disowned her. I guess they were very shocked and reacted this way because of it. Her father was an old school Italian, respect was everything in life. We had totally disrespected them by having a baby out of wedlock. The dorm room we lived in was not a place for a baby so I asked my mother Lucy for help. She happily came to our rescue and took us in. She even scraped up some money and bought a crib for the baby.

The living conditions at my mother's apartment were tight. My Uncle Frank who lived with my mother was not happy with the fact that I was going to marry Marylou. He told me to wait a while before I rushed into it and explained that we were both young and marriage was a tough deal. I told him I had to marry her because it was the right thing to do. Several days later, I snuck into Marylou's parents' house and loaded up a few pillowcases with Marylou's clothes and belongings. I quit college and got a full-time job working at a radio installation shop in Hunts Point. We struggled and knew we needed our own space.

We had no money; I did not know what we could do. A few months had passed by and thankfully, her family had cooled off. Marylou's brother Larry wanted to talk to me. We met at Alex and Henry's a catering hall on 161st street in the Bronx. It was a wedding hall and bar where the neighborhood guys and gals use to go drinking.

It was also the location of my first brush with the law when I was 18 years old. A childhood friend of mine went off to study engineering at Marquette University and had returned to the Bronx on a break. "Tony it's me, Hank", he said. I was startled to hear his voice. It had been two years since I had last seen him. "Meet me at Alex and Henry's" he said. At 8 pm, I arrived to find Hank sitting at the bar with his girlfriend. We started drinking and talked about the old days. We both were avid bowlers and enjoyed playing sports with each other. We grew up on the straight and narrow and the only thing we enjoyed was drinking.

Now Hank seemed to find a different lifestyle while attending college. He was into dealing drugs. "Yeah, bro, that's how I pay my tuition", he told me. He went into his jacket, pulled out a joint, and handed it to me as he told me that the pot business was very good. I nodded my head to acknowledge what he said. "What about around here?" he asked. I stood silent. My friends and I all smoked pot. We would go down to the park on 149th street and College Avenue in the South Bronx. There we would buy a nickel (five dollar) bag when we got the urge and go back to the block to hang out. Most of the time the guys we would sit on the steps in front of "Our Lady of Pity Church", light up and get stoned.

Then sometimes we would all chip in and go down to neighborhood candy store and buy a case of cold Miller beer and play cards. I remember the time my best friend Vinny's grandma played with us. She was a tough old gal and the former girlfriend of Jack "Legs" Diamond, a gangster during prohibition. I forgot the table rule to never raise her in a poker game. One night I did, she became furious and turned to me and said "You should desire your mother." I never forgot that.

Now, at the bar Hank smiled and went into his girlfriend's handbag and pulled out an ounce of pot and handed it to me. "Take this and see if you can sell it", he said. I was taken aback but I smiled, the booze had opened me up. I never could afford to buy an ounce of weed so I gladly took it and jammed it into the top left hand jacket pocket. We continued to drink the night away. Several hours had passed and we were all looped. "Let's get out of here, I want to show my girlfriend Manhattan" he said. The words slurred from his mouth.

We left and walked up the block into the secluded area where his car was parked. As we sat in the car, Hank lit up a fat joint. We passed it around and started talking. Hank reached over, opened his glove box, and pulled out a wallet that contained small white, triangle-shaped paper bags. He slowly unwrapped one of the paper envelopes and a pile of powdered cocaine appeared. Hank opened the glove box and began making lines on its surface. I couldn't believe it and was nervous. I didn't fuck with the hard stuff and I never remembered him indulging in it. I thought about it and knew that he had gone off to college so maybe this was a college thing.

No sooner than I began to relax out of nowhere, suddenly a gypsy cab pulled up and several men jumped out and swarmed around Hank's car. They surrounded the car with guns drawn yelling, "Open the door motherfuckers". We panicked and Hank quickly slammed shut and locked the glove box. White powder flew into the air like a cloud. A badge then flashed in front of my face through the closed window. "Police mother fuckers, open up or we will shoot!" they screamed. I was scared shitless and hesitantly opened my door and the cop grabbed me by jacket and pulled me out.

Hank and his girlfriend also exited the car were then lined up against the wall. "What the fuck are you're doing?" the cop asked. "Nothing officer "I replied. I was shaking in my pants. The cop started patting me down. First, he searched my left top pocket of my jacket and pulled out the joint that Hank I gave me. My heart sunk when he waved it front of my face. "Nothing" he blurted out as he grinned and continued his search.

Out of the right pocket, he hit the jackpot and pulled out the ounce of pot. I had forgotten all about it. My heart sunk. "Oh my GOD" I said to myself. The cop's grin widened and he glared at me and said "nothing huh?" He repeatedly said it as the other undercover cops searched the car. One of them ordered Hank to give him "the fucking key" to the glove box. Hank did pretend to search for the key. One of the cops grew impatient and decided to pried open the glove box where he found the black wallet containing the cocaine. "Nothing" the cop said again, this time slapping handcuffs on me.

All of us were read our rights and were swiftly brought down to the 42nd station house where we were booked. The cops split us up and questioned Hank and me together while his girlfriend was placed in a different room and questioned separately. Where is your girlfriend from?" the cop asked Hank. Mississippi, he replied. The intake cop who was filing out the form asked his partner how to spell Mississippi. "He can't even spell" Hank laughed aloud. I looked at him as if he was crazy. Hank was still buzzed from his Jack and coke drinks and didn't realized the gravity of the situation until the cop reminded him. "Funny, huh, motherfuckers" said the cop who could not spell said as he walked into another room and returned with a shopping bag. He pulled out three pounds of marijuana and slammed the pot on the table. I could not believe what I saw.

Hank was a walking drug store. Now I knew I was really in trouble. The head cop leaned down into my face and smirked as he told me "You guys are in deep shit; you know what you are facing?" He nodded his head up and down. "Life in prison under the Rockefeller Drug Law he said as one of the other cops held up one of the pounds of pot. He opened the bag and a rush of aroma escaped smacking me in the face reminding me of how much trouble we were in.

We were processed and placed in a holding pen until we made bail. When I returned home, my mom called her brother Fury who was a police sergeant in the narcotics division out of the Bronx. Lucy began to cry and pleaded with her brother to help me. She was sobbing. I got on the phone and my uncle began to tell me that I had serious charges under the newly enacted Rockefeller Drug Laws. He told me of the stiff sentences that were a result and that I could do life in prison with all the drugs we were found with. I was very scared and had never heard of the laws because it was my first brush with the law.

I was a good kid and had never been in serious trouble before. When we went before the judge Hank confessed; the drugs were all his and he had bought the drugs to bring back to college so he could pay his college tuition. The Judge gave him a good lecture telling him there were better ways of paying for college. He took in consideration it was the first time we had gotten into trouble and we were all attending college. He decided to throw the case out because he determined it was an illegal search. We all paid a small fine and walked away with violations. I had caught the break of my life and now I was hoping for another break with Marylou's family.

I was nervous when I arrived at the bar where her brother Larry was waiting. I felt I was morally wrong but things happen in life, I thought. I hoped he would understand this. Larry greeted me and I sat next to him. He asked what I wanted to drink and I ordered a beer. We looked at each other pretty intensely, sizing one another up. The first thing out of Larry's mouth made my blood boil. He told me when he heard that his sister had a baby he was going to have me killed.

I immediately went into a defensive mode tensing up and I was ready to fight. I took several deep breaths and managed to keep it together. I knew he was pissed off at me and let him get off what he had on his chest. After he gave me a tongue lashing his tone changed direction. "Look if you marry my sister we will help you out and get you an apartment," he said. My intention was to marry Marylou anyway, so I agreed and soon we were living in our own three-room apartment in the East Tremont section of the Bronx. Her family did the right thing and even furnished it for us. Our good fortune was shot down quickly when I suddenly was fired.

I lost my job at Mid-Town Auto Radio when I slipped while drilling a hole to install a hood-lock in a brand new car. The drill bit went through the surface of the hood and ruined it. My boss got so pissed he canned me on the spot even keeping my paycheck to cover the damage. I was devastated and tried to find another job. It was tough to land one and I tried a few things like driving a cab and working in a car dealership. When these jobs did not work out, I got the idea to start my own business and became self-employed renting out a bay in a gas station and installing radios and alarms. The business was sporadic and at times, I didn't even have enough to pay the bills.

One day the gas station owner demanded the back rent. I knew I had to pay it or he would have thrown me out into the street. When I got home a heated fight between Marylou and me took place when I didn't have the money for our rent. I stormed out of the house and wound up getting into an accident almost killing myself when I crashed into an elevated steel train post after a car cut me off. My head went through my car's windshield and my chest was crushed when the steering wheel fractured my sternum.

It took me a long time to recover. I began popping the prescribed painkillers to kill the pain and started to hang out in a local bar on Pelham Parkway. Bill and Ray's bar was full of barfly's, people who stood there all day and drank their troubles away. I became a regular there at night and use to find escape from my money problems through alcohol and feel good pills.

I knew I needed to find a way to make some real money. To my surprise, I thought I found it when an acquaintance offered me a solution. Polinsky was a gambler in the bowling alleys of Westchester County. He was a real ladies man who drove a flashy Corvette and always had a pocket full of money. His pockets weren't full from gambling alone. He was known to be a big cocaine dealer and he was known to be bad news. Polinsky approached me in the bar of the alley.

I was half in the bag from the pills when he made me a proposition. All I had to do was deliver a package for him and I would make a quick

$500.00. Although I was buzzed, I had the sense to turn him down. Then I got desperate and when you get desperate, you do stupid things. He called again. The timing was just right as I just had a fierce argument with Marylou over money. We didn't have the money to pay our rent. "Ok, I said, what do I do?" Polinsky told me it was simple and all I had to do was bring up a package. He arranged for his drug runner to deliver the package to me.

Against my better judgment, and clouded by the painkillers, I transported the package of 4 and ½ ounces of cocaine from the Bronx to Westchester County. To my surprise, I walked right into a police sting. To make it worse I found out that Polinsky was working for the police. He had been busted and because he was facing life in prison, he cooperated with them. The more people he got involved the less time he got. The cops didn't care who they were arresting as long as they looked like they were doing their job to clean up Westchester County. I did everything I could do that was wrong and eventually, I was sentenced to 15 years to life and sent to Sing Sing.

Now I was free and I was trying to get my life together. I had only seen Stephanie twice and each time we meet it seemed to be a disaster. We did not bond as I thought we would. I had forgotten how to be a father. All those years in captivity had drained the fatherhood from my body and soul. I was ashamed.

Despite how I felt, I was happy. Stephanie was doing well, attending college and pursuing her dream to become a marine biologist. Marylou had done a fine job raising her as a single parent. Things changed for the worst in our relationship when I asked Stephanie to try to reunite with my mother and sister Angela.

She was hesitant to do so because of a family feud that had developed while I was imprisoned. Because of my insistence that Stephanie be reunited with my family, she became distant and our fragile relationship was shattered once again. I felt I was a failure as a father. I was hurt, but realized that the stigma of imprisonment still haunted me and it was so strong it had interfered with my relationship with my daughter.

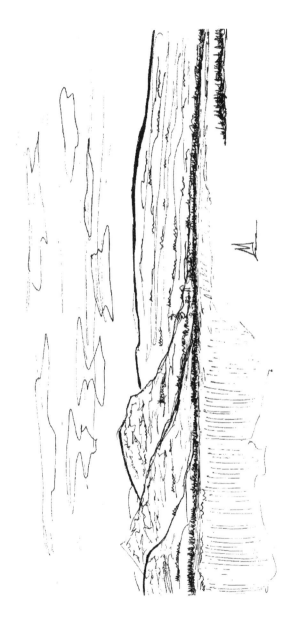

CHAPTER FOUR

Prisoner of the Mountain and Dealing with my Demons

A few days after my release from prison, I participated in a group art show where I was to meet Luciana, the love of my life and my future wife. Gareth Brown, an art dealer, planned the show originally from London, showing "Outsider" art. I met Gareth through a talented writer I knew named Annie Nocenti who was the maid of honor at a prison wedding I attended at Sing Sing. Annie caused quite a commotion when she smuggled in a camera to take photos of her girlfriend Michele who married my friend Les. Cameras were not allowed in prison and the wedding was almost terminated without completion because of this.

Brown came to visit me at the prison about a year before my release and asked me if I wanted to participate in the art show. He was a mellow guy who had worked for HBO in the video department and had a dream to become a famous art dealer. He didn't have a gallery but instead rented the lobby in a performance art space called Solo Arts located on 17th street in New York City. Eventually he bought a house in Long Island City in Queens, NY and converted the ground floor into an art gallery.

My artwork was kept by a friend, Andrea Miller. Andrea lived in Ossining, New York, the town where Sing Sing prison was located. Gareth visited her and took a half of dozen of my pieces to be hung in the show. The plan was to have my artwork exhibited without the possibility of me being there, however, in December of 1997, by nothing short of a miracle, I was granted clemency by Governor George Pataki. My parole officer Joni Johnson managed to pull some strings, cutting through the bureaucratic red tape. I was released two days before the exhibit.

I arrived at the show about an hour late because I went to dinner with David Plant a partner in a law firm that I had met while I was in prison. David would be instrumental in landing me a job as a paralegal with his law firm. When I walked through the door of Solo Arts a huge round of applause came from the crowd. There were a lot of people I knew there that I had met while incarcerated. The group show had quite a spectacular array of artists, if not for their art, then, for sure, their personalities.

There was a mentally ill patient named Tom Carapic who painted on found objects like trashed computer key boards. Then there was 80-year-old Malcolm McKesson who was known to be the Father of Matriarchy. He had authored a semi-autobiographical novel about a boy's discovery of submission and womanhood. My favorite though was Jan Vedra, a former female impersonator whose flashy dress overshadowed his collages. When I met him, he offered to teach me how to draw and at the same time would give me some of his clothing. I pictured Jan in drag, teaching me how to draw, while handing me some used women clothing. I thanked him for the offer and made my way through the crowd.

A pretty girl waiting for the opportunity, took my hand, and guided me to a corner of the room. She flirted with me and we talked for a while. I was having a great time with her until my eyes drifted towards the bar area. Behind the counter top was the most beautiful girl I had ever seen. I was attracted to her wild, crazy curly jet-black hair and chiseled features. She looked like a young version of a singer I liked named Cher. I politely excused myself from the pretty girl and walked over to the woman behind the counter. She introduced herself in her sultry South American voice. "What a pleasure to meet you. "I am Luciana," she said.

I put my hand out to greet her and introduced myself. We started talking and soon we ignored everyone around us. We searched for words that took us deeper and deeper into each other's world. She told me she came from Brazil. As we talked a special, song started playing. It was the great bossa nova classic by Joao Gilberto and Vinicus de Moraes "The Girl from Ipanema." My thoughts drifted back in time and took me to my prison cell where I use to wait by the radio to listen to it. It was a strange place to hear a song of love, sitting on my bed in a maximum-security prison.

Almost every day Mark Simone, a radio personality on WNEW AM radio, played it. This was the only radio station I could get because my radio did not have an antenna. It didn't break off or anything like that. The prison rules forbade you possessing an antenna. When I ordered my radio through a mail order company, I had to request that they remove the antenna. The prison administration said an antenna could be turned into a weapon.

The song touched my soul that contained images of a beautiful girl from the beaches of Ipanema, in Rio De Janeiro, Brazil. Every time I heard that song, love and romance from a distant unfamiliar place filled my head. The song was a tool I used to lift me out of my psychological confinement and bring me to a place I wanted to be. Now, many years later, here I was with the girl I had imagined in the song.

As we talked a tall male continuously squeezed between us, making believe he was searching for something behind the bar. It was obvious he was trying to distract us. "Who's that I whispered?" "Kevin, my husband", she replied. I looked at her in disbelief. "It's OK she said. He is gay." It was then that I found out that Luciana lived with her husband at the performance space and had a marriage of convenience. Kevin had a boyfriend named Shawn, a well know photographer. Together they were a trio, until I entered the picture. We talked for hours just looking into each other's eyes. The timing was just right. She told me she had just broken up with her boyfriend and I was alone looking for that special love. It was such a magical time of my life. Everything was fresh and new, so Zen like. Life was beautiful.

The exhibit closed down at about 10 pm. Luciana shook my hand and said goodnight to me. I looked into her eyes and they told another story. I took the elevator down and waited outside the building on the corner. About 10 minutes later Luciana had exited the building and walked to the corner where I had waited. She was with her girlfriend, Adrian. I was with my friend, Frankie. It started to rain hard. A drunken patron from the art show had grabbed a cab and tried to talk Luciana into getting in the car. She looked at me. I waved and she came. I invited her for a drink. We went to a Cuban restaurant located on the corner of 15th and 6th avenue and sat downstairs near a fireplace. The heat from the burning logs warmed us from the damp clothing we wore. The four of us sat in two lounge sofas. I pulled open my bag, began telling her about my former life, and ruined marriage. She listened intensely to every word. I even took out my divorce papers to show her I was available. She laughed.

We ordered white wine and started to drink. Twenty minutes later she got up to go to the bathroom. I followed and waited outside. When she walked out, I grabbed her arm and gently pushed her against the wall. We embraced and at that special moment, our lips touched. It was the beginning of a romance. I was now lost in her love

Luciana had run away from Brazil when she turned 18. She had a dream of becoming a famous dancer. She was trained in classical ballet and had a dance partner from Brazil named Marcello. Her dream took her to NYC where she met Kevin who ran Solo Arts; it was the home to many upcoming performers that would become famous. This included Janeane Garofalo, Amy Poehler, and the Upright Citizens Brigade comedy troupe.

A few days later, we made love for the first time. Luciana thought I was going to die. My body shook like an earthquake and my breath disappeared. I tried to speak. My lips moved but no sound reached her ears. I had had no intimacy or sex for the entire 12 years I spent in prison. We held each other for what seemed an eternity. I felt so secure in her arms. It made me remember when I wished I could love someone with real arms and lips instead of the paper faces I kissed in Playboy magazines to supplement my non-existent love life while I was in prison. Abruptly my dream like state came to a halt when I heard the elevator door open. My eyes drifted down the 12-foot ladder that I had to climb to reach her loft bed. It was Kevin walking around the space looking for her. He threw his head up and began to sniff the air.

I looked at Luciana and she put her finger to her lips signaling me to be quite. Now, I understood why she told me not to wear too much of my cologne. I use to plaster it on and you could smell me a mile away. He became jealous of our love and wanted to end our relationship. Luciana was the third wheel of his love relationship between himself and Shawn. He did not want to end it. Magically, the love Luciana and I had was strong and I knew it was the end of their relationship and the beginning of ours.

The next day Luciana asked me to go to the movies with her. She took me to the Quad on 13th and 6th in NYC. We saw a foreign film titled "Prisoner of the Mountain". I was shocked at the price of a movie ticket which was eight dollars. The last time I went to one, as a free man, was over twelve years ago. The price was about three dollars and fifty cents. We bought a bag of popcorn and a Pepsi soda. We sat in the middle of the theater. Just before the film started, two guys sat down in front of us. One was very tall, the other was very short. The movie began and I was talking to Luciana. All of a sudden, the short guy turned around and told me not to talk.

This triggered a deep emotional demon. I automatically went into prison survival mode, flashing back to the chapel at Sing Sing where they showed films to the prison population. In that place, everyone had regular seats to sit in no matter what. It was claimed property in a theater full of violence. If you sat in someone's regular seat a fight would always break out. It was a place where people paid the price of admission in blood. Stabbings, drug deals and sex took the place of popcorn and soda in that theater. I snapped back at the guy, "Why don't you move your seat".

My hair curled on the back of my neck. Luciana caught the mood swing and quickly tried to pull me back. She gently placed her hand on my face and said in a stern voice 'Tony calm down". Our eyes met and she managed to calm down the savage beast within that tried to surface rearing its ugly head. I quickly calmed down. It made me realize something important. Maybe it was because I was free now. I didn't have to think about the consequences like I did in prison where my life could be on the line because of a simple incident like this.

This is how I survived in prison. I always thought of my actions. In prison, there was nowhere to run to hide from incidents. They always caught up with you, no matter how small or large they were. A friend, Patty, who was doing time for murder had a small exchange of words with another prisoner in Sing Sing. It was nothing more than a petty argument. Two years later in another prison, Patty was in a shower and seemingly from out of nowhere, the same guy snuck up on him and sliced his face with a razor. This was the way of life inside.

I snapped back to the present and suddenly realized I was still a prisoner of the many years of suppressed emotions that were sitting inside of me that were waiting to be released. I felt humbled by this realization. The short guy looked at me and made a face as if he was a tough guy. He turned away and slumped back into his seat. I smile and looked at Luciana who kissed me on my cheek. She had become my savior. I was falling deeply in love with her.

CHAPTER FIVE

HBO's Oswald Penitentiary

S oon after the group show, Gareth Brown began getting calls from people that were interested in seeing my art. Several of these requests came from organizations that worked with troubled youth who were also ex-offenders. The first was from a woman named Carla White who worked for the Alcoholism Counsel of New York. She asked if I would be able to speak to three groups of graduates from different Alternatives to Incarceration programs. The most rewarding was speaking to about 25 young men who had just completed a shock incarceration program two weeks before.

This event was offered to eligible criminal offenders who had committed non-violent crimes. Instead of being sentenced to prison, they participated in a short-term military-like basic training program that included intensive hard physical labor, drug treatment and academic education. Christopher Wren, a reporter with the New York Times, came with a photographer. He was doing a story on the impact of the War on Drugs and was interested in what I had to say.

As the men looked at my art, they saw powerful images of incarceration; I spoke to them about myself. Since most of them only spent under a year in a program instead of prison, they listened very intently. My paintings really made a connection with them. They felt what

I felt when the prison experience took over my life. Looking at their faces, I actually saw several of these young men with tears in their eyes. I don't think they realized how terrible prison was until they saw the images I created while I was incarcerated. The thought of spending many years behind bars probably never entered their minds. One of the guys got a six-month alternative to prison shock program for drug sale that involved a kilo of cocaine.

Another had a case where he sold eight ounces of heroin. In both of these cases, these individuals could have gotten the same 15 years to life sentence that I had gotten. Instead, they were lucky enough to get a break. They now knew it. When the presentation was over, I shook hands with all of the men. Ms. White told me how she and the men were touched by the experience. It made me feel good.

The next day Gareth got a call from Debbie Sergeant a producer that was part of team creating a new show for HBO called Oswald Penitentiary "OZ". She wanted to come and see my art to see if they possibly could use a piece or two for the credit roll in the show. I was introduced to her by Richard Stratton, a gifted writer and filmmaker who had done some time for a drug crime.

Debbie came by the gallery, liked the work, and asked for a set of slides. A few days later I got a call from her saying that she and her co-producer thought that perhaps just using the paintings would be too bland. She said, "I want to throw this at you". We got an idea for the opening of the show. There is a convict painting in his cell. After a while, he loses it and starts breaking up the cell. He goes over to his easel, picks up his painting, punches his fist through the canvas, then the show starts. How about you playing the part? I was taken back for a while as I thought about it. Sure, I said "why not?' She called me back with more details and told me she would commission me to paint two copies of the painting that help me obtain my freedom.

Debbie saw my self-portrait "15 to Life" hanging in the exhibit. I originally painted the piece in 1988 while sitting in a cell in Sing Sing prison. It depicted the reality of imprisonment, capturing the despair and hopelessness of being incarcerated. At first, I was taken aback by the prospect of painting a copy of it. I had not painted since I was in prison.

I panicked asking "how about if we made a photo print of the piece?" She said a paper copy wouldn't work. "You need to paint it," she said. I hesitated, took a deep breath and thought about the moment I created that piece. I had picked up a mirror and saw an image of man who was to spend the most productive years of life in a cage. I picked up an 18X24 canvas and captured that moment in time.

"OK" I said, I will do it. Debbie said "great" she would talk to her co-producer Chrissy Davis because of a waiver of the actor's equity. Afterward Mark Baker, the production manager, called me and said they would pay me $750.00 dollars for everything. I agreed. It was considerably more than I was making in prison working for 60 cents a day. I told him I would need to buy some art supplies and he asked me how much it was cost. I really had no idea of the cost of materials but took a shot at estimating it and said a hundred dollars. "Bring me a receipt," he said. I went down to Pearl Paint, an art supply store on the lower east side of NYC. When I arrived at the store, I was overwhelmed with choices to make.

The store was gigantic and filled with a tremendous amount of art supplies. It was a completely different experience shopping in person than by mail catalogue; the way I use to get supplies back in prison. Back then, almost every product I wanted was considered contraband because it could be made into a weapon. I picked up two 18x24 canvases, a set of acrylic paints, a palette knife, 3 pencils, and a wooden palette. The best item I bought was a beautiful blue pencil sharpener that was encased in glass. I also wanted to buy some brushes but I didn't because I had already gone over the hundred-dollar quote.

I took a cab from Pearl and went directly to the apartment that Luciana was subleasing from her girlfriend in the lower east side. I asked her if I could paint there since painting at my mother's house would not work. She agreed and went away for the weekend to the New Jersey shore so I was alone. Once I got to the apartment, I set up to paint. I took the palette and filled it with globs of fresh acrylic paint.

I brought over the small wooden easel I had bought while I was in prison some 11 years ago. When I left Sing Sing it was one of the few possessions I brought home with me. I positioned a chair in front of the easel and stared at the blank canvas. I thought it was ironic that I would be painting the same piece that set me free from bondage.

I didn't know if I could duplicate it the same way I did back in 1988 when it was created. To help me do so I got the original painting from my mother's house and set it up in a chair next to the easel. I looked at the portrait. It looked back at me. In a way, I owed my life to it. It was chosen by artist Mike Kelly to hang in his installation "Pay for Your Pleasure" at the Whitney Museum 1994. His curator, Elizabeth Sussman, had contacted the prison and asked if they could borrow a piece of art from a prisoner at Sing Sing. The request was channeled to me and I sent some photos of my art. My self-portrait was chosen and it hung in the Whitney. From this experience, I got tremendous media exposure and it caught the ear of Governor Pataki who granted me executive clemency two years later. I literally painted my way to freedom.

I thought about the emotions that compelled me to create this piece. It was a very sad time of my life. I had lost everything, faced with the reality of spending twelve more years in a 6 X 9 cage. I was alone in the apartment. It reminded me of the solitude of prison. However, something was missing. I started to sweat and went into the bathroom to wash my face. The bathroom was very small.

I looked in the mirror and started to feel the same feeling I had when I lived in my 6x9 cell. Suddenly the answer dawned on me. I grabbed the easel and supplies and set up in the bathroom. It was tiny just like my cell. I set the original painting on the sink and sat in the chair. I shut my eyes and tried to evoke the feelings I had had when I was incarcerated. I thought about the daily deprivation that became part of my reality. When I opened my eyes, I was back in prison in my mind. The walls of the bathroom seemed to close in on me. I felt the pain and sorrow once again; the feeling I needed in order to create. My hands began to move as if they were controlled from the memory of creating the original painting.

With one deliberate and strong movement I dipped my brush into my palette soaking up some mars black paint. I hit the canvas with a sharp stroke and admired the results. I was happy that I began my journey back as an artist in the free world. It took me a day and a half to complete the two pieces. One was a finished piece and the other was half finished to show the stages of creation for the "OZ show. I was proud of my work. It looked even better than the original. I felt powerful to be able to create and paint once again.

A few days later, I went to the studio of the "OZ" production. It was located on the sixth floor in a warehouse on 15th street in NYC. I was met by Mark Baker. He escorted me to the shoot. We began walking through the set. The space was amazing and it looked like a real prison. We stopped along the way and Mark told me of the authenticity or non-authenticity of certain sets.

He escorted me to wardrobe where an intern brought me out a tank top, pair of gray pants and a prison shirt with an ID number. I changed in the booth and walked to makeup. As the makeup artist worked on me, she commented about the scar on my head. She asked if she could photograph it. I asked why. She told me that she had to do a scar for a shoot the week before and had trouble designing it. I agreed and told her if she copied it correctly, she might win an academy award for her work. We both laughed.

As she took photos, I thought about how I got the scar. The original scar occurred in 1979 when I got into a car accident and my head went through my windshield. The result was a one-inch scar on the left side of my forehead. When I came into the system, other convicts were telling me that I could get free medical attention. I decided to try to fix it. What a mistake that was. I went to see the doctor he told me that cosmetic surgery was not allowed. I told him I had a problem with my right eye. This got my foot in the door. When I went to a specialist, I told him my right eyelid was almost cut off an auto accident. This resulted in fluid accumulating in the corner of my eye. The plan was to have surgery done on my eyelid and try to get a package deal when I went before the surgeon.

After several months, I was called out to go on a trip to the hospital. It was five in the morning when a cop came by my cell. "Hey Papa! Wake up, "You're going on a trip.

"Where am I going?" I said all I can tell you is that you're going to a hospital. The transportation officers couldn't tell the prisoners where they were going because of the possibility of a planned escape. This was a breach of security. They led me to the hospital area where a gate was located to the back road that cut through the prison. This is where the facility transportation vehicles were located. Before entering the van, I was secured for travel.

The officer wrapped a chain around my waist and looped it through the handcuffs that were placed on my hands. That wasn't all. When I started to climb into the van the other escort officer called me back out. He told the other guard that I wasn't secured enough. He placed a black box device on the handcuffs. This enclosed the cuffs like a chastity device. So that even if you had a handcuff key you could not open the cuffs. Next, my legs were roped with leg chains. They were so short that I had to shuffle my feet to walk. The two officers sat in the front of the van. Another prisoner sat secured near me but was separated from me by a metal linked fence that was wielded to the ceiling and the floor. It felt like I was in a dog cage. I asked the guard which hospital we were going to.

The guard in the passenger seat told us we were going to Fishkill Correctional Facility to receive the surgery. When we got to the prison I found out that it contained a clinic where they performed medical procedures for prisoners. The hospital was in the center of the facility. I was escorted to the waiting area. There were about a dozen prisoners from prisons all over New York State. To my surprise, most of them were there for nose jobs and wore bandages over their noses. In about two hours, I was called in to be examined. A female doctor examined my eyelid. She told me she could fix it and make it straight again. I told her about my scar. She agreed to fix it.

After the surgery, my one-inch scar was now two inches long. My eyelid was straight, but I couldn't close it all the way. I complained about the botched job. A month later, I returned to get it fixed. The second surgery was worse than the first resulting in my two-inch scar becoming three inches long. On top of that, the horizontal scar had become L shaped and my eyelid was the same.

During the second surgery, the new female doctor noticed the faint scar I had across the bridge of my nose. She asked if I wanted her to repair it. As she spoke, her assistant, a very attractive nurse began rubbing my leg. It felt so good to have so much attention and to feel the touch of another human being. I was in ecstasy and fully agreed, no doubt influenced by her affection and the anesthesia. The surgery was completed and I returned to Sing Sing.

I waited for about a month for the wound to heal and I requested another evaluation from a different doctor. I was sent to Fishkill again where another doctor told me that he could surely reduce my scare. All I had to do was have two balloons placed under my skin in the center of my forehead. He told me that this would stretch my skin so the scar wouldn't stretch while healing. The result would be a reduced scar. At that point, all I envisioned was me walking the yard at Sing Sing and a prisoner slapping me the forehead and blowing up my head. The result would not be too pretty. At that point, I decided to keep the three-inch scar and crooked eyelid. During the years to come, that tough guy look would be a blessing. It helped saved my life.

After makeup, I went to the set where my shoot was to happen. It contained a row of cells, four in total. Each cell had a doubled bunk bed and contained a footlocker, desk and toilet bowl. As we set up in one of the cells, I could feel there was something very strange about the cell. I went over to feel the cell bars and discovered they were made from wood instead of steel. I laughed and told the producer about it. "How did you know?" he said. I told him that being in a cell that was made out of steel for many years I could feel the difference.

The cameraman was crunched in the corner of the bottom of the bunk bed squeezing off shots. I sat in the chair in front of my easel simulating the act of painting. "Action" he yelled. I began to paint and after a couple of brush strokes, I stopped. The camera zoomed into my face while the half-done portrait was switched and in its place, the completed portrait took its place. I stared at the painting again, as my breathing increased. I thought about all the years I had spent in prison wasting away.

I turned around, picked up the chair, and threw it across the cell. Then I went over to the desk and with the back of my forearm started knocking off everything that was on it. I ran to the cell door and grabbed it with both hands while hyperventilating wildly. Then I turned to the easel, walked over and picked up the painting and held it in my left hand.

The camera zoomed in once again as I wound up my right arm and delivered a super punch to the middle of the painting landing the fatal blow dead center. A big thud was heard as my fist bounced off the canvas, instead of breaking through it. "Cut" yelled the camera man. We all stood there in silence as we looked at the painting. "OK" said the director, let's think of what to do. One of the crew suggested we cut the canvas with a razor blade. My teeth started to grind as the thought of destroying my painting came to me. Every painting I ever created became as though it was a child of mine. I had nurtured its growth to see the piece come alive and now I was about to cut its life away.

"What's wrong?" said the cameraman. "Nothing" I said, as two members of the shooting crew held the painting while another made a sign of the cross slice with the razor on the back of the painting. The piece was put back on the easel and the shoot continued. We went through the scene from the point where I held the painting high and then I slowly cocked my right arm back and followed through successfully punching my fist through the canvas.

I froze in time as I looked at the huge hole in the painting that still held my fist and part of arm. I remembered when I painted the original back in 1988 sitting in my cell in Sing Sing. My life was in shambles as I thought about the twelve remaining years I had to serve. I was so depressed I thought about suicide and ending it all. A round of applause from the crew awoke me from my trance. "Great job Tony!" said the producer. You must have done this many times before. "Yeah" I muttered while looking at the broken painting that once helped me paint my way to freedom. No one could understand how important the image was to me. Now it stood there ruined. Let's wrap it up the foreman of the crew told us all. I packed my gym bag with my paints and shook hands with the crew. The two copies of the paintings stood discarded on the floor, in the corner of the cell, as I walked away.

As I headed to the accounts department to pick up my check, I walked through the main set where I saw the famous actress Rita Moreno sitting at a table. She played a psychologist on the show. I walked over to her. "Hello, my name is Anthony Papa and I painted my way to freedom" I said. She smiled. "I know, I heard of you" she replied. I was aghast. "Wow", I said to myself, Rita Moreno knows who I am. I sat down at the table. "I am a big fan of yours". She smiled again. I then pulled my camera out of my gym bag and asked her if she would take a photo with me. "No" she shouted out looking startled.

I thought it was strange that she suddenly became indignant. I guess it was because she had no makeup and didn't look quite as young and pretty as she was when she stared in East Side Story on Broadway many years ago. I smiled and said goodbye to her.

On the way out I was stopped by a staff member that had watched me performing my part. "You were pretty good," she said. "Did you ever consider acting? I could introduce you to someone who might be able to get you on the show". I froze when I thought about giving her an answer. It was one of those moments in time where the answer could affect the rest of my life. I just got a job with a law firm as a litigation paralegal. It was a steady job that paid the bills and even provided medical insurance. I really knew nothing about acting. The only experience I had was in elementary school where I played a slave in a play called Amal and the Night Visitors. I tried out for the lead role and didn't get it. I then tried out for the role of the slave and screamed out all my lines because I was angry I didn't get the lead.

My teacher interpreted the screaming as significant attribute for the role and she thought I would be perfect. I got the part and got rave reviews for my acting. Despite my success in my acting role as a kid, I now turned down the offer to try to get me a part on the show. "No thanks" I said, short and sweet. It was a decision I was to regret many years later. "Oz" went on to become a big hit on HBO. The piece shot for the opening of "OZ" was cut, but a small piece was left in the new opening credit sequence of the first season. I watched myself in the title opening each week of the first season and wondered what my life would be like if I had tried my hand at acting.

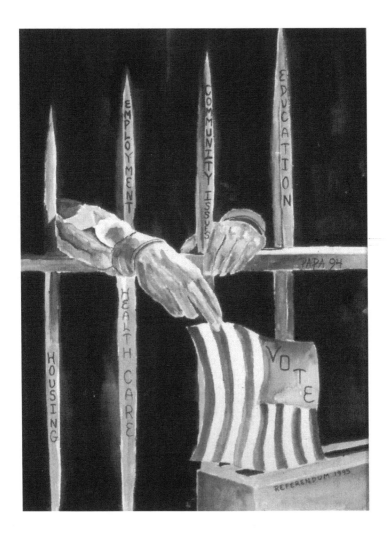

CHAPTER SIX

The Vote

O ne of the most important things I wanted to do when I was released from prison in 1997 was to vote. In prison, I had lost many of my civil rights including the ability to vote. I remember while I was in Sing Sing I addressed this issue by painting a piece titled the "Vote." It was an 18 x 24 watercolor of a pair of hands protruding cell bars while holding a voting ballot hovering over a ballot box. The cell bars were adorned with descriptions of issues that affected my community like housing, employment, and taxes. It was a powerful piece of art that I displayed in Albany at an annual art show for prisoners.

Now I was free, I had a place to live and a good job. My next move was to finally cast a vote. It had been many years since I had voted. But when I went to register to vote I was told I was not eligible to vote because I was on parole. This totally disappointed me because at that time my South Bronx neighborhood was deteriorating and there were many community issues I wanted to voice my opinion on through voting. I experienced the pain of felony disenfranchisement and felt I was being punished further from the crime I had committed despite paying my debt to society. I was told I had to wait five years until I got off parole to cast my vote. I thought that the ability to vote was very important because it was part of the rehabilitation process. This was because it would show I was being accepted back into society as a citizen. I waited five long years and then when I became eligible to vote in 2003 I contacted reporter Ellis Henican an award-winning journalist for Newsday who agreed to write and publish a story of me casting my first vote in a piece titled "Ex-Con Free to Vote His Conscience":

He walked into the polling place in a dark-gray coat and nicely shined shoes. Voting clothes. This was a little after 9 o'clock yesterday morning at PS 78, the Robert Wagner Jr. Elementary School, which is tucked into the first floor of one of the new high-rises by the water in Long Island City. The bright lights were humming. The sign said "Election District 19." Children's drawings were taped to the walls. "Anthony Papa," he said to the woman at the table. "Papa. P-A-P-A." "Pappas?" the woman asked, looking up from her computer printouts. "Papa," he said again. "Like Mama. Papa." The woman nodded and ran a finger down her list of names. "Here you are, "she said. "Sign your name and take this card to the man over there." After 17 years - 12 in prison, five on parole and one false start in September - Anthony Papa, painter, ex-felon and dedicated drug-law reformer, was finally exercising his constitutional right to vote. As far as New York State is concerned, he's finally paid his debt and is permitted to vote again. That may not sound like much to some people. This is a country, after all, where two-thirds of the people don't even bother voting in most elections.

But try telling that to a man who's had his right to vote taken away. Watch him turn into a voting zealot, right before your eyes. "Actually, I tried to vote in the primary in September," Tony Papa said before he stepped inside the big booth yesterday. "I had trouble with the machine. It was kind of embarrassing, actually." But that wasn't going to happen again. Papa's troubles go back to 1985, when he went to prison under New York's Rockefeller drug laws. It was his first - and his last – criminal conviction.

"I met a guy in a bowling alley where I used to bowl," he recalled. "He asked me if I wanted to make some money. He said he heard I was having a tough time, which I was. "Business was slow. I had rented space in a garage, installing car alarms and radios. I was behind in my rent. I had a wife and a young daughter. "This guy told me, 'Bring this envelope to a place in Mount Vernon. You'll make 500 bucks.' I went into the place. Must have been 20 undercover cops came out of nowhere." Papa went to trial - stupidly. He was convicted after two days. Obviously, he was a tiny player in the drug business. But under the mandatory sentencing of the rigid Rockefeller laws, the judge had no room for mercy.

He sent the defendant to Sing Sing for 15 years to life. Papa did his time productively. He found inside himself the talent to paint. His artwork was praised by serious critics. He painted a gut-wrenching self-portrait he called "15 years to life." "I looked into a mirror one day and saw an individual who was spending the most productive years of his life in prison," Papa said. "Seven years later, that painting was hanging in the Whitney Museum of Art." That amazing prison achievement got some pickup in the media. Art dealers wrote letters, asking about other work. Pressure began to build. He was a first-time nonviolent offender. He had all this talent. Wasn't 12 years enough? On Jan. 23, 1997, Gov. George Pataki signed a clemency order, releasing the artist-inmate three years early. Papa stayed busy. He went to work as a legal assistant at a large Midtown firm. "From the Rockefeller Law to Rockefeller Center," he liked to say. He joined the fight to reform the Rockefeller drug laws. He lobbied in Albany. He traveled to Washington. He helped to create a group called the New York Mothers of the Disappeared, adding the voices of family members to the drug-reform debate.

But reform has been slow. Pataki courted Papa and his friends, promising big changes. But the proposals from the governor's office added up to tiny reforms. "If he wanted to change these laws," Papa said, "Pataki could go into an office with Shelly Silver and come out in an hour with a compromise." When the governor's race heated up, Tony Papa made a commercial for Tom Golisano, the rich businessman from Rochester who wasn't a natural fit on many issues - but was dead-on with the issue of drug-law reform. His drug-reform commercials brought the issue millions of dollars in publicity. Now it was time for Tony Papa to vote. He stepped into the booth. He pulled the curtain. He was in there for several minutes, making sure he did everything right. Then he pulled the curtain back.

"Some people have said to me, 'The governor gave you your freedom. How could you not vote for him?' It's a good question. "I thank him for my freedom," Tony Papa said. "But he's been selling us nothing but a dream. It really breaks your heart to see these old women on a cane or a walker, dying while their son or daughter stays in prison." So many other people are counting on us. I couldn't waste my vote."

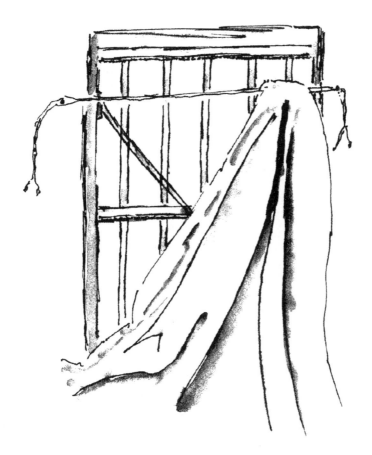

CHAPTER SEVEN

Artistic Dreams

In prison, I discovered my talent as an artist. In reality, art saved my life and helped me retain my humanity. More importantly, it became a cathartic tool by using my canvas to paint away the pain of my imprisonment. Prison wasn't the most conductive venues to paint in. For one thing, most of the materials used were considered contraband. Oil paints and paint thinner were not allowed because they were considered to be materials that you could make bombs out of.

Privacy was an issue. It eluded me because of the way of life in prison. You were confined to such a small area that you rarely had moments to be alone. You had to work to create ways to have private time. One of the best for me was the old "curtain over the shoelace routine", a technique that sent an automatic "stay away" signal to unwanted visitors. Imagine three well-worn sheets splattered with paint, hanging over a pair of old shoestrings, stretched like a clothesline across the front of my cell. This was a simple but effective tool for keeping away individuals and making the space I needed to be creative. It worked most of the time. The unwritten social rules of prison dictated that when one saw that a curtain hung across a cell it meant privacy was needed. It was the equivalent of a do not disturb sign. However, some people couldn't read or didn't want to grant privacy to others.

One guy in the housing block in which I lived had no respect for closed cell doors or curtains. It was this big, six foot two guy who was doing ten to twenty for armed robbery. His name was Juice. Well it was really Arthur, but he hated that name. He had a bad habit of coming by and wanting to have a conversation when I wanted to be alone. Every day at about 3:30 in the afternoon, Juice made his presence known. Every day he would walk through the big iron gate of the housing unit we lived in and yell "Honey I'm home." He told me that it was to check up on me, see if I was all right. I thought it was abuse, but he'd argue it was concern for my wellbeing.

One day I had my curtain in its usual position. It hung high above the eye level of the traffic that passed back and forth. I was busy painting a magnificent work entitled "After the Whitney." It was a surreal view of my life after having my work exhibited at the Mike Kelly retrospective at the Whitney Museum of American Art in 1994, while I was in prison.

It was created one night while sitting in my cell, three years into my sentence, I picked up a mirror and saw the face of an individual who would spend the most productive years of his life in a cage. I then picked up a canvas and painted the image I saw. The painting was foreboding and dark, and captured the total agony of imprisonment. It became my greatest masterpiece.

Several years later, the piece, titled "15 to Life," was exhibited at the Whitney Museum of American Art. Now I stood there in front of my sink looking at the painting I was working on. It took me almost 3 months to develop, and like a flower in bloom, my canvas was finally coming alive. Everything was merging together, growing like a living organism. "Yo, you in there!

He yelled. I did not answer. Maybe he'll go away, I said to myself, absorbing the beauty of my painting and watching the hard lines drip into softness. "Yo man, I know you're in there," he said, in a high wail. It was the kind of noise that could crack solid concrete.

"I know you're in there! Answer me, do you miss me?" He yelled. I hated those words. Every day he come by and asked that same stupid question, do you miss me? He never left until I responded. I ran to the back of my cell, hoping to escape, but realized there was no place to go.

"My God", I said. "What can I do?" I looked around my 6 x 9 cell and sized it up and down. There was nowhere to hide.

I'd have to respond or he would never leave. One time he had stood there, for two hours, waiting. "No! I shouted. I don't miss you!" "Now get the fuck away from my cell, I'm busy!"

"Awwwwww come on - you know you miss me!" "Look!" I screamed. "I got no time for this bullshit! I'm painting!" No response. Not even a peep. He knew I meant business. Painting was my life. It's what I lived for.

"Thank you God" I said, out loud, looking at the cross hanging over the doorway. I started to paint again, totally absorbed in the sensations I felt while stroking my brush against the creamy surface of the canvas. "I KNOW YOU MISS ME"! He shouted. Now I was really pissed! "Hit the road you jerk! Beat it! SCRAM! Get out of my face!"

He replied through the curtain, which fluttered. His breath, just like a dragon's, so hot it almost ignited it. "Look", he said. "I told you about dissing me, man." "When I talk, you respond!" "You'd give an aspirin a headache, you big, stupid jerk! I told you! I'm busy! Hit the road! Vamoose!" As I continued to paint, I listened for a response. The corner of my eyes noticed an unsightly invasion. An oversized brown hand reached through the curtain and tugged on the shoestrings. They snapped. The sheets fell. I lunged to catch them, and tripped on the leg of the chair. I lost my balance. My hand slid across the wet canvas. The sheets were on the floor in front of me. I felt naked, exposed. There he was standing in front of me baring his teeth. "You see," he gestured, "you're not busy at all."

I turned, and looked at my painting. In the middle of the canvas a muddy streak appeared in the place of well detailed area that took me 6 weeks to complete. It was an abstract curve that tucked and dipped in an attractive fashion. I was steaming and the sweat rolled off my brow and down my nose. I bit my lower lip. My heart pounded. Adrenaline started to circulate causing my mind to spin. I turned my head and our eyes met. We stared each other down. "Do you miss me?" he said. I looked at him in disbelief. I was crushed. My head hung, looking at the curtains on the floor, and I said, softly, "Yeah, I miss you. Would you get out of here now?" When Arthur left my cell, I sat on my bed and started thinking about him. Arthur needed to have a friend. He chose me whether I liked it or not. That's the way it was in prison. You had limited choices in the things you did the food you ate and the friends you had.

While in prison, because of exhibiting my work at the Whitney Museum, I developed interest from several art dealers who wanted to represent me. One of them was a businessman named Steve Kirsh who was part owner of the Hudson River Gallery in Ossining NY. Steve had read about me in the local paper and contacted Andrea Miller who lived in the town and was the keeper of my art. He was interested in giving me a show of my art. Several months later, I had a one-man show at the gallery. Although I was absent from the show it generated some press along with more interest in my work.

Since I knew very little about the art world, I contacted a famous artist named Larry Rivers. Rivers was an American master, who I had read about through my studies. I met him through Dave, one of my students in the art class I ran at Sing Sing. At first, I didn't believe he knew Rivers, but he proved it when he brought photographs of them together. Dave was quite a character and totally out of place at the prison. He was from East Hampton and in a drunken daze kidnapped a lesbian that stole his girlfriend from him. It would have been comical if not for the 10-year sentence he got for the crime. Besides his big mouth, he flaunted his privileged background and dropped famous names when he shouldn't have.

He refused to acknowledge he was in a place where your life could end because of a misplaced statement. I saved Dave's life when he dry snitched (inadvertently told) on himself and the landscaping crew, he worked with. The administration found out about the availability of their tools, which were being used as weapons. This put heat on the crew and resulted in several of them plotting Dave's demise. When I found out about this, I asked Big Don to intervene and he stopped it.

Here I was hoping to jump-start my art career. I began canvassing around the galleries of Manhattan with the hope of getting my work shown at a leading "Outsider" art gallery. Anne Nocenti who introduced me to Gareth had invited me to go to the Puck Building in NYC where they were holding a huge Outsider Art Exhibit with dozens of galleries from across the country participating. She wanted me to meet gallery owners in the hope I could get someone to represent me. I was nervous and didn't really know how to make a connection. Anne told me to watch her as she introduced herself to an art dealer from Chicago.

She then called me over. I held my breath and tried. I walked over to the dealer and introduced myself. We had a conversation and I walked away with the dealer's card, he had said to give him a call. "You see" she said with a smile, "it's easy". Yes, it was. I felt relieved in knowing that I had the ability to try to push my dream of being an artist in NYC. Everything was going well and my self-confidence was beginning to build. I had talked to several art dealers who seemed to have an interest in my art.

Then I saw her. It was Phyllis Kind, a big New York City dealer who had been in a New York Times article that featured me. It was written by Donatella Torch titled "Survival Found on the Tip of a Paint Brush". The article talked about my art saying how it was a means of strict survival and described my reality as a canvas of rage and sorrow, fear and hope. She went on to talk about how art had flourished in prisons and some art collectors had become increasingly attracted to self-taught artists like me.

Donatella stated some of the leading galleries in NYC including the Phyllis Kind Gallery. Ms. Kind was quoted as saying that the art had become a way of life for prisoners and that people in prison are more content when pulling something out of themselves. She said she was fascinated by imprisoned artist's obsessive involvement. I'm in I thought! There was no one I knew that had more obsessive involvement in my art than myself. I was on a roll and I approached Ms. Kind, "Hi", I said, "I am Anthony Papa". I made my mistake when I told her she was in "my" NY Times article "Survival on the Tip of a Paint Brush".

She looked at me as if I had just insulted her saying the NY Times story was about me – not her. She abruptly cut me off. "I don't care," she claimed in a very loud boisterous voice. I don't have time to talk to you. I couldn't believe how rude she was. I walked away with my tail between my legs. It was a wakeup call and an example of the reality I faced in trying to show my art in NYC.

Luciana and I continued to hit the gallery scene in the Chelsea section of Manhattan. One day I walked into Ricco/Maresca Gallery. It was a well-established gallery featuring Outsider Art. I spoke to a guy at the front desk named Steven. He told me to leave a set of slides there and he would talk to the owners about me. Two weeks later, I returned to find out if they had any interest in my work. Steven returned my slides to and told me that he doubted that the gallery would help me. He told me the story of how one of the owners had tried to help another ex-con that was released from prison. It did not work out and soon after the owner's life had been threatened by the ex-con he was trying to help. At that point, my dreams of exhibiting with the Ricco/Maresca Gallery went up in smoke. I continued to try to find representation in a major New York gallery. After experiencing rejection after rejection and running out of money, I decided to abandon my dream and look for a job.

PAPA 92

CHAPTER EIGHT

C- Span and Issues that Feed Mass Incarceration

D on't move motherfucker! You're under arrest!"
I was thrown to the ground and a pair cuffs were tightly slapped on my wrists by the undercover cop who told me I was going away for a long time. It was the day I got arrested that led to my imprisonment of a 15 to life sentence. I would never forget that moment. Now I was standing in the corridor of Bronx Supreme Court, watching the court officers taking away my client in cuffs, I squeezed my wrists with my hands. It brought back bad memories of my brush with the law.

It had been two months since my release and I had landed an unpaid intern position with the Fortune Society as a court advocate in their alternative to incarceration (ATI) program. I was being trained with the possibility of obtaining a paid job if I did well. The non-for-profit agency provided an array of re-entry services for both criminal defendants and ex-offenders. I was a liaison for those trying to stay out of prison and worked with lawyers, prosecutors and judges in trying to broker a way of preventing them from entering walking the road I had walked. I enjoyed traveling to courthouses in different parts of New York City but found it difficult in watching court proceedings.

One day in the Supreme Court of Bronx County I was interviewing a client in court before he had to appear before a judge. He had a substance abuse problem that I thought could be negotiated with a treatment program instead of putting him into a jail. About an hour later, to my surprise, they led him away to a holding pen where he would eventually go back to prison. This was too much for me to handle, because it brought back horrible memories of my arrest. I realized I was too wounded from my own experience to help others in similar situations, so I decided to look for another job.

At that point, I contacted David Plant, a senior partner at his law firm. I met Dave in prison where he belonged to a prison ministry program out of Rye Presbyterian Church. The members of the program visited graduates of the New York Theological Seminary program once a month and shared in dialogue. Dave invited me to go see his law firm with the prospect of possibly landing a job there. Fish & Neave was a boutique intellectual property firm and had been around for over one hundred years. It was one of the nation's most respected law firms in its field. It specialized in patents, trademarks and copyrights.

The firm had a track record of serving some of the most illustrious American inventors, including Thomas Edison, Alexander Graham Bell, Edwin Land, and the Wright brothers. By catering to clients in such fields as nuclear energy, fiber optics, computer technology, and telecommunications, it played an important role in the modern history of science, technology, and business. When I stepped into the firm's reception area, I felt like a fish out of water. The ride in the elevator to the 49th floor had taken the wind out of me. I felt embarrassed by the fact that I had hesitated in pushing the buttons on the control panel of the elevator because of its high tech look.

This was a recurrent problem I had with any contraption that was unfamiliar to me. The receptionist smiled and introduced herself as I approached her. I told her who I was and she handed me a standard employment form and asked me to answer the questions on it. The reception area was lavishly arranged with expensive furniture and amazing glass displays that contained inventions that the firm represented. There was even a model of the first airplane invented by their clients, the Wright Brothers, I looked around and was in awe. What blew my mind was the majestic view from its oversized glass windows where I could see all of Manhattan. I sat down on a couch and began answering the questions.

Everything went smoothly until I reached the line where it asked if I was ever convicted of a crime. There, on the application, was a box I had to check that indicated yes or no. I panicked, thinking about how it would look answering "yes." After all, I was a convicted felon. A panic came over me and made me think should I answer the question or not? I wondered how many ex-offenders have lied about their past when applying for a job. I knew from the information I had gathered sitting in the parole office where I talked to many former prisoners who told me that as soon as they answered that question truthfully their interviews were terminated. Many employers were very hesitant to hire ex-felons.

My parole officer talked to me about this problem and said most of her parolees would not be considered on equal status with other job applicants because of their criminal records. She thought it was unfair and said that a way to solve this problem would be to conduct a criminal background only during the final interview process if it is being relevant or required for the position. From her experience, she saw one of the biggest barriers for individuals re-entering society from incarceration is finding employment and one of the main reasons the rate of recidivism remains so high.

A lot of her clients told her that when filling applications, they had to check a "yes" or "no" box if they have ever been convicted of a felony and had had no opportunity for them to provide an explanation of the crime, the circumstances or date of the conviction, or any rehabilitation that has been completed since being charged. It was a no win situation for them.

I thought about my situation. I was recommended for a job by one of the big partners of the firm. So, the firm would know about my past anyway. I checked the box yes and even squeezed in additional information which told of my 15- to-life sentence for a non-violent drug crime. I handed the form to the receptionist and left feeling as though my past would prevent me from ever getting a job. The next day, to my surprise, I got a call from the firm telling me I had been hired on a part time basis. I was happy beyond belief!

Things at the firm went smoothly until I made a mistake of exposing my checkered past through the media. I was invited by C-Span to be a guest commentator on a special they were doing about the history of the formation of the American penitentiary. The show was taped on C-Span's specially equipped bus that was a television studio on wheels. It sat on property that faced opposite Sing Sing prison in Ossining NY. Before the interview, I had a confrontation with a guard on the tower that tried to stop me taking a photo of a gun tower. I had walked to the wall and was intrigued by the shape of the tower and how it looked from the outside of the prison after years of looking at it from the inside. The prison rules were against taking any photos on the grounds of the prison because it was a breach of security. I took one anyway and panicked, the tower guard screamed at me and ran inside the tower to get his rifle. I ran for my life and managed to get into the bus just in the nick of time and avoided being caught by guards in a van dispatched to the area.

I was scared to death because if they found me I would have violated my parole. I sat down and was hyperventilating, thinking of the consequences of my actions. I could have been in custody and would have probably lost my freedom. As I looked around the C-Span bus, I was astonished. The bus was loaded with high tech TV production equipment. It was a studio on wheels which contained robotically controlled TV cameras, recording decks and electronic gadgets that looked like they were from a spaceship for a scientific expedition. The producer handed me a glass of water and asked me to come to the back of the bus.

I passed by a glass enclosure that had an entrance in it. Behind the entrance was a table and a chair. In front of the table was a camera and to its right was a wall with two television screens. The producer asked me to sit down and the camera man began to adjust it so he could get a clear picture of the view directly over my right shoulder looking out of a window. Through the window you could see the gun tower that almost cost me my freedom. The bus had been tilted on an angle so that its right side was higher than its left, which enabled the camera to view the prison over my shoulder while I spoke. It added to the intensity of the moment and was good TV.

As I looked straight into the camera above it I could see myself on the monitor. The producer clipped a wireless mike on my shirt and stuck a jack in my right ear. He told me he was connecting me to C-Span founder Brian Lamb in Washington DC. After the connection, Lamb introduced himself and explained what he wanted me to do. I was to look at the television screen on the right hand side of the camera where they were going to roll footage they shot when they went into Sing Sing the week before. He wanted me to comment to the viewers on what I saw.

The program would focus on the past, present and future of the U.S. Penal System using Sing Sing as an example. Brian also told me that I would be having a discussion with James Gondles, the Executive Director of the American Correctional Association, about the continuing debate between rehabilitation and punishment, we would take phone calls from the television audience. I thought it would be a perfect opportunity to use my story as a prime example of the insanity of the War on Drugs and the use of mandatory sentencing laws.

I told him I would do my best. As I looked around, I caught a glance of myself on one of the TV monitors. There I was looking scared and angry. The incident with the guard on the tower awoke many suppressed feelings of the dehumanizing experience of imprisonment. As I thought about this, my eyes focused on my white shirt and the tie I was wearing. My co-worker Roberto from the law firm gave me his special tie to wear. He told me that in order to make a good impression I should wear his red power tie.

"Red" is the color of power, "Go there and be powerful." He said. Roberto was a good guy and had taken me under his wing to show me the ropes at the job. He reminded me of my friend Indio who taught me how to paint and do time when I got to Sing Sing. I stared at the necktie and thought about what he had said. I was going to be on national television. What people would see was not only me. I was going to represent hundreds of thousands of prisoners incarcerated in the United States. I had to represent a former prisoner in a positive way that would convince the viewing audience that prisoners were human beings and deserved a second chance in their lives. I was going to be interviewed live and they couldn't sensor what I was going to say.

I had to carefully balance my feelings of oppression in order to achieve my goal of changing the brutal drug laws that imprisoned me. The prison was about fifty yards away from the bus. Close enough to make me feel its past, but too far away to control me as it did for all those years.

The show opened up with Brian Lamb announcing what the program would cover. He told the audience the names of his scheduled guests, but surprisingly he didn't mention my name. Instead, he said he had a surprise guest sitting in the C-Span bus. I think this was because C-Span did not want the prison to know I was going to be on. They too felt intimidated. Maybe it was because of the incident I had with the tower guard. If the prison had any idea I was involved with the show they would have tried to stop it.

C-Span announced to the audience that they were going to show some footage of the prison that was shot 2 weeks prior and warned people that the e garbage bags. People live in these cells for ten to twenty years at a time with no access to any type of modern appliances. Almost everything is considered contraband. No metal wood or glass is allowed. Your cell comes equipped with a metal cot with a mattress and a small footlocker." I said. The camera then focused in on the toilet bowl in the cell. It was wrapped in a brown towel to make it look fancy.

I said, "I knew some guys who used their toilets as refrigerators. Lambs face dropped in horror. That's how bad it got in there. But on the other hand, in the world of prison, believe it or not, this was considered living good in prison." I knew as I spoke that the general population had no clue of what life was living in a maximum-security prison. It would be an eye opening experience for most of them.

Brian Lamb knew this and was pleased with my commentary. He then asked Jim "How does Sing Sing prison compare to others you've seen?" Gondles said, "Well, this prison again is an old prison. It's over a hundred and fifty years old. Many cell sizes are larger today. In New York State, they are having a terrible situation with scenes they were about to show which were graphic. Lamb even suggested that if children were around the footage might be too strong for them. Suddenly the monitor I was watching was flooded with scenes from the C-Span camera crew-walking pass the A – Block yard. It was a startling scene to see dozens of prisoners cursing and swearing behind the fences that held them. I guess it was typical of prisoners to voice their anger at their confinement to the media. Based on my personal experience I could not blame them. To my puzzlement, now a free person sitting on the other side of the fence, they looked as though they were wild animals out of control. The scene shifted to another part of the prison when the camera crew traveled inside of the A Block housing unit. The noise level was tremendously high with prisoners yelling and cursing at the C-Span crew from their cells.

"Motherfuckers suck my dick" one prisoner yelled as they showed him pointing to his crotch. It looked downright scary and made me think how in the world I ever survived that hellhole. After a few moments passed, the scene changed once again when the cameras took the viewing audience to the outside area behind the prison chapel. It showed the complete opposite of the mass confusion inside of the prison. It was now suddenly peace and quiet with the viewing audience looking at a very sober and quiet shot of the prison surrounded by lush green grass and the beautiful Hudson River. The shot eventually faded away and returned to its host Brian Lamb.

Little did the audience know that the chapel was home to extraordinary violence and corruption. It housed several different religious groups including Catholic, Jewish and Muslim denominations, however, religion did little to stop the horrible conditions of imprisonment.

It seemed that even God could not save the chapel's participants from the prison's unhealthy and perverse environment. I remember in 1988 a female guard was busted giving a convict head in a room in the chapel. Upon an investigation, the prison administration found the guard to part of a female prostitution/drug ring that operated in the prison. Violence was also prevalent there and raids were routinely made; finding stashes of weapons hidden behind statues of saints and pews.

Brian Lamb then introduced his first guest who was James Gondles of the American Correctional Association. Gondles explained that his organization was an association that represented correctional professionals mainly throughout the United States, formed in 1870. It was one of the oldest continuously existing associations in the United States. Lamb then introduced me and asked me to comment on some footage of the prison that was being shown to the audience. This is why I was chosen to be on the show. Who better could explain in detail what was being shown to the TV audience. I had spent twelve years at the prison and knew it inside out. I was honest and explained that the footage showed a prime example of the overcrowding of New York State's prisons.

They were literally bursting out of its seams, mostly filled with non-violent Rockefeller Drug Law offenders who had committed low-level drug crimes. I looked intensely into the camera and listed a torrid of problems I saw with the system. My voice was stern and steady as I said that there were over seventy thousand individuals locked up in NYS prisons. There were no college programs, limited education available and that even vocational training had been taken away. It was unbelievable, society is in this punitive mode of justice and it was not the answer. As I continued to list the atrocities of imprisonment, Lamb stopped me, and said "Tony Papa hold on a second and let me interrupt you. I want to get Jim Gondles in on this, Jim you been listening to this what reaction do you have?" Mr. Gondles responded and brought up an age-old question that has never been answered and had plagued our criminal justice system since its inception. He smiled and said, "Surprisingly I don't have a major amount of disagreement with Mr. Papa over the question of programing in a prison. I think Papa said something 'like everyone wants to do away with programs in prisons". Maybe a majority of our leaders throughout the country do. I think there are many correctional professionals, certainly in our association that realizes the value of programs. Education opens doors for people, it doesn't close them.

The question always becomes what is more important, is it more important to educate kids which are six years old that have never done anything wrong or offer education to someone who is in prison that is eighteen to twenty-five years of age. We, the American Correctional Association, advocate the use of programs within correctional facilities. I would argue too that one of the reasons for prisons is not solely for reforming the person, it's for punishment. Many people want to punish offenders and society needs to be protected from some individuals. Some folks need to be there for a long period of time." "Jim Gondles use to be the sheriff of Arlington County," said Lamb.

"Where is your home originally?" Gondles replied "Oklahoma, born and raised and educated there". "Tony Papa where are you from" asked Lamb. "Bronx New York", I quickly shot back. Lamb leaned back in his chair and poised a question "What are you going to do now since you are out of prison Mr. Papa." "Well Brian, frankly speaking I'm going to go on a rescue mission to save the lives of others I left behind in prison. Lamb looked amused and then asked his viewers to call into to ask questions. Brian went on to say they were going to show some video of the prison cells and asked me we to describe what I saw.

"Mr. Papa how many hours a day did you spend in that cell?" he asked. The screen showed a camera man slowly walking into a prisoner's cell and I cringed when I saw the footage. It brought a sickly feeling to my stomach. The windowless 6x9 cell was practically empty except for a small cot and a desk. It wasn't fit for a dog, no less a human being to live in.

"I would say I spent about 12 hours a day in my cell and what the viewer is now seeing is A-Block. It resembles a giant airplane hangar with stacks of cages, three tiers high, with about six hundred and seventy men locked in cages like animals. There was mass confusion and systematic dehumanization everywhere you looked. The place was like a jungle where you didn't know for certain if you would live another day." The camera zoomed in with a close up of the inside of a cell where it focused on about a dozen garbage bags near a toilet bowl.

I hesitated and said, "What you see here is someone's life long belongings in 'suitcases" provided by the Corrections Department. In my judgment, they are doing an admirable job, a fantastic job. There are 69, 400 inmates in the New York system today as I speak to you. The New York taxpayer is spending one point four billion dollars there. At an average cost of twenty-seven thousand dollars a year per inmate. I understand that sometimes the conditions are not always like they are on the outside. They are not supposed to be. People have been put there because they have been adjudicated and found guilty by either a judge or a jury. One of the reasons they have been put there is for punishment. I would co-state that we firmly believe in programs and rehabilitation. Mr. Papa is an excellent example of this and it should show the nation that people can turn their lives around and we need to give them the tools in order to do that."

I wanted to respond and tell Gondles that although I might be a good example, but there were many men and women that have fallen through the cracks of the criminal justice system and are rotting away in prison with no chance of returning to society because of the War on Drugs. Before I could speak these words, Lamb took another call. "Ok now let's take a call from Greenville North Carolina 'Good evening' caller".

The viewer responded, "I have a couple of concerns about the prison system. I guess I'll qualify this by saying that I am a black man. You know one of the things I have discovered since being an elected official, when I speak out on the issue, even if it's an environmental issue, say I'm talking about trees, most of the population feels that I'm only concerned with the black tree and I am not even concerned with the green trees. As a black elected official, I have to speak out about the prison system, especially when it comes down to the use of inmate labor." This practice has grown to be extremely popular and what has happened as a result is that I think we are producing an entire inmate generation of slaves, because their pay is about seventy cents a day, if they get paid at all. Not only that, they are depriving jobs for law-abiding citizens. Mr. Papa represents, I think, the make-up of most young black men that wind up in prisons, petty drug crimes, petty social crimes that are filling up our jails. No rehabilitation; they are released out here on the streets and expect everything to be okay and expect them to be reformed. It's not going to happen the way it's going." Brian Lamb then asked me if I was paid for work while I was in prison and if so what I did. I told him that I had various jobs. I made top pay in the entire prison when I worked as a jailhouse attorney for one dollar and fifty-five cents a day. I went on to tell him that the basic rate in New York State was about sixty cents a day. There were many kinds of jobs that were available throughout the prison, such as porters, clerks, and electricians.

It was much cheaper to maintain the prison through inmate labor. In fact, in NYS they have CoreCraft where prison labor is used to produce products sold to the public. A question was then asked to Jim Gondles by Lamb, "Do all prisoners work for a living?" Gondles replied that it varied from state to state. The federal government's bureau of prisons requires all healthy inmates to work. They are paid a wage that is not very high, but it is a source of income for many individuals that would have no income at all. There is no question that the pay is much less than it would be in a free society.

Brian Lamb then told the audience that he was going to show some video tape of the telephones at Sing Sing. Lamb then asked me how often prisoners get to use the phones. As the cameras rolled in on the phones I remembered when I witnessed a confrontation between two prisoners over the use of a phone. One prisoner complained to the other that he was on the phone too long. In response, the older black prisoner stabbed the younger one several times in the chest. Over and over the blade penetrated his body as he screamed for mercy. As I thought about this, I explained the procedure that was used for making a call. You couldn't use the phone directly, but instead had to use a system that only let you call collect to numbers placed on the caller's personal phone list. The prisoner would have to go through his counselor to add or delete the 15 phone numbers allowed. All the calls were monitored. This was because of security. I hated to use the phones.

It was nothing but trouble "Let me take a call from New York City" barked Lamb "Yeah Hi" the caller said. "I just like to say that I believe that Mr. Papa definitely turned himself around and he seems like he is going in the right direction. He got the education in prison. Is that correct?" I knew at this point that this caller would be trouble. I had been challenged on the issue of my getting a college education in prison before. "Yes" I replied. "I got three college degrees while I was in prison."

The caller said "that is such a tremendous advantage to an individual. I don't believe you paid for that education, did you?" "The taxpayer paid for two out of the three degrees," I answered. The remaining Master's degree from New York Theological Seminary was paid by donations from concerned Christians. "I paid a lot of money for my education" the caller replied. "I'm sure it took me longer than it probably took you. I just don't think that's such a good issue. I mean I'm still trying to pay my college tuition off and you got a free ride." The blood quickly rose to my head but I maintained my composure and I shot out my reply instantly. "I didn't get a free ride. I spent twelve years in a cage like an animal. I did everything I could to rehabilitate myself in the best way and I took advantage of education available. It was there and I took it. I'm a better person now than I was twelve years ago. I think this caller makes the point I want to make. There are walls of silence that are built around the prisons of the United States. These walls in turn build barriers that blind the public about the truth about the prison experience. I think this is a perfect example. There have been surveys that said that education reduces the rate of recidivism. Now, doesn't it make common sense to give someone in prison an education so that person can return to society and be a contributing citizen in a positive way?"

"Let me ask Jim Gondles about this on a nationwide basis" said Lamb. What is the recidivism rate? How many people get out and go back?" Gondles replied, "Well, about a third of new commitments in state systems are violations of probation or parole or a repeat crime" The two last callers make an excellent point of view. That's what I said in the very beginning of the show. It's a balance whether or not the public should be able to have the advantages of free college, for instance, verses inmates. I'm not here to debate Mr. Papa. Many of the things he says I totally agree with. On the other hand, I think things ought to be put in perspective from time to time. Twenty years ago, when I started to work in a local correctional system there was one jail jack for a phone for about twenty inmates for maybe a five to ten-minute period of a week. Almost every institution in the country now has telephone service for the offenders in those institutions to use much more than they did twenty-five years ago".

Brian Lamb then cut to some video of the recreation yard in A-Block and asked me to describe what I saw. I then explained that the prison was broken down in several sections that maintained housing for prisoners. Each of them had the opportunity to go out to the yard three times a day. Many guys found solitude when going to the yard. There were no windows in the cells inside and it's a very terrible atmosphere. So, recreation is another way of coping with imprisonment. People who were thrown into this environment have to find things to do this time in a positive way. Many guys exercise and workout with weights. It makes you feel better to go out in the yard.

"Let me take a call from Hartford Connecticut" said Lamb. The caller said "Two things. One, Mr. Gondles and Mr. Papa seem to have very sanitized versions representing their respective constituencies. I have noticed something, I have a comment and a question. The comment is I have been watching the show and I want to say that I have seen more toiletry in those prison cells than I was able to afford as a student in upstate New York at Cornell University paying cash for my education, delivering society back the benefit of getting good grades. Second, the question is what good is a system if the punishment doesn't deter and the reform doesn't reform?"

"Thanks caller" said Lamb. I smirked, thinking what an asshole the caller was. I bit my lip but kept quiet. Instead, Jim replied, "That's a question that has been asked for two hundred years. It's a question that correctional professionals are asking. I don't know what you mean when you say a sanitized view that I am representing here. I am trying to represent correctional professionals. We believe in programs because they are beneficial. We also believe there has to be a balance in America. We have to do things for people who are free who haven't committed any crimes, who haven't been convicted, in order to take advantage of what society can give them. We also believe we ought to have the tools to give to them so they don't go back. When you're cutting programs and when you're cutting education and when you're cutting class rooms and teachers, cutting exercise equipment, when you're cracking down, so to speak, you're not accomplishing much of anything except more turmoil and problems for the future within the prison system within the United States".

Brian Lamb then told me that he was going to show some video of the mess hall where prisoners ate. He then said "Tony Papa tell us about the food you ate". I gave the worst look I could make, as if I swallowed poison and stared into the camera and said, "The food in prison is terrible". In the background I heard Jim Gondles laugh. I then said,

"That is actually an understatement. I went on to condemn the menu and said we ate the same food year after year. You got limited portions and most of the time the food was cold. You get four slices of bread and they stuff you with a lot of rice. It's supposed to be a balanced meal, but I don't think it is".

The camera then zoomed in on a plate of food sitting on a table in the mess hall. The plate was overflowing with steaming hot rice with a healthy portion of meat. It reminded me of one of those TV commercials trying to sell the viewer on the product. I said, "What you're seeing once again is the cameras. When the cameras roll in here, they clean the place up and make the food look real pretty. It's not like that. Everything is chaotic in prison. Many times, when people go into the mess hall there are fights and stabbings. It's a really terrible place. It looks really clean now. Cleaner then when I was there for twelve years. I guess they like being on TV."

"Let's go to Lima Ohio," said Lamb. The next caller was unsympathetic to what he had witnessed, "I don't understand how he thinks we should feel sorry for those prisoners. From what I see they are living better than I was in my first struggling years of marriage" said the viewer. "We have a guy here in Allen County Ohio that pled guilty to murder. He also has a form of cancer and in the short time he has been in our county jail, our county has spent twenty-five thousand dollars on his medical bills. That's more than I earn in a year and I work 52 hours a week. Why should we feel bad for them being paid small amounts of money for the work they do?"

Lamb asked Jim to answer the question. Jim responded "Obviously if you don't take care of them medically, it would be cruel and unusual punishment", which is clearly unconstitutional, again, it's a question of balance. I don't have all the answers about whether we should spend the amount of money we do. Medical costs, no matter where you are, are very high, whether you're a citizen or you are incarcerated in the United States. I understand that the gentleman on this program is complaining a lot. When I was in college I said the same things about the meals that were served to me in my University. I never heard too many people incarcerated anywhere in the United States that don't do things like complain about the food, complain about the lack of programs, complain about the lack of exercise equipment, complain about this and complain about that. Correctional professionals do the best they can to represent them in a professional manner.

I think the prison system in the United States is well operated and I am proud of the people that do operate it. We don't have a number of riots and murders that are disproportionate to the amount of people we are taking care of. Because if we did it would be on the front cover of every newspaper every day and TV cameras would be camped out like they have on the few isolated incidents we have had in the past. I just happen to believe that we are running very constitutional prisons and jails in the United States. I am not proud of the fact that we incarcerate as many people as we do, however, once again, it's a question of balance over whether or not they should receive medical treatment better than someone on the outside.

Brian Lamb then said "Anthony Papa, my statistics show that the population of Sing Sing is about 2300. The racial mix is about 85 % percent black, Hispanic, and about 15% white. Is that accurate, and if it is, what impact does it have on the relationship among the races in the prison. I replied, those stats are about right. When I was there everybody got along as best as they could. Prison is a very violent world. I don't think color really matters that much. It's disproportionate because of sentencing in reference to certain drug laws. A lot of people are from the inner city that get convicted under the current drug laws, over 80% percent of individuals in NYS prisons are somehow drug related in some way. The issue is very deep, very complex and I really can't give you a short answer on this."

Mr. Lamb then told the audience that I was celebrating my 43rd birthday. I understand that you have a website that people can check out your art. I told him I did and that the audience could take a tour through my art and feel imprisonment without being incarcerated. Brian then asked Jim what kind of people belonged to his organization.

He replied, "Professionals like wardens, correctional officers, doctors, nurses and teachers in correction facilities, probation, parole and administrators that span the world of corrections. Lamb then asked "how many members?" He answered, "We have over twenty thousand members".

Brian Lamb then told the audience that before he took the next call he wanted to show a still of the comparison of how many prisoners in prisons in the United States and how many there are in other countries. He held up a chart and explained that it showed the international incarceration rate from 1993, the latest statistics that we have, per one hundred thousand people. "You can see on the list Canada 116, France 84, Germany 80, India 23, Russia 558, Sweden 69, and the U.S. 519. What does that say to you Jim?" Gondles answered, "I have newer statistics that tell us the estimates for 1996. They are 615 for one hundred thousand in prison for the U.S. We have the highest rate of incarceration in the world. We lock up many people for fairly long periods of time.

Lamb took another call from L.A. "You're on the air, what is your question?" The caller said, "I have a comment and a question. First, my comment, you know I have really grown tired of the people of this country being so angry in saying lock people up and throw away the key. I have done a lot of reading on prisons and I would suggest to anyone so angry, go to your local bookstore and find yourself a book about the reality of being in prison. By the time you finish that book you will find that Mr. Papa's experience is the one that we need to go with. Taking away educational programs and putting more weights in the yard is going to cause people victimize themselves and each other over and over. I realize that the previous caller was angry because he had to pay more for his education than Mr. Papa did. Well I guarantee him that Mr. Papa would have come out a violent criminal when he went in a non-violent one. People get so angry and we feel so victimized over and over again. If people educated themselves about what was really happening in prison they would find that giving someone a book as opposed to them a ten-pound weight, it's going to make the biggest difference in their own personal safety. I really think what Mr. Papa said about the walls of silence being up around prisons is so true. Because those walls of silence keep us from hearing what actually goes on inside and they convince us that we know, when we really don't. We as the public have no idea what actually is happening in there and if we did, we would change our opinion."

From my perspective, I saw that the show was very informative to those who viewed it. I was proud of the fact that Jim Gondels had agreed with me on most of the things I said. In closing, Mr. Lamb asked me what my plans were now. I told him that I was on a mission to inform people of what the reality of imprisonment was and to fight for changing the mandatory minimum sentencing laws. This applied to both State and Federal law. I was not a unique case. There were many men and women that were fully rehabilitate and ready to return to society as contributing citizens, however, they could not because they were stuck in prison because of the existing laws.

The show was the start of my political activism and the beginning of the realization of the stigma I wore because I was an ex-felon. This was brought to my attention by a senior attorney at the firm who saw the show. He called me to his office and suggested I should curtail my media participation. It made me recall a time in Sing Sing, when a counselor at the prison told me the same thing. The warden of the prison had told the counselor that he wanted to take back the recommendation he gave to the governor's office in support of my executive clemency application.

He was angry at me because I was using the media exposure to tell of the horrible conditions of imprisonment and the draconian drug laws that had imprisoned me and many others. Without his support, it would have been unlikely that my clemency would have been considered.

I did not stop speaking out and because of this I was punished and transferred from the safety of my locked maximum-security cell to the medium part of the facility. In many ways, the lesser security part of the prison was much more dangerous. I lived in an open dorm area that contained open cubicles instead of cells. I was attacked on several occasions, and robbed multiple times when I was asleep.

Now here I was speaking my mind once again. Soon after, people at the law firm suddenly changed their attitude toward me and became distant. I was even subjected to a background check by my office mate and at that point, I realized I was burdened with being labeled an ex-felon.

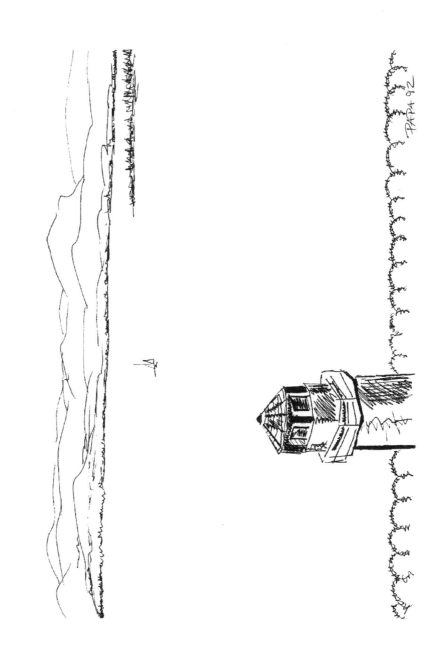

PAPA 92

CHAPTER NINE

This Side of Freedom

T ony, I need you."

It was Benny. I had been free for three years, this was the first time I'd heard from him. I had met Benny years before, in a parenting class for men at Sing Sing. My daughter Stephanie and I had drifted apart, and I wanted to try re-establishing our relationship. I went to a prison counselor, who suggested I enroll in the Family Works program, a comprehensive fatherhood program that included parenting education and family counseling. Benny and I bonded when he gave a passionate speech about his five-year-old twin girls. Many of the things he said about being a parent in prison touched my heart; he shared the same struggle I was going through with my young daughter.

"Walking the yard" with someone, a very private and ritualistic act, is a typical occurrence in prisons across America. Often used as an aid for cleaning the soul, protocol dictates that the person you walked with should be trusted enough for you to reveal and discuss thoughts that lay heavily on your mind. After many months of walking the yard with Benny, we opened up to each other about our deepest problems and concerns. We became tight. He took me under his wing, and taught me everything he knew about Benny invited me to the law library, where he taught a paralegal program for prisoners. He was king of the hill there, and had a good reputation as a jailhouse attorney, writing successful legal motions for prisoners. These motions could sometimes open the prison gates, and lead to a prisoner's eventual freedom. On the scale of importance in the hierarchy of prison life, a successful jailhouse lawyer is at the top, bar none.

The law library was a place where prisoners found solace in trying to overturn their criminal convictions. You could get a criminal appeal drafted in no time for the right price. However, you had to be careful when hiring a jailhouse lawyer, because many of them didn't know what they were doing. Typically, you had one shot to file a legal remedy, if the argument was poorly written, you were done. There was no such thing as asking the court for a do-over. So, prisoners were always desperate to hire someone who knew what they were doing.

Although being a jailhouse lawyer could be lucrative, at times it was also downright perilous. I remembered a time when a client lost the legal motion that Benny had prepared for him; he slammed Benny in the head with a law book and threatened his life if he didn't refund his money. Benny did, because he didn't want the prison administration to find out. If so, they would charge Benny with extortion, and send him to solitary confinement.

Benny was an excellent writer, and so gifted in verbal persuasion that he even managed to convince several leading New York criminal attorneys to visit the paralegal program he ran at the prison. I got to know him well when we talked about our lives during our frequent walks in A-block yard. We talked about how we wound up in prison, about our families and the tribulations we went through while doing hard time.

Benny helped me to walk through my case, and he knew how to write legal motions to challenge my conviction. It made a huge difference, and I was forever grateful. I felt indebted to him.

Yet, despite his genius in practicing law, Benny couldn't control his addiction. He got high whenever he could get his hands on some heroin. It was easy for him, because the law library was a hub of illegal activity. It was flooded with drug dealers looking to peddle their goods: you could purchase any type of drug you wanted if you had the money (although you had to pay three to four times their street value). Drugs came into prison several ways.

Most of it was brought in via drug mules; a female drug mule visiting the prison would put the drugs in balloons and then hide them in her vagina. Once inside the visiting area, the drugs were passed off to prisoners, who then brought the drugs into the prison via their anus or by swallowing the balloons. Drugs were also smuggled in through packages of food sent to prisoners. Cans of coffee, cereal boxes and jars of peanut butter were common choices. More often, though, drugs were smuggled in by prison guards, who dealt drugs as a way of supplementing their income.

Upon release, Benny managed to flip his criminal lifestyle into a respectable one, landing a good paralegal position at the Bronx Defenders, a nonprofit agency that gives free legal representation to indigent clients. For extra income, he also wrote parole briefs for a former New York State parole commissioner, at a thousand dollars a pop. He'd come a long way from prison, where he would hustle in the law library and push out the same work for a ten-dollar carton of cigarettes.

Benny's good fortune became his worst nightmare. The extra cash flow soon provided Benny with the means to become deeply hooked on heroin again. It was a habit that ruled his life, no matter what he was doing. In prison, the habit was curtailed because of limits on the money he had access to, but now, on the outside, it was another matter. Benny was spending every dime he made on supporting his habit.

Making the transition from imprisonment to the real world is no easy matter, and for someone with a severe drug addiction, it is even harder. It is inevitable that sooner or later the "get high" bell would ring and that person would return to their old ways. Benny's drug addiction was the reason he was sentenced to 10 years in prison (for robbery) in the first place. The hard time he did didn't mean a thing to him now. He was desperate for a fix and needed to get right, even if it meant jeopardizing his freedom.

For some whom return to the real world, this side of freedom is just too much to handle. The resulting shock would generally cause them to revisit the lifestyle that led them down the road to imprisonment. This is what happened to Benny.

"Tony, I need you. I need a fix, bad. I need money and I need you to tag along." I would do almost anything for Benny but I had reservations over giving him money to score dope. I didn't want to contribute to his addiction. In any case, I definitely wasn't prepared to tag along with him. "Why do you need me to go?" "It's the East Bronx. It's a bad hood. I need someone to watch my back." "I want no part of this! I said, what if we get busted?" " I'm not going to violate my parole and go back in." "I hear you, that's the last thing I want. It's not going to happen. All you need to do is stand nearby and watch out for the cops. You'll be down the block from me. Even if something goes down—which it won't—you won't be anywhere near me."

As I listed to Benny, I thought about my life I was doing good. I was employed, with great benefits and had my own apartment. I had been reunited with my family and found true love. It had been a long way since prison, where I had lost everything important to me. In reality, I had beaten the odds, which dictated that I should have returned to prison. Benny kept talking, trying to convince me to go with him.

My better judgment told me not to listen, because if anything went wrong I could lose everything I fought so hard to get, including my freedom. He must have sensed that his plea was just floating by me and I was not taking him seriously. "You owe me," he said. My body went stiff. Those words sunk deep and hit me hard. They neutralized my pending fear of going back in that hellhole of a prison. If it wasn't for Benny, I might have never regained my freedom. He had been instrumental in teaching me the law and using the tools I learned to fight my criminal case. I admitted to myself that he was right. I did owe him. I paused, and responded, "OK. Where do you want to meet?"

We arranged to meet at a diner at the corner of the Pelham Parkway train station in the Bronx. I knew the diner well because I used to hang out at Bill & Ray's, a neighborhood bar right down the block. I used to go to Bill & Ray's to unwind after putting in a hard day's work at the radio shop I owned before I went to prison. When I got to the diner, I saw Benny sitting in a booth facing its window. As he sipped his coffee, he was nervously tapping his three middle fingers with his other hand in a methodical pattern.

He looked sickly, his face pastel-white and the skin under his eyes swollen. He sat slumped in his seat, looking as if the entire world sat on his shoulders. When Benny saw me, his face lit up with happiness, as though he had seen his savior. He jumped up to greet me and gave me a big bear hug. "Hey bro, glad you came," he said, as he squeezed me tightly. He quickly paid his tab and rushed me out of the diner. "We'll catch the crosstown bus right on the corner," he said. I was startled; I hadn't been prepared for a journey. "Cross-town?" I asked.

The words squirmed out of my mouth. Benny sensed the fear returning to me. He put his hand on my right shoulder to comfort me and assured me that everything would go smoothly. Minutes later, we were sitting on the crowded bus traveling to a seedy area of the Bronx, not far from the community college I attended as a teenager. As we got closer to the drug spot, Benny kept talking to keep me comfortable. The words kept pouring out, bringing me deeper into his world. He talked about his daughters and that he had, recently, written a parole brief that won his clients' freedom. "Hanging out with you is just like the old days," he said. Benny put out his hand to slap me five. As my hand slapped his, it jarred loose a memory of our past in prison. I thought about the law library, where Benny and I spent an enormous amount of our time. We spent most our time in the book room, where we both worked as paralegals.

One-day Benny threw a surprise birthday party for Devine, an old-timer that had been down for thirty years. He managed to get someone who worked in the mess hall to make a real pizza pie topped with pepperoni. We put a bunch of matchsticks in the pie to substitute for the lack of candles, which were considered to be contraband. The officer in charge looked the other way when out of the blue one prisoner pulled out a thermos filled with jailhouse wine.

Paper cups were passed around full of the potent hooch, made from fermented fruit. Prisoners collected the fruit from their daily trips to the mess hall, and usually stored them in a sealed plastic bucket used to wash clothing. The bucket was then stashed for many days until the fruit turned into wine. It was a risky business to do this because if the bucket wasn't sealed properly, the odor of the wine saturated the air. If the guards caught you with the contraband, you would go to solitary confinement, losing your freedom within the prison.

I remember chugging the wine, swallowing it as fast as I could, because of its nasty taste. In just moments my head began spinning, making me feel a quick high that helped me to mentally escape my imprisonment. This was the reality of doing hard time. You tried to find ways to cope and transcend imprisonment, one of those ways was to get high on anything that would do the trick. Now in the present, my eyes rolled back and my head mimicked the spinning movement of my past. It began swirling in a circular motion. "Hey, snap out of it!" Benny cried as he nudged me.

My chin shifted to the left and my head popped up. I was back to reality. The bus had started out very crowded, but had made stops, letting people off. I found it strange that no one was getting on the bus. As we got closer to our destination, the bus was empty. This brought on an immediate sense of doom and with one last effort brought on by my sense of survival, I suggested we turn back. "No man, we're here already. Let's go," Benny said.

We walked for several blocks, passing a bunch of used car lots under the elevated train line near Fordham Road and Jerome Avenue. The tracks loomed large, blocking the sky and making the streets look dirtier than they really were. The neighborhood looked different from the last time I walked its streets many years ago. Back then, I was a young man attending college, with dreams and aspirations. The area was affluent. Now broken down tenement buildings adorned the sidewalks.

It was 5pm. The autumn weather was nippy. I wore jeans and a black windbreaker that covered my t- shirt. Despite the chill, Benny wore just a thin blue shirt that was tucked neatly in his dark dress trousers. I started getting nervous again. Benny assured me once again that everything would be fine. "Wait here," Benny said. He pointed to a Latino bodega on the corner. "I am going to make my move now. If by chance I run into a problem with someone, I'll waive to you. You then acknowledge me and put your hand in your pocket like you're reaching for something."

The store was about 25 yards away, close enough for someone to see me make a move for something in my pocket. In the drug street game, this was known as "fronting" on someone. In plain English, it was making believe. I hesitated to answer, thinking about the possible negative consequences of reaching for an imaginary weapon. This was especially dangerous if it turned out to be an armed robber. It was common knowledge that thugs roamed these streets looking to rob drug-buyers of their money. It suddenly occurred to me that this was the real reason Benny wanted me to come with him. He was afraid of being robbed.

The first thought that came to my mind was, what if a confrontation with one of them actually occurred, and my bluff was called? Forget about the fear I had about losing my freedom; far worse, I could get shot dead. I was already deeply in the situation and I had told Benny I would watch his back. I just wanted this to be over quickly so I could get the fuck out of there. "OK," I said, "just be careful." He nodded and shook my hand. "No worries," he said, and coolly walked away.

I started getting nervous as I watched him enter a street littered with drug steerers, workers who direct potential buyers to drug pushers. Benny's assurances did not help at all. I did not have a good feeling about the situation. I could not believe that he had talked me into coming along with him and that I might get into a situation that could spiral out of control. I was now petrified and wanted to run.

Benny stuck out like a sore thumb among the people that populated the area—they were all young Blacks and Latinos; Benny, on the other hand, was 43 years old, 6-foot-1, and had pale white skin. If you saw him on a good day, minus the sickness, he looked like he might be a police detective. The style of his clothing didn't help either.

He was conservatively dressed, while everyone around him wore baggy pants that hung low exposing their rear ends. I thought for sure we were going to have a problem. Cops in this neighborhood were not welcomed. I knew from my experience that the majority of those imprisoned for drug crimes were Black and Latino.

Over 93 percent of those locked up in prison were there because of the Rockefeller Drug Laws. Now here I was, in the middle of the neighborhood that kept those prisons filled. I started to think up an excuse to leave. Maybe I could say that it was getting late and I had to meet Luciana. He knew I was struggling in my relationship with her. Before I could yell out, Benny had already made his move. He walked toward a crowd of people hanging out in front of a rundown looking building, he yelled something in Spanish.

A Latino kid ran up to him and they greeted each other. He gave the guy a high five, embraced him, and they walked into a nearby building. A minute later my heart started to race when a police car slowly passed by. The cop in the passenger seat looked my way and gave me a long stare. I tried to be cool, gripping my chin with my right hand as I acknowledged his look. Our eyes met. I knew if I broke eye contact, the cop would get suspicious. I nodded my head and the cop returned the greeting with a slight nod as the car drove away. I was relieved--temporarily.

Benny had been gone for almost 30 minutes. I started to have bad thoughts, thinking something had happened. Could it be that Benny was being ripped off? It happened all the time. The streets were full of drug dealers that did this. I remembered Chino from seven building housing block at Sing Sing. He was doing a 25 to life sentence for murdering a drug dealer who sold him a dummy bag. This was a 10-dollar bag full of baby powder instead of heroin. Enraged when he found out, Chino returned to the dealer and demanded his money back. The dealer told him to go fuck himself. Chino pulled out a gun and shot the guy six times.

My thoughts of Chino were suddenly broken when I saw Benny reappearing in the doorway of the building. He looked totally fucked up as he stumbled down the stoop. As he walked up the block toward me, an unmarked police car came out of nowhere and stopped him. After an exchange of words, the cops slammed Benny's upper body on the hood of their patrol car. My heart beat violently as I panicked, and ran into a bodega. Several minutes later, I came out. The car was gone, along with Benny.

On my way home, I thought it was a sure bet the cops had arrested him, and that they would soon be knocking at my door. As I sat on the train, I became terrified; I suddenly went into a repetitive mantra, whispering to myself that I did not want to go back to prison. I thought of what a fool I had been to help Benny. My entire life was about to go down the drain once again. I became delusional from the fear, sweating profusely and feeling lightheaded. As I placed my hands firmly on the seat to keep from falling, a passenger asked if I was all right. I nodded yes, although I wasn't.

The middle door of the train that separated the cars suddenly slid open. A skinny homeless man appeared dressed in a black garbage bag He made his way down the car and started to sing a song that was off key, but very familiar. It was the theme song to *Annie*. He sang: "The sun will come out tomorrow, bet your bottom dollar that tomorrow, there'll be sun." It was the same song I used to sing with my young daughter, Stephanie. It brought back memories of a time of innocence, where I enjoyed the comfort of my wife and child. The melody became so soothing that it enabled me to shake off the fear of being arrested.

When I got home, I was relieved. I fell to my knees and kissed the living room floor. It felt good to be home instead of a jail cell. I knew that feeling all too well. When I was arrested, I sat in a cell and was asked by a cop to hand over my shoelaces and belt. "What for, I asked. The cop grinned and sarcastically responded, "This way you don't try to hang yourself." I couldn't believe it, but a few hours later, the thoughts of suicide flooded my mind. I prayed that would never happen again.

The next day, my phone rang. It was Benny. I was relieved, and shocked, when he told me that everything was all right. The cops had held him for a few hours and searched him. They found no drugs because he had shot up all the dope at his connection's house. That lucky break enabled him to talk his way out of the situation. That was Benny. He was such a smooth talker that we all called him "golden tongue" in prison.

I was lucky that the incident with Benny did not put me back in. My life at that point was normal, built around my career at the law firm. I was litigation paralegal at a leading New York City intellectual property firm. I controlled millions of documents, which were used in lawsuits-or-I should say, they controlled me. I worked 50 to 60 hours a week, including weekends, and sometimes on holidays. Bottom line: I did grunge work for well-paid attorneys.

Although I was very grateful, I had a job it was repetitively boring and was sucking the life out of me and curbed my artistic talents. When I came out of prison, I wanted so badly to be an artist and use my art to change the world. Now my love of art had practically disappeared from my life. I could not believe it. I had been trapped off by taking a job that took over my very being. Soon I discovered the office politics of work reminded me of the gulag in many ways. There was a hierarchy of order like prison. Partners in the firm were on top, followed by attorneys, patent agents, secretaries, paralegals, and at the bottom of the heap were the copy and mailroom employees. In prison drug dealers ruled, followed up by jailhouse lawyers and stick up kids.

You had to know where you stood in this hierarchy in order to survive. The unofficial office committee tried its best to keep up morale by constantly calling for keg parties and after work happy hours, which promoted alcohol use. My day of reckoning came one day when a fellow paralegal, Mike, had given me an impossible assignment. He was bucking to become a senior paralegal, which would mean a big pay raise and a bump in status. Mike was in a bind. The hotshot attorney he worked for needed a project completed by the next day. I helped him with his assignment, which meant doing a name search of 20,000 documents by hand. In this case, I had to search each document for 120 individuals. The average name search was from five to 10 names)

After a day of work, skimming thousands of pages of documents for names, my left eye suddenly saw a bolt of extreme bright light. Afterwards, dozens of black spots floated in my left eye. The next day I went to an eye specialist, who told me that my eye was damaged; the retina had several holes in it, causing me to need eye surgery. Maybe it was coincidence, or maybe not, but I knew for sure that my job was taking a toll. Sure, it paid the bills, but it also was eating up my entire life. My creative energy was at its lowest point; I was not painting and I was not living my life the way it should have been lived. I needed some advice, and tried to seek out guidance from a couple I had met through a church program in prison.

Bob and Nancy Steed were members of Rye Presbyterian Church, and leaders in the church's criminal justice program. One Sunday afternoon I was invited to come up to their home to break bread with other former prisoners that had graduated from New York Theological Seminary in Sing Sing. At the gathering, I was happy to see Julio, who did years with me at Sing Sing. Julio had also helped me when I first got out, reaching out to guide me with my transition.

Julio had grown up poor in the South Bronx, and saw, as his role models all the neighborhood drug dealers who drove fancy cars. At 14, he started selling marijuana and eventually learned the drug trade. He rose in the ranks, elevating himself to become a leader of a drug gang that distributed drugs in Albany. Medina had everything he could have wanted; endless cash flow, luxury cars and an expensive condominium. His world drastically changed when he got arrested and was sentenced to seven-years-to-life under the Rockefeller Drug Laws. Julio was at the lowest point in his life when he discovered Jesus. Through religion he turned his life around. The change compelled him to try to better himself by getting an education and seeing the world in a different way. In prison, he got both a Bachelor's and Master's Degree.

Julio had schooled me on how to be free again. In his talks with me, he admitted that the transition from prison to the real world was one of the scariest things he had ever faced. Coming home for him was a kind of rebirth, where he had to re-learn how to be a human being again. He told me that was one of the most important and difficult tasks I would face as a free man. Julio was turned down a dozen times for jobs before he became a substance abuse counselor.

Also at the Steed's home was Tommy Chiodi. Tommy was a former postal worker whose crack cocaine habit landed him in prison. He served an eight-year sentence for robbery. We were locked in prison together in Tappan, the medium-security section of Sing Sing. Tommy approached me. He looked as sharp as a tack in his brand new suit. "Papa, how ya doing?" he said. We shook hands and talked about our days together in prison. "Those days of struggling are over," he confidently assured me. He started to brag about how good he was doing. I was impressed. It seemed as though he was really doing well. He asked me for my contact information and said he would be in touch. I gave him my phone number. I soon realized that this was a big mistake. A week later, the phone rang at 2:00 o'clock in the dead of the morning. It was Tommy.

"Tony, you gotta help me out," he said, "I'm stuck with my car in a gas station not far from you. I need to purchase a battery but don't have any money on me. Can you loan me the money and I'll pay you back next week?" In bed, I turned to Luciana. "Baby, it's Tommy Chiodi. He's stuck with his car, I gotta help him out." Luciana was half-asleep and gave me an unsympathetic look. She reached for the alarm clock and placed it two inches from my face. "It's 2 o'clock in the morning. He's gotta be kidding." I reminded her that it was the right thing to do.

She mumbled something back and quickly turned and jammed her pillow over her head. Silence followed. For me that was the signal that it was all right to go. I quickly got dressed and took a cab to the gas station. When I exited the cab, Tommy was waiting for me in front of his broken-down caddy. "Thank God you came," he said as he shook my hand furiously.

As I paid Chiodi's bill he thanked me over and over and swore he would pay me back. I told him it was no problem. It was the least I could do for a friend. A few days later, he called and told me to meet him downstairs in front of my building. He handed me a check for three times the amount he owed me.

I told him it was way too much. Chiodi smiled, "Well, if you got 70 or 80 bucks in your wallet it would be okay. You can have dinner for you and your girl on me." I agreed and pulled out 70 bucks to hand over to him. He smiled, looking like he had just hit the lottery. "Thanks a lot," he said.

Days later, the check bounced. I called Chiodi; his phone was shut off. I called his job and he had been fired for not showing up for work. I made additional calls, and found out that Chiodi had hooked up with the former wife of a prisoner we both knew. She was a crack addict and had turned out Chiodi, who then became hooked on crack again. When Luciana found out about the bounced check, she was mad as hell, and swore up and down that if I ever got involved helping out an ex-con again, she would leave me.

"Please help me," the voice cried out on the phone. "I need to borrow some money." I shook my head in disbelief as I listened to the voice on the other end of the phone. The cry for help had now become a repetitive motif in my life. I guess it was because I was known to be a soft touch.

It was six months later, and it was Benny again. "I need a fix—bad," he told me. In the background, I could hear him puking his guts out. Because of his severe drug habit, I had stayed away from him. Benny's addiction was out of control. I last heard about him from his Latino girlfriend, who told me that he was at the end of his rope.

"Okay, don't do anything stupid. I'll help you out," I said. "I have to go to the Museum of Modern Art with my girlfriend, but I'll meet you on the corner of 54th and 6th at six." Luciana and I arrived at the museum at about half past five. We walked hand in hand, enjoying the exhibits until about 6 p.m. As planned, I went to the corner and called Benny on his cell but he neither answered his phone nor showed up. I returned to the museum and continued touring the art. At 7:00 p.m., I was startled to hear myself being paged by the museum. Benny was waiting for me near the information desk. He looked all strung out, and was having an argument with a security guard. I grabbed Benny by the arm and dragged him away.

Benny swore, "I will pay you back. I'm getting paid the day after tomorrow." I shook my head in disgust and looked at Benny. I saw a man who could have had a bright future. He was so full of talent. The dope had taken him down and dragged him through a mop wringer. I held Benny by the shoulders and looked him in the eye. "You gotta get it together. If not for yourself, do it for your daughters." Benny bit his lip and agreed.

I went into my wallet and handed him the $200. He left the museum, giving the security guard the finger as he left. Luciana had witnessed the entire incident, including the transaction and wanted to know why I gave him the money. I explained the situation to her and she blew a fit. She reminded me of the last time I helped out a former prisoner.

Now the incident with Benny cemented her promise. When we returned home, as soon as the front door of the apartment opened, Luciana ran into the bedroom and began to gather her most prized possessions. I stood there watching her packing, and tried to reason with her. "Baby, please don't do this. You know I love you." She snapped back, "If you loved me, you wouldn't be hanging out with guys like

Benny. He's a lowlife and you know the old saying; if you lay with dogs, you'll get fleas." I stood there and scratched my head, trying to think of something that would make her change her mind.

"But he's sick and he helped me get my freedom back," I said. She stopped momentarily as she stuffed her tattered backpack with clothing. Luciana was a low-key woman and spiritual person, however at that point the devil had gotten into her. She almost never argued with me, but when you crossed her path, she exploded with rage. She screamed at the top of her lungs:

"That's the PROBLEM WITH you – you are still in prison in your mind!"

With that said, she left. I dipped my head down low and thought about what she said. She was right. All those years of doing, hard time was still with me. I was free, but in my mind, I still was a prisoner of my past. Benny was part of the life I was supposed to leave behind when those gates of prison shut behind me. Here in my freedom, those memories I needed to forget had managed to control my existence. Because of this, I was about to lose the love of my life.

"Benny is dead. "I froze. It was Benny's mother on the phone. It had been about four weeks since I had last seen him. My hand tightly squeezed the phone and my throat became dry when I tried to respond.

"Oh my God, what happened?" I asked

"He died of a massive heart attack."

My first thought was that he was too young to die. My voice barely audible, I responded, "I'm so sorry to hear this." At first, I was very shocked; Benny was only 45 years old and he had so much to live for. After a few moments, I knew deep inside that the probability of his death was surely drug-related, most likely from an overdose. I thought about the incident at the museum and how I had lent him money. Could I have been partially responsible for Benny's death? Should I have denied lending him money to support the habit that finally did him in? My mind raced and tried to calculate the timing of his death.

"When did he die?" I asked. "I buried him a few weeks ago," she said. I exhaled deeply, feeling guilty. The timing sounded about right. Maybe I should have tried to help Benny get some treatment instead of lending him money. I put the thought aside as we continued with some small talk.

"How are the twins?" I asked. The line went dead for a long moment. "His twin girls," I repeated. She quickly responded, "He has no twin girls." "Are you sure?" I asked. She responded tartly, "Of course he doesn't. I would know--since I'm his mother." My mouth dropped open and I was speechless. I couldn't believe it. For all those years, Benny had lied to me about having children. He had spoken so convincingly about having twin girls. It blew my mind to think that he would lie about this. "Maybe I misunderstood him," I told her, as I said goodbye.

When I put the phone down, I really thought hard about Benny's lying to me. Maybe he was justified in his actions, in that he needed to create that fantasy to keep him going while he was imprisoned for those 10 years. Prison is a cruel place, and you have to make up ways to bring you to the next day. You need to find meaning in your life in order to survive. I guess it doesn't matter whether it was true or not.

The thought of my contributing to Benny's death came back to haunt me. I began to feel responsible for his death, and fell into a deep depression. I started to drink heavily and smoked marijuana. It took a toll on me. Soon I came into work with terrible hangovers. My friends covered for me, giving me assignments I could do in my office. I shut my door and spent most of the day recovering at my desk. My guilt was destroying me, and leading me onto a path of destruction. To add gasoline to the fire, I got a letter from Luciana.

She told me she went back to Brazil and was living on the family farm in the countryside of Sao Paulo. Her love for me was still there but she couldn't deal with me living in the past when I should be in the present. I missed her so much. I felt trapped by my past, but what could I do? It was not easy to forget the years I spent in prison. Now with the death of Benny, coupled with the failure of my relationship with Luciana and my daughter, I was also coming to the end of my rope. Was I about to follow in Benny's footsteps?

The answer to my question came soon enough. The day after a big hangover, I received a message on my answering machine from my parole officer (P.O.) The voice on the machine said: "Mr. Papa, it's been weeks and I have not seen you. You must report for a drug test the day after tomorrow." "Oh my God," I cried, as I fell to my knees. I screamed to the ceiling. "Please God, please, don't let me go back!"

I knew my urine was "dirty" and I would fail that test. An all-consuming feeling of doom blanketed my being. I totally freaked out. My heart began beating wildly and I prayed that I would not return to prison. I had heard that the majority of prison admissions came not from arrests for new crimes, but from probation and parole violations, like "dirty" urine tests. Nationwide, roughly two-thirds of parolees fail to complete parole successfully and returned to prison. I did not want to be one of them.

I knew prayers alone would not stop me from being caught violating parole. After I calmed down, I thought about what I could do. Maybe I could call my parole officer and tell her I was sick and couldn't come in. No, that would not work; not showing up could in itself be a violation. My mind searched for an answer, and then I remembered an old trick that cons used to beat drug tests. I ran to the sink and began consuming an enormous amount of water for the next two days. My kidneys were almost bursting from consuming the water to flush out the marijuana.

The day I reported to my parole officer, I was scared to say the least. If my test results came back positive (indicating drug use), my P.O. could put me back in. I sat in the waiting area as I waited for her to call me. Two hours passed by as I watched dozens of ex-cons get called in by their prospective parole officers. The door swung open and out popped my P.O., Ms. Brown. "Papa, front and center!" she called out. I entered her office and sat in a metal chair facing her desk. After exchanging some information, she opened her desk drawer and pulled out a zip lock bag that contained a plastic bottle for my urine. She then made a phone call and got a male parole officer to escort me to the bathroom, where he would watch me piss.

As I stood there holding the bottle in front of my penis I couldn't help but think of how I had fucked up my life. How stupid could I be, putting my freedom on the line? I was responsible for my actions, and now I would have to pay the price. I filled the bottle up and handed it to the parole officer. We went back to Ms. Brown's office. I took a seat and watched her put on some plastic gloves. They looked like the same ones used by the guards to conduct contraband searches back at Sing Sing prison. Prisoners used to find the discarded gloves and cut off the fingers to make condoms.

My P.O. then opened the cap and tilted her head back as she caught a whiff of the urine. She placed a test strip into the piss, and I sank back into my seat. *Please God, don't let me go back in.* I also prayed to St. Anthony and Mary mother of God. After the longest minute of my life, Ms. Brown pulled the stick out of the urine and held it above her head, facing me. "You're clean," she calmly said I let out a sigh of relief that caught her attention. "You're not fucking around, are you?" she asked. "No, Ms. Brown," I quickly replied. "Good," she said. "Report back in one month." "OK, thank you," I said. I felt a tremendous boulder lift off my shoulders.

As I walked out of her office, I vowed never to put myself into that position again. It was a lesson learned that made me realize how precious—and precarious—freedom was. To my astonishment, the lesson I learned meant nothing to prevent my freedom from being in jeopardy again. Little did I know that through the chance meeting of someone, my freedom would be on the line many times over.

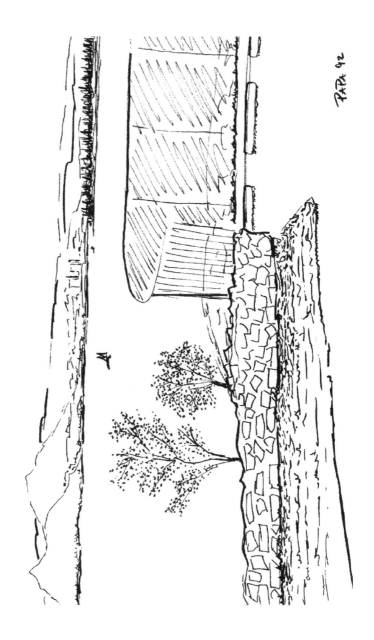

Chapter Ten

Randy Credico and Mothers of the New York Disappeared

Sometimes in life, you meet people that will change you forever. This is what happened to me when I met Randy Credico, a political comedian and activist who directed the William Moses Kunstler Fund for Racial Justice. I don't know if it was destiny or by chance that our lives crossed paths. All I know is that our partnership gave birth to a street movement that challenged the laws that put hundreds of thousands of low-level non-violent offenders in prison for many years. My partnership with Randy brought me on a different path in my life. Sometimes that path walked the road of danger, jeopardizing my freedom through the pursuit of justice.

Most of the time I walked a line steady toward changing the draconian laws that had destroyed many lives. God was with me and my return to prison was not on his agenda. One night as Credico was flipping the channel of a television in a sleazy motel in Florida as he was drying out from a cocaine binge he stumbled upon me on C-Span television talking about the Rockefeller Drug Laws and the conditions of imprisonment I faced. He was so moved and impressed with what I had said that he vowed to get involved to fight the injustice of New York State's drug laws.

Credico tracked me down and invited me to the "Monkey's Paw," a famous west village bar where he regularly performed comedy.

I soon discovered that not only was Randy funny but he was also a questionable eccentric who was quite a character whose zany actions sometimes bordered on the insane. He was born and raised in Pomona California and became involved with show business at an early age. Credico was influenced by his father Bill who ran a multi- entertainment complex in Southern California, which featured world-renowned entertainers like Louie Armstrong and Bobby Darin.

Bill also did a ten-year stint for bank robbery, which influenced Randy to become a fighter for justice. Credico had performed on the comedy circuit for twenty years making regular appearances in Las Vegas. His career reached critical acclaim when he appeared on the "Tonight Show" at the age of 27. At that point, he decided to combine his love of comedy and activism and began to fight for justice on behalf of those less fortunate. He spent much of the 1980's in Central America with the peace movement and organized and led a group of comedians through the region. Randy returned and was credited with catapulting the son of teamster Jimmy Hoffa into the teamster presidency through "Humor for Hoffa."

His political activism was cultivated when he became friends with the legionary civil rights attorney William Kunstler. Credico met him when he asked for Kunstler's help for Credico's girlfriend at the time, singer and actress Joey Heatherton, who had gotten in trouble with the law. A strong friendship developed between Credico and Kunstler. And after Bill had passed on, Randy founded the William Moses Kunstler Fund for Racial Justice along with Bill's wife Marge Kunstler. As director, he targeted issues of injustice that affected communities of color. One of the issues he concentrated on was the nation's War on Drugs.

When I met Credico, I just had gotten out of prison and I was hell bent on going on a rescue mission to save others I had left behind. Fresh out of the gulag I started making trips to Albany New York along with other activist organizations to talk with politicians about repealing the laws that put me away. Most of the time I talked to them I saw that it was a typical reaction for them to yes me to death and almost always do nothing in following up when they did agree to help out. When the novelty of meeting with politicians wore off, I saw that all I was really doing was spinning my wheels in trying to get something done with them.

This was not working for me and I knew that the problem would have to be approached from another angle. It seemed that Randy could provide me with one. When I met him, he wanted to know what his organization could do to fight the drug war in New York. This went hand in hand with what I wanted to do. Some might call it a match made in heaven. Whatever it was, I knew that my friendship with him would lead to my dream of changing the horrible laws that had put me away, along with tens of thousands of low-level non-violent drug offenders.

Our first meeting I was invited to a meeting at the "Monkey's Paw" a bar where Credico had thrown a party for Geronimo Pratt, a former high ranking member of the Black Panther Party. The party was the result of a project the Kunstler fund did with the Black Panthers where they provided them with video cameras in order to patrol Harlem to curb police brutality. Pratt had spent 27 years in prison for murder and was freed in 1997 when his conviction was vacated. He was targeted by the FBI as part of their counterintelligence program (COINTELPRO) aimed at neutralizing Pratt and other Black Panthers. At the party, I met a host of characters, including other Panthers and celebrities like actress Marlo Thomas and her husband talk show host Phil Donahue. The most interesting person I met there was minimalist artist Brice Marden who had designed an award in metal that was given to recipients of the William Kunstler award for Racial Justice. When I was introduced to him, I was very excited to meet such a famous artist. I gave my pitch to him and told him how I used my art to paint my way to freedom. He was impressed and gave me encouragement and told me to keep painting.

After several meetings where we racked our brains to come up with an idea how we could challenge New York's drug laws we finally hit pay dirt. We came up with the idea of organizing family members of those imprisoned under the Rockefeller Drug Laws in a manner modeled after the 1970's Argentina mothers of the disappeared - who regularly took to the streets, protesting the government's "Dirty War" of torture, murder and disappearance of accused left-wingers. We figured we could start a street movement that would convince politicians to do away with these horrible laws. In order to form this group, we decided to put the word out with the hope that those affected by the Rock Laws would join us.

We started by creating a flyer that was a call for offenders to spotlight their cases in our campaign. Since we needed to get to those prisoners in NYS gulags, we targeted their family members. We passed these flyers out at midtown Manhattan and 59th street Columbus Circle where buses departed to several NYS upstate prisons.

Every weekend we went there to recruit the dozens of passengers that were headed for prisons like Attica, Auburn and Clinton. I stood there pushing the flyers into the hands of everyone while asking the same repetitive question. I asked "is your man in prison for drugs? If he is, we'll help him profile his case and use it to change the Rockefeller Drug Laws". Just bring this flyer to the prison you are going to and ask whoever you are going to see to pass it around throughout the prison." The flyer contained information about how we were going to profile prisoners convicted under the Rockefeller Drug laws. It also contained a short questionnaire asking details of their cases. For example, it asked if they were first time offenders and if they had a drug habit or were there any violence in the crime they were charged with.

Credico even got Juan Gonzales, a columnist with the NY Daily News, to do a piece on our canvassing at Columbus Circle. We hit pay dirt with that and pretty soon we began to receive dozens of letters from prisoners telling us about their cases. We took the best ones to profile and built a coalition of people that wanted to support our cause. On May 8th 1998, the NY "Mothers of the Disappeared" staged their first rally at Rockefeller Center in NYC. About two dozen family members held signs with photos of their loved ones who had disappeared because of New York's drug laws. This simple but dramatic gesture led to amazing media coverage. We knew, at that point, we had given birth to a street movement that was able to reach out to citizens because it put a human face on the War on Drugs.

We chronicled amazing stories of courage from our members, including a ten-year-old girl whose mother was sentenced to 15 to Life, who became the "Shirley Temple" of our drug law movement.

Numerous advocates have joined our ranks. They include celebrities like comic actor and TV host Charles Grodin, religious leaders such as Cardinal O'Connor and former politicians.

Through Credico, I met an array of characters from show business. It was through this relationship that I met Lara Kightlinger. She was directing a documentary on Credico called "60 Spins around the Sun". The film centered on Credico's activism and it documented his involvement with the Rockefeller Drug Laws and the Mothers of the New York Disappeared. The film won 'Best Documentary' at several film festivals including the Boston Film Festival. It was there that I met actor Jack Black. He was Laura's boyfriend and he banked the documentary.

The most memorial moment of the tour was when I went to the Beverly Hills screening and bumped heads with Larry David of Jerry Seinfeld fame. I was sitting in the audience watching the film and Larry was sitting directly behind me. To my ignorance, I did not recognize who he was. He was making rude comments during the screening which prompted me to turn around and give David a piece of my mind. When Larry's eyes met mine he was quick to slump down into his seat. At that end of the film Larry appeared on screen, wishing Credico would die because he had robbed a handful of very expensive cigars from his humidor when he had invited Credico to take only one or two. I was pretty embarrassed and afterward apologized to David.

It wasn't all glamour and big stars in my relationship with Credico. In the beginning of our friendship, I started to hang out at the bar he regularly performed. A multitude of sleaze balls appeared including Frank the drug dealer who found out about my past and tried to convince me to deal cocaine for him. For me it was simple to refuse getting involved with something that had already tried to destroy my life. Reverting to past life- styles was a repetitive problem that existed with most ex-offenders. This was why the rates of recidivism were so high. When prisoners are released from incarceration they struggle with their existence and find solace in returning to the comfort of their past way of life. For some it's all they know in order to survive.

I saw the easy money that Frank made and I thought back to the day that changed my life forever. Years back, I met a drug dealer who asked me to deliver an envelope of cocaine for the sum of $500. At that time, I was desperate and needed money to pay my rent and support my family. I was young and stupid and I agreed to do it. When I delivered that envelope of 4 ounces of cocaine for $500 bucks, I walked smack into a police sting operation. My life flashed in front of me when the cop's 38 revolver was stuck squarely in my ear. "Don't move mother fucker, your life is over" he said.

The cop was right and I did everything I could do wrong and was sentenced to 15 years to life. I had learned my lesson and had no desire to go back to prison; I told Frank no thanks. Several weeks later, we got the news that Frank was arrested and ironically, he was sentenced to prison under the Rockefeller Drug Laws.

Together we battled the laws and forged a partnership that brought us a multitude of rich experiences, which led to the release of many of the prisoners we advocated for. We knew we were facing an uphill battle taking on a bad law that had stayed in place for many years backed by the political power of the 62 District Attorneys of New York State.

This was coupled with a police presence always looming over us because of the nature of our work. It became a dangerous situation for me because I was on parole. Any negative police contact would bring on a parole violation, sending me back to prison. Because of Credico's tendency to verbally confront the cops, sometimes our rallies and protests led to disorder and chaos, with people being arrested. I disappeared from many a protest when I thought my freedom was in jeopardy. I developed an uncanny sixth sense that helped me to stay out of trouble. Even State Senator David Paterson (now governor of New York State), joined the reform movement with us and in an act of civil disobedience, got arrested at a Rockefeller Drug Law protest in 2002 in front of Governor George Pataki's Midtown office.

With a small group of about 25 dedicated individuals, in five years we managed to shift public opinion and changed the face of the drug war in New York State. Once this occurred many elected officials spoke out, putting aside their fears of political death that had been traditionally associated with drug reform. Finally, in 2001, Governor Pataki along with the Assembly and Senate, called for reform of the Rockefeller Drug

Laws. Both houses submitted bills with their own version of what changes should be made.

This triggered an ongoing battle that ended the legislative session in a deadlock. This pushed us even more to fight for change. Since an election year for the governor approached, we decided to use the Mothers of the NY Disappeared of the Disappeared to respond to the fact that many non-violent drug offenders sat in prison rotting away while politicians wallowed in debate.

An ad campaign was developed that targeted the Hispanic vote in New York City. We had stinging ads portraying the governor as the main reason why 94 % of drug offenders in New York's prisons were Black and Latino. The governor's popularity among this population suddenly plummeted which forced him to seek us to stop airing the ads. For this mission, he sent Chauncey Parker, his newly appointed Director of Criminal Justice. A meeting was set up; Parker met with family members of those incarcerated under the A1 felony provisions of the Rockefeller Drug Laws. Parker pitched the governor's proposed bill to an audience of about 20 people. For the most part no one really understood the technical aspects of what he said. After a while, an elderly Hispanic woman who was in very poor health spoke out. She asked Parker how the governor's new law would help her son who had been incarcerated for the past 12 years.

Chauncey stopped dead in his sentence and answered her. He told her if the assembly would approve the governor's bill, he would be eligible to file a motion and request immediate release from prison. The woman in response smiled as though Parker was her savior. Another black woman asked the same question. Parker analyzed the situation based on what information she told him. "Immediate release" was his answer and with a pause added, "If the governor's bill was passed". Everyone in the room started to ask the same question. Parker went around the room and answered with the same response. The room was now full of happiness with the hope that they would be reunited with their incarcerated love ones.

The meeting left everyone with the idea that all the hard work they have been doing for years had begun to pay off. Freedom was so close, but yet so far off because it was in the hands of politicians who, through the rhetoric of crime and politics, were forgetting the human aspect of the drug war.

There was only a month left in the year's legislative session. Hope was dwindling fast. A week later Randy set up a two separate meetings. The first one was with head counsel for Sheldon Silver the assembly leader. The second meeting was at Governor Pataki's New York office with Chauncey Parker.

We rounded up members of our group. It was getting harder and harder for us to get them to take the very long ride to the New York State Capital in Albany. For years, these family members were promised that we would secure freedom for their love ones. We arranged for the 3-hour trip and met the group, telling them this was the trip that was going to change the Rockefeller Drug Laws. The bus ride up was full of hope and anticipation because of this. The riders were all veterans of our protests and had heard this line before. When we got to the Capital, our first meeting was with the Assembly leader Sheldon Silver.

Silver had been supporter for many years and had advocated for reform of the Rock Laws. When we walked into Silver's office, his staff greeted us. Several of our members were confined to wheelchairs. Others limped in holding onto their canes tightly. It was a sight to see us all line up squeezing in his office. Silver then greeted us and went into a speech on why the Governor's proposed legislation was not good for us. He told us not to endorse Pataki's bill. We all agreed.

The next stop was the governor's executive chambers for our historic meeting. The night before, the Governor had pushed through the Senate an additional bill that would affect only Class A-1 felons. This would allow about two hundred prisoners to be eligible for immediate release if the Assembly passed the bill. Not surprisingly, most of those incarcerated who would be eligible were family members of the Mothers of the NY Disappeared. A dilemma of moral proportions arose. Would we take the proffered carrot by the string and support the governor freeing our loved ones, even though all of his legislation fell far short of true reform?

On June 12, 2002, we arrived at the location and checked into security. We were all given badges to wear. We brought a camera-man to document our meeting. Because of security, we were told that the camera could not be brought in. We told the governor's staff that we would only use the footage for our group to show others who were not healthy enough to make the long trip to Albany. The staff looked at us up and down seeing the wheelchairs and people who were in bad health. We looked like veterans that had just returned from war. They agreed to let us bring in the camera only if we kept the sound off.

We entered the executive chambers and were amazed at the size and elegant surroundings. A huge conference table that must have been 20 feet long sat in the middle of the room. As we sat and waited for the governor, Chauncey introduced us to his staff. An undercover state police officer sat quietly in a chair carefully checking us out. After 20 minutes, Governor Pataki entered the room. As he approached us, I stepped forward and put out my hand to greet him. The governor passed me right by ignoring me completely. Who could blame him, after all, he granted me my freedom and to thank him I began a campaign against him to change the Rockefeller Drug Laws.

The governor thanked us all for coming to the meeting and went into the reasons why we should support his bill. Hope was dwindling fast as both sides could not come to an agreement. We listened as Governor Pataki blamed the Assembly for not cooperating with him. After he spoke, we had an opportunity to respond. I was the first to speak out. Can I say something? Pataki said sure. "Governor I want to take this opportunity to thank you for granting me my freedom. I acknowledged that three others were in the room who had also been granted clemency. Gov. Shelly Silver said that your proposed bill addresses half of one percent of people inside affected by the Rock Laws."

The Governor responded and told us "this bill addresses the most egregious cases by far". I shook my head in agreement and asked, "My question to you is that we came away from the meeting with Silver with the knowledge that he is not going to pass your bill. So, we stand here today and came to present you with a question. How about using the vehicle of executive clemency? We know for me and others in this room, it saved our lives. There are many people in this room here today that represent others that are eligible for clemency. The governor quickly responded, "I know and we will look at

We have exercised clemency and we will continue to go through that process, but it's a long process. I just can't sign a blanket order for everybody to get clemency. We go through case by case and it does nothing now for those who are sentenced to 15 to life going forward.

After the meetings, which both parties blamed each other for the failure to compromise, we realized that both parties were 90 % away from reaching an agreement that would change the existing laws. This was absolutely amazing considering only a few years ago I was sitting in a cell at Sing Sing praying for my release. Now here I was part of the process to reform the same laws that incarcerated me. The meeting lasted for over an hour. When we left, we were part of a press conference in which New York Assembly leader Sheldon Silver blamed the governor for not cooperating with the Assembly. At the conference, Randy told the press that our message to Governor Pataki, the Senate and Assembly was a simple one.

We would not take a position and support any pending legislation. I told them to please put aside any political rhetoric of crime and politics and realize that there is a human element involved. Then when this was done, maybe we all could walk hand in hand on common ground to change the Rockefeller Drug Laws. We listened as our dreams of changing the Rockefeller Drug Laws began to fade away. The 2002 legislative session ended with no resolution, leaving us in anguish for being so close, yet so far in reforming the laws.

In 2003 fresh off of a staggering defeat that took most of the wind out of our sails, we tried our best to regroup. Each year was getting harder to keep together the Mothers of the NY Disappeared. For many of the group's members 2002 was the final straw that convinced them to give up fighting for the release of their love ones in prison. Several members of the group had formally quit. The empty promises we once gave them were no longer effective. It became so bad that the only way members would come to protests is that they had to be bribed.

Credico developed the idea after he offered to pay a poor mothers jacked up phone bill because of a phone scam that the Department of Corrections was pulling with the phone company, MCI. They were charging outrageous amounts of money to prisoners and their families for phone use. For many the phone became the only vehicle for them to stay in touch with loved ones who could not afford transportation fees that were too costly. A trip to an upstate from someone living in the inner city could run hundreds of dollars in expenses in bus, taxi and hotel fees.

Despite the fact that people were tired and our luck was bad, we did not give up and continued to find ways to keep the issue of Rockefeller law reform alive. One day our prayers to find a source of energy to reignite our movement were answered. In March of 2003 Andrew Cuomo agreed to join us to speak at our annual May 25th Rock Law anniversary protest in front of the NYS governor's office on 43rd and 3rd street. I got to know Andrew when I helped him put together a press conference in his first run for Governor of New York the year before in 2002. Credico and I reached out to Cuomo and went to meet with him at his NYC office. I brought along a limited edition of a poster I created that featured my famous self-portrait "15 to Life." Andrew was very impressed with my art and my story.

So much, in fact, that he used them as a vehicle to launch his Rockefeller Drug Law repeal bill at a press conference for his 2002 run for governor that I helped him put together at a church in Harlem, New York. The "Church of the Living Hope" was located on 116th street. Its pastor was Rev. Lonny McCloud who, in his past life, had done hard time with me over at Sing Sing.

McCloud was also a graduate of the NYTS Seminary Master's program in the prison. I arranged the use of the church through Julio Medina who ran Exodus Transitional Community, a re-entry organization that helped ex-prisoners, that was located upstairs from the church. At the press conference, a load of media showed up, as they were interested in hearing what he had to say.

Cuomo talked to the press while standing near an easel that held my self-portrait. As he called for the outright repeal of mandatory minimum sentences for nonviolent, low-level drug offenders, I was proud to be standing next to him along with Jan Warren who also served 12 years under the laws. He offered an alternative plan for the sentencing of low-level drug offenders that went as far as to take for task his opponents for not doing more to roll back the Rockefeller Drug Laws. He even accused his Democratic opponent, H. Carl McCall, and Gov. George E. Pataki of failing to change the "antiquated criminal justice system." Cuomo called the existing laws "probably the most personal, the most human manifestation" of Albany's failings.

Although both of his opponents supported some sort of reform Andrew took it a step further and called for the outright repeal of the Rockefeller Drug Laws. The NY Times reported that by going further than his two major opponents in his opposition to the Rockefeller drug laws, Mr. Cuomo was clearly trying to capitalize on an issue that has resonated with traditionally Democratic voters, but primarily with Blacks and Hispanics, who account for more than 90 percent of the 19,000 people in prison for drug offenses. Whatever the reason was, I felt confident that Cuomo was really supporting our movement and wanted to see true repeal of the laws. Andrew's bold attempt to run was cut short when Assembly leader Sheldon Silver backed Carl McCall forcing Cuomo to withdraw from the race. His political career suffered a tremendous blow. We were sad to see Cuomo go but soon after Credico was contacted by the people for Tom Golisano who was also a candidate for governor running on the independent party ticket. Golisano was a Buffalo businessman and philanthropist who was the founder of Paychex, the second-largest payroll processor in the United States. This was his third run for the governorship after failing to win in 1994 and 1998.

This time Tom, who had an endless cash flow, had the genius of Roger Stone behind his campaign. Stone was a veteran political consultant and lobbyist who was chief strategist in many political campaigns. He has worked with Tom Kean, Bob Dole, Ronald Reagan and Lee Atwater. The New Yorker magazine had described him as a political trickster and others have called him a force in the world of politics.

A strategy was developed wherein Golisano was going to attack Pataki's record on Rockefeller reform. It was fantastic for us since we wanted to continue to make the Rockefeller Drug Laws a political issue for the race for governor. I was called to Roger Stone's NYC office where I met Carl Gingsberg, a television producer who was doing PSA's for Golisano's campaign. Gingsberg thought my story was moving and he wanted to use me for a 30-second spot going after Governor Pataki in regards to his dancing around the issue of the Rockefeller Drug Laws.

The commercial was made and aired in the NY market between five and seven p.m. on WPIX and WOR TV. The first night it aired I actually got nervous when I saw the commercial continuously airing. After all, I was still on parole and I could be pulled in for any little violation. Every time I flipped the channel between the two stations, I was calling out Governor Pataki.

I sat there in front of the camera and told the audience that I spent twelve years in prison for a first time non-violent drug offense under the Rockefeller drug laws. In a smooth and convincing voice, I said, "When I was a young man I made a mistake. It was the only time I got in trouble with the law, twelve years in a 6x9 foot cage. These laws waste money, destroy lives, and break up families. Gov. Pataki's plan to change these laws is not true reform and he knows it. After eight years of talk, it's time for a change. Tom Golisano's plan is true reform and that's why I am supporting him for governor".

It was a very powerful commercial that made a point. On my way to work the next morning, a young guy sitting on the subway steps as I stood waiting for a train pointed his finger at me. He yelled, "Hey man, you're that Rockefeller guy, keep up the fight"! I was taken aback, startled to say the least. I waved to him and shook my head yes. Afterwards a warm feeling came over me. I was happy thinking I was making a difference by publicly calling out the Governor Pataki. At the same time, I thought about how I was jeopardizing my freedom in taking on the most powerful man in NYS. Not to mention he was the one who gave me my freedom.

Golisano went on to spend 70 million dollars in his campaign. It was to no avail and he and McCall were easily defeated and Gov. Pataki was re-elected to a third term. The good thing I got from the campaign was the fact that I had cemented a relationship with Andrew Cuomo that would become very important in fighting to change the Rockefeller drug laws. About a year went by before I was reunited with Cuomo. A situation developed when one of his staff members reached out to me and said she was doing research on the Rockefeller Drug Laws.

Ashley had stumbled upon my website "15 to Life" and from this chance meeting via the web we agreed to have Andrew speak at our yearly Rockefeller Drug Law anniversary protest we held in front of the governor's office in midtown Manhattan. Cuomo was happy to help us get exposure to our movement and even offered to get his friend hip-hop businessman, Russell Simmons, involved in our struggle to repeal the Rock laws. I knew Simmons was a powerhouse and with him we would finally have the ability through his organization, the Hip-Hop Summit Network, to reach a new and unexplored audience. In 2000 in an attempt to bring light to the issue of education, Simmons gathered over 100,000 people to fill the streets; this produced a tremendous amount of media coverage.

We set up a meeting with Simmons and his right hand man Ben Chavis, former president of the NAACP. The first time I met Simmons I knew he didn't like my aggressive style. I showed up with my signature poster and a 15 minute VHS tape I had put together promoting my story. This was a continual problem I had when I got out of prison. I was so used to trying to sell myself to generate support for my executive clemency application, that when I was released it took me many years to shake off the often-overpowering approach I had. I guess what I was trying to do was compensate for the negative label I wore as an ex-con. When we left Simmons, we had a good feeling and knew he was going to be a powerful force. Randy was especially happy because Simmons gave him a brand-new pair of white Fat Farm sneakers, part of the clothing line that Simmons owned.

From that initial meeting, we set up weekly meetings which were conducted over Russell's offices at Fat Farm on 37th street and 7th avenue. A strategy was developed where we agreed to create a national coalition of groups and individuals that would speak out against the Rockefeller Drug Laws at an event planned for June 25th, called the "Countdown to Fairness". The event would demand that the Governor act within 30 days to repeal the Rockefeller Drug Laws. Simmons began his magic and enlisted the biggest names in the rap music industry. Public service announcements were created by entertainers like Jay-Z, 50 cent and Mariah Carey. Credico even got billionaire Tom Golisano to contribute $125,000 dollars to the planned budget of $300,000 dollars for the building of a Broadway stage near City Hall in downtown NYC. To get the campaign rolling a letter was widely distributed that was written by Andrew Cuomo. It read: A letter from Andrew Cuomo"

Dear Friend,

On the 30th Anniversary of the Rockefeller Drug Laws, I along with Russell Simmons & the Hip –Hop Summit Action Network and the Mothers of the New York Disappeared, announced the formation of the Countdown for Fairness to pressure Governor Pataki to repeal these laws during this legislative session. The culmination of our Countdown is a rally planned for June 4th at 2:00 in Foley Square in Manhattan. Since the announcement on May 8th, we have put together a growing national Coalition including Senators Hillary Clinton and Charles Schumer and Congressman Charles Rangel. In New York City, we have additional support of 30 New York City Council Members, including Speaker Miller, Public Advocate Betsy Gotbaum, and the Borough Presidents from the Bronx, Brooklyn and Manhattan.

The Countdown for Fairness is strengthened by the diversity and vitality of its membership. I am writing to you today to ask you to join our Coalition and participate in the June 4th rally. Let's show Governor Pataki and other leaders in Albany a vast Coalition that demands action now. After 30 years, it is clear that the Rockefeller Drug Laws are a failure. They have led to the unfair lengthy incarceration of tens of thousands of non-violent drug offenders. These laws waste precious resources on the wrong target –low-level non-violent offenders – instead of fighting large-scale drug pushers and violent offenders. New York State cannot wait another year to repeal the Drug Laws.

We must restore sentencing discretion to trial judges now. While we face the worst budget crisis in years, cutbacks, and layoffs, we need to find creative solutions for saving. According to the Correction Association, New York State could save nearly $245 million annually by repealing the Rockefeller Drug Laws. After 30 years of failure, it is time to repeal the mandatory minimum laws and stop wasting precious resources! I have attached a current list of our ever-growing Coalition. Please contact us to discuss your participation at 212-981-5265. I hope you will join us June 4th and support the Countdown to Fairness.

Sincerely, Andrew Cuomo

COUNTDOWN TO FAIRNESS Mothers of the New York Disappeared. Russell Simmons & the Hip-Hop Summit Action Network & Andrew Cuomo

Supporters and Endorsers:

- Senator Hillary Clinton
- Senator Chuck Schumer
- Congressman Charles Rangel
- Congressman Elijah Cummings
- Congresswoman Maxine Waters
- Congressman John Conyers
- Congressman Gregory Meeks
- Congressman Ed Towns
- Congressman Major Owens
- State Senator David Patterson
- State Senator Eric T. Schneiderman
- State Senator Liz Krueger
- Assemblyman Jose Rivera
- Assemblyman Jeffrion L. Aubry
- Assemblyman Sam Hoyt
- Former Senator Carol Mosley Braun
- Kweisi Mfume
- Tom Golisano
- Rev. Jesse Jackson
- Rev. Al Sharpton
- Sean P. Diddy Combs
- Damon Dash
- Rev. Run
- Doug E. Fresh
- Cash Money Crew
- Beastie Boys

- Ludacris
- Red Man
- Method Man
- Steve Rifkind
- Kevin Liles
- Keith Murray
- Cam'ron
- The Diplomats
- Ghost Face
- Tony Maranda
- Frank Garcia
- Dennis Rivera
- George MacDonald
- Terrence Stevens
- Catherine Crier
- Anthony Papa
- Jan Warren
- Jann Wenner
- Borough President C. Virginia Fields
- Borough President Adolfo Carrion
- Borough President Marty Markowitz
- Public Advocate Betsy Gotbaum
- Ossie Davis & Ruby Dee
- City Council Member Joel Rivera
- City Council Member Bill DeBlasio
- City Council Member Yvette Clarke
- City Council Member Larry Seabrook
- City Council Speaker Gifford Miller
- City Council Majority Leader Joel Rivera
- City Council Member Helen Foster
- City Council Member Hiram Monserrate
- City Council Member Bill DeBlasio
- City Council Member Yvette Clarke
- City Council Member Christine Quinn

- City Council Member James Sanders, Jr.
- City Council Member Charles Barron
- City Council Member James Davis
- City Council Member Maria Baez
- City Council Member Leroy Comrie

Organizations:

- Congressional Black Caucus
- National Urban League
- NAACP
- Hip-Hop Summit Action Network
- NYACLU, Donna Lieberman
- Drop the Rock Coalition
- Rolling Stone Magazine
- National Latino Officers Association, Tony Maranda
- Bronx Hispanic Association, Frank Garcia
- Nation of Islam--a minister was there
- National Action Network
- PUSH/National Rainbow Coalition
- The Doe Fund
- 1199 SEIU New York's Health
- and Human Service Union
- NYS Association of Substance Abuse Providers (ASAP), Roy Kearse & John Capolla
- Samaritan House
- Justice Works Community
- Conscious Movements Collective
- Families against Mandatory Minimum Sentencing (FAMM)
- CURE-NY (Citizens United for the Rehabilitation
- of Errants)
- StopTheDrugWar.org: The Reform Coordination Network

- Students for a Sensible Drug Policy
- Brennan Center for Justice, NYU
- Prison Family Community Forum
- Correction Association of New York, Bob Gangi
- Tulia Legal Defense Fund
- Center for Constitutional Rights
- William Moses Kunstler Fund for Racial Justice Project

P.E.A.C.E

The pressure was on Pataki but it became apparent the governor was not going to agree to the request. The event was finalized and the biggest drug war rally in the history of NYC took place. Over 50,000 people showed up that day to hear speakers like P-Diddy and Susan Sarandon and many other celebrities and entertainers. Security was maintained by Louis Farrakhan's army of Muslims and levels of security were created to prevent the crowd from entering the stage area. The Mothers of the NY Disappeared had front row seats at the event and several members spoke and told their stories to a cheering crowd. The event was unbelievable and I swore on that day that something good was going to happen but I was wrong.

The event was successful and showed the power we had with Russell Simmons taking charge and getting national and international attention to the issue. What happened next was something we could not imagine. A struggle broke out between us and Russell in what would be considered to be positive reform and two camps of thought emerged.

On one side of it, the diehard activists that had worked so hard for many years to fight the laws were calling for full repeal. It was thought that this was the only way negotiating meaningful changes would be implemented. This was the original position Simmons took in the beginning of the campaign, but now he had jumped ship and joined those who thought that repeal was a farfetched idea and would never happen. Instead, he wanted to try to get a watered-down version of change in the way of incremental change. Simmons wanted to make a deal and it was clear he wanted to be known as a major player that would be the first to change the laws that had existed for thirty years.

During a weekly meeting, it was revealed that Russell had set up a meeting with the governor at his NYC office. We found out that Deborah Small of the Drug Policy Alliance had become Simmons secret advisor and convinced him to abandon his repeal position. Simmons had been seeking a way to get back face after Gov. Pataki refused to change the laws, then agreed with Gov. Pataki and adopted his reform position. This was totally against what our Coalition originally wanted to do. Now, because he was leading our movement, we wanted it to be clear we did not support Simmons.

We leaked our disappointment to the press and the Village Voice captured our thoughts clearly in a piece that was published on June 10, 2003 titled "Movement Hijacked by Hip-hop?" Activists Fear a Compromise on Rockefeller Repeal by Dasau Allah.

"The Countdown to Fairness Coalition's June 4 City Hall rally may have failed to attract an astronomical turnout, but the hip-hop-infused initiative has attracted attention in Albany and brought higher visibility to the decades-long war to repeal the notorious Rockefeller Drug Laws. However, along with the new momentum, there is concern among longtime repeal advocates that mixed signals from the coalition's leadership may blight political negotiations and result in a meaningless makeover instead of a significant overhaul of the disputed legislation. The Countdown to Fairness Coalition, led by Russell Simmons Hip Hop Summit Action Network, (HSAN) the Mothers of the New York Disappeared (MNYD), and Andrew Cuomo, also includes such notables as Tom Golisano and Sean "P. Diddy" Combs, and is the latest offensive in the ongoing battle to overturn the ironclad drug legislation enacted in 1973 under Governor Nelson D. Rockefeller. The laws' mandatory sentencing schemes, which eliminate judicial discretion, have long been criticized as draconian and are credited with unnecessarily inflating state prison populations at enormous taxpayer expense. Last month, the coalition issued an ultimatum to Albany to either repeal the Rockefeller drug laws by June 4 or face the wrath of the hip-hop community, later announcing the date would either serve for celebration of the laws' repeal or protest against the politicians' inaction.

Organizers anticipated upward of 100,000 to attend the event, but inclement weather appears to have frustrated expectations. Sources place attendance between 20,000 and 50,000, although HSAN charges that people were turned away by police. "It was a good event," said Drop the Rock spokesman Bob Gangi, "If there had been greater numbers, I think the event would have been even more effective as a strategy. Still, it's the largest drug law repeal rally that has ever been held.

Plus, there were a lot of people who got educated about the issue." "It's not about how many came, but who is listening," said Simmons backstage, and that is precisely why there are concerns within the campaign's leadership.

Since the countdown began, there has been a whirlwind of activity around changing the laws. This whirlwind has been both a blessing and a curse to the coalition. There are opposing viewpoints and tensions in the group over ultimate objectives, and who should be at the negotiating table. At the rally, Randy Credico, director of the MNYD, said: "There's been some infighting here among some of the organizers about the message up in Albany. Some of the people involved in the negotiations are promoting reform. We are demanding repeal." The repeal vs. reform debate is the main point of contention within the coalition. "Everybody agrees that the optimal goal is repeal," said Cuomo, "but everyone also agrees that the shot at getting repeal is the shot of me waking up tomorrow with blond hair, blue eyes, and a small nose. It ain't gonna happen." Credico sees it differently. "The problem is we set our sights too low," he said. After giving an account of the long and arduous struggles veteran activists have faced, an impassioned Credico added: "For some of the people involved who appropriated the negotiations to call for reform and accept reform, I consider that treasonous. They are saying repeal is not possible and they'll have to answer to us . . . "

To the dismay of these activists, HSAN and Deborah P. Small of the Drug Policy Alliance have emerged as the chief negotiators with state lawmakers. "We should all be involved in the negotiations," said Credico. "[Simmons] can't be involved by himself." "Russell is sexier to talk to," said Cuomo. "Let's be honest. Meet with the Mothers of the New York Disappeared or with the Correction Association, you don't get a story. You meet with Russell Simmons, the governor looks like an enlightened activist sitting down with everybody." There is a sense that the momentum gained by ties to the hip-hop community has eclipsed the activists who were the movement's catalysts.

More importantly, activists are worried that lawmakers will just offer the new negotiators the same compromise deals that have been rejected in the past. The assembly has already presented the same legislation offered last year; Gangi called it old wine in a new bottle. "I think that there is a concern," said Gangi, "that out of this momentum could come a 'deal' or 'compromise' that is very limited and that would be worse than no deal at all; that the governor and the legislative leaders will use the cover of Simmons's intervention to come up with a half-baked compromise that doesn't really advance the cause." Simmons says that he is not alone in the negotiations, and progress is being made:

"Deborah Small is doing negotiation. She's been working on this for many years. She's committed to closing. I'm committed to closing. We have a draft of something that we are going to circulate from the governor," said Simmons. "A lot of people are calling it a jailbreak or saying what they want to say about it, and there are other people who are saying that it's too much of a compromise, but I'm a deal maker and I want to make a deal." But it is just this rush on Simmons's part to make a deal that has activists fearful. "There's a mixed message out there," said Credico. "Someone says that he'll take any deal. He's a deal maker. Well, you got to talk to the people you are making that deal for." Simmons reacted strongly to the tensions that have arisen since the rally. "I've heard a lot about that. I don't give a fuck about them.

All I care is that I appreciate their hard work and they are the true heroes," said Simmons. "I love Randy Credico's work. He's been excellent. But to criticize somebody for coming and adding to your effort, creating awareness of your effort— I'm not saying he's done that, but anybody who does that is missing the point. I don't give a fuck. I want to get people out of jail. That's my only objective. Get people out of jail and make the laws more fair."

"There was a breakdown in communications to Russell Simmons," said Anthony Papa, MNYD co-founder, who served 12 years under the Rockefeller laws. "Russell's a businessman. I have nothing bad to say about him. What he did was take as his adviser Deborah Small to see the governor, and we don't agree with her philosophy. She wants to make a deal; we call it a sellout because it's watered-down reform."

Although Simmons has gone on record as saying the difference between repeal or reform is semantics, he appears aware of the nuances: "What does total repeal mean, anyway? That no law exists at all? We know that we want to return some discretion to the judges and we know that we want to send people home retroactively. We want to get thousands of people out of jail now."

Papa says recent budget concerns will bring 800 prisoners home, so there are higher stakes involved in changing the laws to stop others from just taking the places of those who are released. "We want the judge to have [full] discretion to look at the totality of facts," said Papa, noting that state prosecutors have hampered efforts at true reform out of their own personal interests. The current makeup of the drug laws allows prosecutors of A-1 drug felonies to control the outcome of the case. "Prosecutors live and die by their conviction records. This is not a case of what's just and what's the correct thing to do. It's about judicial economy. This is not about a business deal. This is about people's lives."

Sources close to all parties involved said that other high-profile coalition members are dissatisfied with the direction negotiations seem to be heading, but remain silent for fear of sabotaging the current chance to change the Rockefeller laws. "Understand, there may be tensions and disagreements among the overall coalition," said Gangi. "That is often the case. And that doesn't mean that we trash each other or stop talking to each other." At press time, a draft resolution was being prepared by legislators to be circulated among all parties. "If we can't get repeal, which nobody believes we're going to get," said Cuomo, "there may be a divergence depending then on the deal. But you're going to have to wait and see. There may be a deal that everyone can take."

Soon after the piece appeared, we found out that Simmons was invited to meet with the Governor Pataki and the republican and democratic leaders Joe Bruno and Shelly Silver. The meeting occurred on June 20, the last day of the 2003 legislative session. A seven-and-a-half-hour meeting took place with Simmons emerging and swearing to the press that a deal was cut, but was very disappointed that the next day there was no deal made.

I actually felt bad for Russell because they had fooled him. I breathed a sigh of relief and was almost glad watered down reform did not materialize. But then again it was another year repeal of the Rock laws had passed us by. I wondered if we would ever get reform of the Rockefeller Drug Laws.

CHAPTER ELEVEN

Brazil and my Life Changing Trip to Argentina

My wife Luciana (Lila) called me from Brazil and asked when I was going to be with her and our son. "Baby, soon" I said. Her daily calls had gently prodded me to come there to start a new life with her. I had told her for almost two years now that I would leave my life, as I knew it, to join her. I was obsessed with reforming the Rockefeller Drug Laws. It had become the center of my life. The question of me leaving my life in America for love in Brazil always lay heavily on my mind. I realized that in life you face choices that can drastically alter your existence.

I thought that most of the time we do not act on positive choices in our lives, because we did not want to alter the balance of our lives. This was especially true if we have some measure of comfort. Luciana had returned to Brazil to give birth to our son Anthony and decided she wanted to stay in Brazil to transform Jatoba, the family farm, into a yoga retreat. The plan was that I would come to Brazil to join her. However, in reality, I was afraid to act upon the words I spoke to her. I had lived in America all my life and the thought of leaving everything behind was incomprehensible.

My weeks of apprehension turned into months and then years. Luciana had become impatient. I had traveled to Brazil to be with her whenever I could. The short two-week trips were not enough for her. I knew in my heart she needed a husband and my son needed a father. Then one afternoon in central park, I heard a presentation from the Dalai Lama. He talked about learning to letting go of the rope in order to take new steps in life. Now after the heartbreak of being so close but failing to reform the Rockefeller Drug Laws, for two successive years in a row, I came to the realization that changing the laws was not going to happen anytime soon. Then I had an amazing realization. Since I could not change the Rockefeller Drug Laws why not just change my life? Maybe this would compensate for my failure and at the same time, I could be a father and a husband once again.

Suddenly like a brick that hit me smack in the head, I got it. I got the courage to change my life. After years of disappointment in trying to advocate for meaningful reform of the Rockefeller Drug Laws, I decided to abandon my quest, and follow my heart. I resigned my position at the law firm and cashed out my pension to pay off my credit cards. I also sold my famous painting 15 to Life for a ton of dough to an art collector and left America to be with my family in Brazil.

Luciana had done a fine job building a life in Brazil with our son. Jatoba was a beautiful peaceful place that sat on two hundred acres of land. Its name came from the Jatoba tree that stood tall in front of the main house. It was planted five feet high, on top of a circular mount that was made from old stone. The nine-room home was grand. Lila used the main house for work utilizing the living room as a place for yoga sessions and meditation. The additional rooms housed guests who stayed for her various workshops and retreats. On the grounds outside were a half a dozen single rooms, along with a very large space located in another house. Beside the second house, about twenty-five yards away stood a lake where water supplied to the farm was born.

This was priceless, because this is where life began from the nurturing water that ran throughout the farm, running into a second lake in the front of Jatobas property. Behind the lake was another house where Aldelso and his wife Rita had lived with their four children. They were the caretakers of the property for many years and had followed her father Joe there from Aldelsos old town of Bahia. The farm was full of creatures including horses and cows that roamed the fields along with wild animals and insects of all kind. Lila loved nature and was very compassionate towards all the life forms that lived on the farm.

Luciana's favorite animal was a dog named Om. It was a huge black Rottweiler. He had become the love of her life. When he was a pup, he fit into the easy and simple life of the farm. When the dog grew into a very large and aggressive animal, it became another matter. The dog suddenly did not fit into the world that Luciana had built. His instincts took over and the dog became wild and uncontrollable, attacking anything that moved. Luciana tried to cope with it, even when Om chewed up one of the kittens. Her patients slowly eroded when Om had run away and returned several days later dirty and full of caked up blood. We found out from Adelso that neighboring farmers were looking for a black dog that had killed several calves from their herds of cows. Before she could make a decision whether or not to give him away, he put his faith in his own hands.

The next morning, I was awoken by a tremendous chatter outside of the front of the house. I ran to the window to catch a glimpse of Om shaking something viciously with his jaws. At first, I thought it was another small dog that lived on the farm. But when I got outside I found lying dead next to Om, was a fifty-pound anteater. The animal wandered onto the farm in search of food like many other creatures that would visit Jatoba. But this creature had the misfortune of meeting Om. And by the same token, Om had crossed paths with a wild animal that had mortally wounded him.

He had a large gash in his chest cavity inflicted by the razor-sharp claws of the animal. Om died several days later. I was pretty shaken up but I remembered what my father in law Joe had told me about the farm. He warned me about nature and the sounds of silence at Jatoba. After a few weeks, I realized what he said was true. I had been a native New Yorker all my life and was accustomed to living in a city filled with all kinds of sounds. But now, the sounds of the big city were gone and dead silence had taken its place. There were no sirens and sounds of traffic, just pitch-black silence that began to drive me batty.

I started losing sleep and found myself staying up all night waiting for any type of sound to materialize. I remembered one night past midnight, I had waited for hours for a sound. Suddenly out of nowhere, the silence of the night was broken by the sound of a frog croaking. At first, the repetitive sound of the frog was a welcome change, but as the night went on the croaking became unbearable. The voice of the frog had changed into a wail, soon sounding like the cries of a human being. I shut all of the windows of the house, but the sound penetrated the walls. The darkness of the night added to the intensity of the horror of the sound.

The sound and darkness became familiar, bringing me back to my cell in Sing Sing. It was there I inched my way to the front of my cell where I pressed my face against the cold steel bars to listen to the cries that woke me from my sleep. Moments later, the prisoner next door told me not to worry, and informed me that the cries were not human, but those of a cat being fucked by a madman. I could not believe my ears when he told me that a crazed prisoner purchased the cats that ran wild on the prison grounds. The administration allowed the cats to flourish to control the rat population at the prison. The cats were everywhere, and soon I developed an affliction every time I saw a cat, bringing on a queasy gut wrenching sickness in my stomach that overpowered me.

I couldn't take the sound of the frog anymore, grabbed a broom, and ran from my house into the field toward the sound. I climbed over a wooden fence and reached the water trawl that was the home of the frog. The sound began to intensify and it compelled me to strike down at the water over and over again. Splashes of water began to violently bounce into the air. A wild frenzy came about. After a few moments, the sound of the frog croaking stopped, and I stood there staring at the shimmering shadows of light from the full moon, when a black cat appeared. The cat stared at me and I froze in my tracks.

The sickness quickly came and I ran from the field back into the house. The incident would become a repetitive occurrence at Jatoba, sometimes overpowering me, causing me to lose control. I told Luciana about it and she told me to ask for spiritual guidance from the shaman couple that often visited Jatoba and consulted its residents. Rita came from Rio with her husband Rico and two children, to hold healing sessions several times a year. At first, I was hesitant to approach them and ask for help. But I knew I desperately needed some help in order to live on Jatoba.

The night after Rico had performed a fire dance I asked Lila to ask him for a consultation. Rico did not speak English so my wife had to be our interpreter. We sat in the kitchen of our house and Rico did a reading of my palm. I was intrigued to find out that in my prior life I was a nomad of some sort, who had roamed the land and never stood in one place for a long time. He told me that my past life would run into my present life and that to my surprise, this was the last life of my soul. At the end of the session, he also told me that I needed to stay busy in order to cope with my life in Brazil.

I was hesitant to see Rita because of the power she had. The last trip to Jatoba she healed a client, but at the same time used unethical actions. Rita had read the mind of a client whose dead father had spoken to her. She told the client that his father was mad at him for not publishing his writings. His son had promised him before he passed on. The son was astounded by this and she became his advisor in his affairs. He brought his entire family and friends

But a problem arose when we found out that Rita had tried to convince the client to give up his worldly goods to her, including the family internet business. I went to Rico with my problem and he read my horoscope, and told me many things that amazed me. This included the information that this was the last life of my soul. I was taken aback with this. He told me in order to survive my new life at Jatoba, I needed to stay busy in order to cope. If not, my life would be doomed there.

No sooner than he told me that I began plans to build an art studio. I enlisted the help of a builder named Gordo, which translated into English, means fat man. He was the boyfriend of Rosy who worked part time doing housekeeping work at Jatoba. Twenty yards from our house, we rebuilt an old worn down horse stable into a magnificent studio. I had always dreamed of having my own studio where I could create my art. It was generous in space and was full of natural light. The studio became part of Jatoba program, when Luciana asked me to conduct art classes for guests. I developed a method of teaching the creation of spiritual mandala paintings.

Because of Luciana's business of maintaining a yoga retreat, the farm had an array of individuals from around the world visiting. This included Zen Buddhist monks, mystical Shamans and those that wanted a relaxing place to do their yoga practice. Luciana's description of Jatoba was honed in on the concept that it was a place where you had a distinct opportunity to live Yoga.

Luciana's philosophy was that through the practice of yoga you would experience simplicity and beauty. And you would be in harmony with the body, mind and spirit. She believed that everyone already was at peace with themselves because it was our natural state. Through yoga, you would learn how to bring out this natural state as a way to live in the present moment. At Jatoba she offered an opportunity for you to discover that place within you that is beyond external change. Like the sky, Jatoba was always beautiful and bright. Luciana had it right when she recited me a poem whenever I was in doubt with myself. She said "Yesterday is history, tomorrow is a mystery, today is a gift, that's why they call it the present."

One night my wife, son and I were sitting in the living room watching a film. I went to the kitchen to wash my face and my wife let out a shout "Oh my god". I ran back in the room and she pointed to the ceiling of our refurbished barn. The white ceiling was almost black in its center, it was covered with hornets. I immediately freaked out and told her to take Anthony down stairs to the other house. I ran into the bedroom and put on two sweaters and a jacket, a scarf, a hat, my gloves and my thickest boots. I was ready for war. I then ran outside to my studio grabbed a broom, took a pair of Joe Boxer underwear and wrapped it around the bristles. I doused the boxer shorts with a ton of kerosene and ran to the house.

I grabbed some matches and lit the broom. A flame three-foot high came alive. I jabbed the tip of the broom to the top of the ceiling. In a flash dozens of hornets began dropping. I followed them while cursing madly. Suddenly, I turned around and saw that the rubber from the bristles had landed on our cloth sofa, causing it to catch fire. The same thing happened to my favorite leather leisure chair, and the bottom of our front door. The floor was covered with dead hornets and black melted plastic droppings from the broom. I had almost burnt down the house, but I did my duty as protector of our home.

Soon after my art studio was completed and I began to paint full-time, creating a body of work that was influenced by my new life in Brazil. I meet an array of individuals from around the world. This included Zen Buddhist monks, mystical Shamans and others, all seeking to share their wisdom. After speaking to them, I became torn between the life I left behind and my current life. I desperately sought to find an answer to my situation. I wanted to be with my family, but my true calling was reforming the horrendous laws, that put me away for so many years. I had a tough decision to make.

Through a deep meditation, I recalled a time when I had to make another tough decision. I was locked in my cell and Tutee came by. He was part of a crazy Puerto Rican crew that I had been hanging with. Tutee was their recruiter and wanted me to join them. He took out his blade and cut his finger and stuck his hand through the bars. He wanted me to cut my finger and bond our two fingers together, so I could officially be inducted in their crew. This is how you survived in prison. There was power in being group. If you messed with one, you were messing with the entire crew. It was a good way to secure my safety in the dangerous world of Sing Sing. I looked at Tutees finger dripping with blood and weighed the consequences of the situation. I thought hard, questioning whether or not I should join the gang. We stared each other down, and through this eye contact, my better judgment made me say no. Thank God I refused, Tutee wound up dying from AIDS, just like many others at the prison who had shared dirty needles.

Tragically, the grass was not greener for me in Brazil. I found that the stigma of my imprisonment had followed me. When people found out about my past life as a convict, their friendly attitudes disappeared. I thought maybe it wasn't about me being an ex-con. Maybe it was because I did not understand their culture, nor speak their language. I wanted to believe this, but I had experienced this before in New York. I felt it in my bones that it was the stigma of being an ex-offender

It was at that time, I got a phone call from Randy Credico. It had been over a year since I last spoke to him. He made some small talk then said, "I got a great idea. Let's take a trip to Buenos Aires, Argentina, to pay homage to the Argentinean women of Los Madres de los Desaparecidos". My first reaction was no way I was going, but as I listened to him trying to convince me, Credico was making sense. After all, these women were the inspiration for the formation of the organization we co-founded, the Mothers of the New York Disappeared. I told him I would go but only under the condition that I could bring my wife Luciana, and he would foot the entire bill. Credico readily agreed. He was desperate for me to go with him.

Little did I know the trip I was about to embark on, was to set in motion, a dramatic change in my life. When I told Luciana, it would good for us to get away and see Argentina she was hesitant because Randy had left a bad impression on her. Luciana had a standing joke she use to tell, about me and Randy, and our attempt to change the Rockefeller Drug Laws. Most of our planning was done over cocktails, and at the end of the strategy sessions, Randy couldn't stand up and I couldn't see straight, after consuming a shit load of margaritas. Neither one of us could walk a straight line, yet we trying to do the impossible. She was right. But one thing she had overlooked was the dedication we had, to reach the impossible task. This flame always remained strong in us, whether or not, we were sober or drunk.

We met Credico in a hotel in Buenos Aires Argentina. He had arrived along with Alice, a photographer who doubled as our interpreter and Julie Colon an activist. Marge Kunstler was also there, who was the wife of legendary civil rights attorney William Kunstler. He had already set up meetings with three different groups of Madres. The first was with Juana De Pargament, President of Association of the Mothers of the Plaza de Mayo on February 5, 2004. We met at the their newly built coffee shop. But when we got there and toured it, we realized it served as a multi-purpose home for its 2,000 members to study and meet.

The association had acquired two adjacent buildings that featured a library, theater and an area for study and seminars. As we walked to her office, the walls of the buildings were lined with works of Karl Marx and Leon Trotsky. When we entered her office, her walls were full of photographs with political figures and celebrities like Che Guevara and U2s Bono posing with her. Juana looked like a sweet elderly looking, well into her sixties. Her thirty-year-old son had disappeared during the reign of terror in Argentina by the military dictatorship that overtook the country. But we didn't know at the time, she was a tough cookie, and a well-known radical who was quoted as saying that America deserved the 9/11 attack and when it occurred, she felt happiness.

In our meeting with her Credico introduced Julie Colon. Her mother Melita Oliviera had served thirteen years of a fifteen-to-life sentence for a first-time non-violent offense for the sale of cocaine before she was granted clemency two years prior by Governor George Pataki. Julie told Pargament her story and how she had fought for her mother's freedom. "My mother had made a mistake, and she paid dearly for it," said Colon. I am here to join with other mothers and family members to share the pain of losing someone dear. Although it was not finite, the act of her being taken from my life for all those years was devastating to me." This was because Julie was placed in foster care.

Her case is representative of many others in the NY group including Arlene Olberg, whose baby was born in prison while she was serving time under the Rockefeller drug laws. We had arranged for Pargament to reach out to her contacts to try and arrange for some media coverage of our group marching with their group at their weekly march at have marched on Thursday afternoons in front of Government House, where Argentina's president lived. It would be good press for her organization and the movement.

The next day we met with a second group of mothers at their offices. They were known as the Madres Plaza De Mayo Linea Fundadora. It was a much smaller space they situated than the other group. As I walked around their space, I was amazed when I saw a wall that contained photographs of the group's history. My eyes were fixated on a black and white photo of a group of mothers shouting at men dressed in military uniforms. The faces in the photos represented the struggle that they had experienced when they went through the agony of having their country taken over by the military in Argentina's "dirty war" which lasted from 1976 to1983. Over 30,000 individuals had disappeared.

Any individuals who were considered subversive against the military were kidnapped and murdered. In a corner of one of the rooms, I came upon stacks of signs that were used when the group would stage protests.

As I flipped through the stacks of posters, I read the vivid descriptions on each of them, all detailing the demise of the victim. One poster had a news article that was attached to it dated from 1987. It described how the Mothers of the Plaza De Mayo had started a campaign that collected signatures on handkerchiefs.

The lettering above the article had the words "Carcel A Los Genocidas" which meant jail to the murderers. It felt eerie holding the posters, and I was surprised how similar they were to the signs we had created used in our weekly protests in NYC. Although no one was murdered in New York, the creation of the drug laws led to the social death of hundreds of thousands of individuals that were sentenced under the Rockefeller Drug Laws.

The delegation of women introduced themselves to our group. One by one they told us of their stories which all shared the common fact that their children were taken away from them and murdered. Since they spoke no English our interpreter translated for us. It was sad indeed and our group which included my wife, Julie and Marge Kunstler started to cry. Randy and I soon joined in on the sobbing and the entire room was moved to tears. After we all regained our composure, the leader of their organization, Taty Almeida, spoke to us. She turned out to be a charmer. She and half dozen members were chosen from her group. They were much friendlier than Pargament, and because of this, Credico took a liking to them. After the meeting Taty suggested we go to a reporter she knew at the local Associated Press office. Credico did not hesitate; he was a media junkie by heart and knew that the show must go on. After the meeting, Credico went and touched base with the reporter. The very next day a big story appeared in the local paper about the historic march that was to take place with the Linea Fundadora group and the Mothers of the NY Disappeared.

On Feb. 5, 2004, the historic march took place at the Plaza de Mayo circle. For over twenty-five years, Argentine mothers had come to the circle every Thursday to protest against the disappearance of their love ones, from the despicable acts of the military dictatorship of Argentina, which formed in 1976. In our meetings with the two groups, we told them that we came to Argentina to pay homage to them. They had inspired us in our seven-year struggle against the Rockefeller drug laws of New York State. Now here we were groups of mothers, from worlds apart, united against the violation of human rights.

It was a bright, sunny day at the circle where dozens of elderly women marched through the plaza, praying that their dedication might somehow bring justice to the children of the disappeared. Proud and strong women from several groups participated. They began the march waving bright blue flags proudly displaying their logo. One banner read "Ni Un Paso A Tras!!" -- "No Step Back" The banner was held tightly in their frail hands. A sea of white handkerchiefs adorned the heads of the Argentinean mothers, gracefully marching in protest against atrocities that were committed against them and their families. Tens of thousands of people were kidnapped and murdered in a reign of terror. Some 500 young children and babies were born to mothers who were kept alive long enough to give birth.

Then the babies were given to the families of high ranking military officers and their accomplices, thus robbing those children of their true identities and families. There were approximately three hundred fifty detention centers and concentration camps, some large and some small, spread throughout the entire country. Where over 1,000 military personnel were involved in the abduction, physical and psychological torture and murder of the disappeared occurred. These activities were sanctioned and planned by the military.

In 1973, a similar reign silently began in New York State where the draconian Rockefeller drug laws sentenced thousands of men and women, many non-violent offenders, to life imprisonment. They were "disappeared" from the roles they played in society. These laws devastated and destroyed families. Although the acts of the New York legislature were not of the same caliber as those implemented by the Argentinean dictatorship, the enactment of the Rockefeller drug laws was similarly a violation of human rights. Over 94 percent of the population incarcerated in New York State prisons were people of color.

As I watched the mothers marching, I felt the connection the groups had through the pain of losing someone dear. I thought to myself as I marched that this is what ties the American families who have lost sons and daughters to the Rockefeller drug laws with the Argentinean families who lost members to the brutal dictatorship.

I began talking to Laura Estella de Carlotto of the president of the Abuelas de Plaza de Mayo. These were the grandmothers of the disappeared which was formed on October 22, 1977, and who were dedicated to finding the children that were stolen from them. She told me that in an attempt at political repression, the dictatorship would kidnap pregnant women and put them in concentration camps where their children were born. Then they were murdered and their children were put up for adoption. She had told me that through her program 77 children have been found through DNA testing. Estela a soft-spoken woman in her 70's sadly told me the story of her losing her daughter on November 26, 1977. Laura Estella de Carlotto had been a militant student at the university. Estela had warned her daughter of the danger, but she did not care and wanted to change the country. Nine months after she was kidnapped the military police called Estela to tell her that her 21-year-old daughter had been assassinated.

She told us that protesting the kidnappings "was dangerous and that many of her friends were kidnapped and assassinated." But their perseverance paid off when she said that the government annulled two immunity laws of those who committed the atrocities, allowing the law to be able to prosecute them. Estela said that their new president had opened doors to us all the time because he belongs to the same generation of the children that disappeared."

As the women marched around the plaza, I began taking photos of the event. I noticed that the different groups of mothers never marched with each other and instead made sure a huge gap existed separating the groups. This seemed odd to me and I asked a local reporter if he knew the reason why.

The reporter told me that the reason for this was that the two groups hated each other. It seemed that Taty's group was getting government funding and the other group said that this was selling out to the government that they had been responsible for the murder of their children. Whatever the reason was, the two groups did not get along. It reminded me of the strife that existed among organizations that fought the drug war in the United States. Many of them competed with each other for funding and this led to the same kind of friction.

After the march, we were scheduled to appear at Pargaments place to speak about our group. Before going there, Credico went over to the tables that were set up by groups that sold souvenirs. He chose Pargaments group and bought one of everything they had. When we arrived at their place Credico looked comical wearing his array of souvenirs. He had a cap on along with two tee shirts he slipped over his sports jacket. In his left hand, he held a coffee cup, and his right wrist, was adorned with several colorful bracelets. But all these souvenirs could not buy away the anger that Pargament had when Credico approached her. She was as mad as hell that Credico had double-crossed her when he met with Tady's group and appeared in the newspaper with them. She explained to him that they had made an agreement to appear in the paper with her group and he did not abide by it.

Credico tried his best to sweet talk his way out of this but she was not buying it. The tension in the air was thick as we walked towards the hall where we were scheduled to talk. A small frail woman came up to me dressed in a traditional Madres headgear, a white handkerchief covered her head. She began to scream at us in English, telling us how we could associate ourselves with Tady's group who were sellouts. After that confrontation, I saw that the situation might escalate and become dangerous. The members of the Association of the Mothers of the Plaza de mayo were pissed off. I wanted to leave. Credico who was nervous as hell insisted that I stay. He wanted to address the group. I told him he was fucking crazy and I was leaving. I took Luciana and we left the coffee house and walked the streets for about an hour until we returned.

When I got back, I had envisioned a scene where a group of the toughest seventy-year-old Madres had overpowered Credico, hog-tied him, and took immense pleasure taking turns waterboarding him. But that wasn't the case at all. When I walked into the meeting hall there was Credico on stage doing his act mimicking the voice of President Ronald Reagan wisecracking on his administration's war on Central America. I had forgotten Credico' past as a standup comedian in Las Vegas where he faced situations like this all the time with drunken patrons that booed and heckled him during his shows. I guess that animosity fueled his creativity in his comedy. Randy had won over the crowd and actually got most of the group to like him. It was an amazing feat considering they were looking to hang him from a tree a few hours prior.

We soon left Argentina and Luciana and I returned to Brazil. I tried my best to fit into the lifestyle that Luciana wanted me to live, but struggled greatly. After my experience in Argentina, I was motivated again by my activist calling. Meeting the Madres had ignited the fire that had I thought had been distinguished.

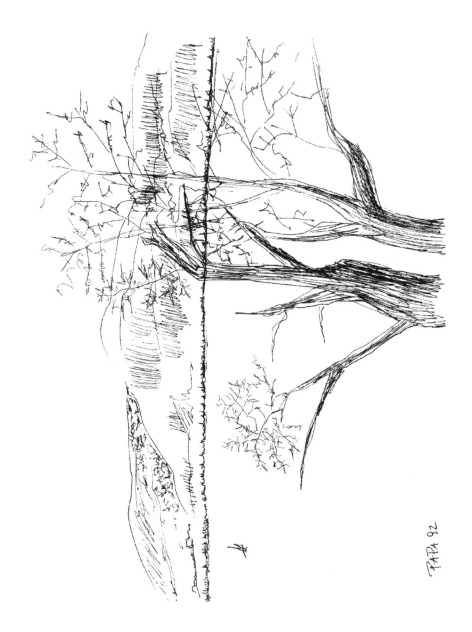

PAPA 92

CHAPTER TWELVE

Andrew Cuomo Gets Me the Whitney Museum

A few months after Argentina my publisher Adam Parfrey of Feral House contacted me and told me, he was ready to publish my memoir. I had written it before moving to Brazil and was very excited that my story would be available for the world to see. I had worked on the book for over five years and developed an idea that my book would bring to light the Rockefeller Drug Laws and become a vehicle that could be used to fight for meaningful reform of the laws. I began making the final edits of the book from Brazil and sending it to my publisher. We went through a series of edits until Adam gave me a final deadline. The book was completed and in the hands of the designer and a projected date of publication was made.

Feral House was a small publishing company and didn't have the where-with-all to really promote the book. I knew I needed to be involved with the process. Although I was in Brazil, I knew I had the ability to make a big splash with the media in America. I had a similar experience when I was in prison and successfully planned and put on an art exhibit in the free world. And I did that from my 6 x 9 cell with the help of some friends on the outside. It was 1996 and New York Theological Seminary's president invited me to show my work at their 29th street offices. They had a rotating exhibit showing the work of various artists. When the show went on, we got tremendous media coverage including the NY Times with a piece titled "Survival on the Tip of a Paint Brush." This brought media attention to my case and helped me bring my case to the governor's attention where he eventually granted me my freedom through my art.

I knew I needed to have a big book opening that would turn out the same media attention that would propel my book along with the issue of the Rockefeller Drug Laws in the limelight. I started reaching out to individuals and organizations I worked with in the past including the Legal Action Center (LAC) and The Fortune Society. These organizations had also worked to fight for changing these laws.

Pretty soon I started receiving responses from my request. Almost all of them said they were happy for me but could not help me out. My dream of somehow getting attention for my book was slowly dying. Then several weeks later out of the blue I received an email from Ashley Cotton from Andrew Cuomo's staff. I had worked with her in the past with Andrew on Rockefeller reform. She told me that Andrew was interested in helping me and to give him a call. I was excited to say the least and called Andrew Cuomo, a former U.S. HUD Secretary (currently the Governor of New York). I had helped Cuomo with his 2002 run for governor when Andrew used my story and art to support his Rockefeller reform platform.

Andrew and I had a conversation and he told me that he would like to throw a book party for me at the Whitney Museum of American Art. I was elated, but I doubted this would ever happen. I hesitated when I told Cuomo of a possible conflict of interest with the Whitney. He asked me to explain. I told him short and sweet the startling truth that when my self-portrait was shown at the Whitney in 1994 I had to lie and tell them I was a convicted murderer in order to get into the exhibit. I explained that after my painting was chosen; the curator told the prison administration that the artist chosen needed to be a convicted murderer, in order to fit the artistic/intellectual criteria of the art installation it would appear in. It was my last hope, since I had exhausted all of my legal remedies. Only my art could save me and set me free.

There was a long moment of silence on the phone. I guess Andrew was startled by this and was in a somewhat state of disbelief. My heart pounded as I waited for a response because this was something that I would never ever think could happen in my wildest dreams. Suddenly Cuomo responded and said, "Let me see what I could do". I thanked him and waited nervously for several weeks. During that time, I relived the Whitney experience that had occurred when I was in prison. It was the happiest moment of my incarceration when my self-portrait was displayed there. It was also the saddest when I almost was excluded from the exhibit because I was not a convicted murderer (This is explained in detail in my first memoir 15-to Life.)

To my surprise, I received a call from Cuomo's people and they told me they had gotten the Whitney. I happily made arrangements to return to New York City to attend the book party on October 11th of 2004. Luciana arranged to sublease her friend's Suzy's apartment in Long Island City for our stay in New York. We arrived a week before the planned event and a meeting was set up with Andrew at his NYC office.

The plan was for me to come to meet with Andrew who was working at a hedge fund company in NYC. Andrew worked as an ambassador of goodwill of sorts for Andrew Fargas who is the chairman of Island Global Yachting and founder and Chief Executive Officer of Island Capital Group (ICG). (Fargas eventually became Cuomo's financial manager in his successful run for governor in 2010). When I got to their offices in midtown Manhattan IGC I was greeted by a very attractive receptionist and was escorted to their conference room where Andrew Cuomo soon appeared. We shook hands and embraced. The last time we had saw each other is when we had appeared a year prior at the Countdown for Fairness, the largest drug war rally ever held in New York City.

It was a campaign to repeal the Rockefeller Drug Laws that was hosted by Russell Simmons the Hip-Hop entrepreneur and co-founder of Def Jam records. Over 50,000 people attended the event that featured the broadest coalition ever assembled on the issue. This included hip hop artists and record company executives like Sean P. Diddy and Jay-Z and Jason Flom. National Civil right leaders like Reverend Jesse Jackson and

Al Sharpton. And movie stars and celebrities like Susan Sarandon and Mariah Carey. Andrew sat me down and told me his plan for the event.

He said that the event would be hosted by HELP USA, an organization he founded, when he worked as the director of HUD under the Clinton administration. His sister Maria Cuomo Cole, who was married to designer Kenneth Cole, was now running the organization. HELP USA was a non-for profit organization whose mission is to help those who are homeless and others in need to become and remain self-reliant. Since 1986, they have provided homes and jobs to many individuals.

Andrew wanted me to meet someone who would be funding the event. His name was Larry Goldfarb, who was a San Francisco hedge fund wizard. Larry was the CEO and founder of LRG Capital group. He was a respected and well-known fund manager that was involved in many charitable and non-for-profit foundations.

When I walked into the conference room, I was surprised to see that Larry did not look at all like I pictured him. He was dressed in blue jeans, was tanned, and had shoulder length hair. Larry looked like a rock star. When he spoke to me, he was full of enthusiasm and told me that he had read my book and was really impressed with my story. We talked about prison and I told him about the laws that put me away. Larry assured me that the book party would be an extraordinary event and I was assured that nothing would be spared. It was to be a class event and they even planned an after party to be held over Larry's apartment at the prestigious Waldorf Astoria located on Park Ave in Manhattan.

I soon found out that Larry was not kidding. Larry had footed the bill for the entire event which included the 20,000 dollars it cost for the use of the Whitney. He even bought 300 books that were wrapped in donated black Kenneth Cole designer bags to give as gifts for guests. I could not believe that this was happening. It was a dream come true. Helping us plan the event was Ashley Cotton who introduced me to a director from HELP USA who walked me through the program they planned.

The Whitney agreed to let me hang five of my paintings at the event. Anymore would have triggered the union getting involved and would have added an additional cost. I picked five paintings that would best describe my prison experience. This included my famous self-portrait 15 to Life. The painting was graciously loaned to me from a friend who purchased it several years prior. John Payne was an old bowling buddy that had lost touch with me before I went into prison. I reconnected with John through a chance meeting with his lawyer Jacob at a restaurant that was on the corner of Governor George Pataki's NYS office. Jacob was one of many professionals in the legal field that frequented DOCS restaurant at 43rd and 3rd street in NYC.

We got to know the place and became regulars there from our protests for reform of the Rockefeller Drug Laws that we staged against the governor. Retired Supreme Court Justice Jerome Marks, Randy Credico and I meet for dinner there every Friday night. It was the boy's night out where we would discuss various subjects including the world of politics and especially how we were going to reform the Rockefeller Drug Laws.

The Judge would supplement the good time we shared by reciting poetry attracting many of the restaurant's patrons. One of them was Jacob, who actually practiced his trade in the Judge's courtroom when he was on the bench. One night at the bar Jacob mentioned to me, that one of his clients knew me many years ago and wanted to talk to me. I asked him who it was and I was floored when he told me it was John Payne who I had not seen for over twenty years. Jacob arranged for us to meet at the bar. When I met John, he could not believe I had served twelve years in prison and was so moved with my story he wanted to buy my self-portrait for a large amount of money. I guess John had felt terrible about it. He had been the one I called up to ask for a loan when I was going to trial. I wanted to borrow some money so I could run away. I was afraid and did not want to go to prison.

But John did not lend it to me and instead tried to talk me out of running. I never forgot John's words when he asked me, "What you going to do run forever? Because of this, coupled with the fact I was dead broke, I did not run. The next day I was found guilty and I was taken into custody to serve my 15-to-Life sentence. But now, here I was, returning to the Whitney Museum along with my painting. What a great feeling that was.

Luciana arranged to sublease her friend's apartment for our stay in New York. We arrived a week before the planned event. There I met many influential people including Senator David Paterson (who became Governor of NYS in 2008). I gave a tremendous speech to an audience of 300 individuals about the drug war and its impact. The responses to the book party were amazing. It opened the eyes of many rich and famous individuals that now wanted to get involved with reforming the drug laws of New York State. Soon after I returned to Brazil with Luciana but felt the presence of the Whitney book party. I went back to Jatoba and felt homesick for the city I grew up in.

This homesickness was taking its toll on me and I knew that because of this my relationship with Luciana was being tested. Then on December of 2004 while surfing the internet I got an email that blew my mind. After many years of our struggle, the Rockefeller Drug Laws were finally reformed. When I realized what changes occurred I became very upset. To me, at that time, I felt as though the changes were nothing more than watered down reform. We had fought for years for meaningful changes, and now sitting in the middle of nowhere out in Brazil, I felt helpless to do anything.

I read a news article that really pushed my button. It talked about Russell Simmons and how he stood by Governor Pataki when the 2004 Rockefeller reform bill was signed into law. The piece pointed out that Simmons had said how happy he was because the governor had given him the pen that he used to sign the bill. I totally blew my top and couldn't believe what I was reading. All the hard work we had done for years to get real drug law reform, and now instead, watered down reform was happening.

I then shot a paragraph that summed up how I felt and sent it to few reporters in New York. I guess it was a way of letting off steam. A few days later, I got an email from Ashley who worked for Andrew Cuomo. It was short and sweet. She wished me congratulations and asked me how did I make the article happen. I didn't even know what she was referring to and did not pay it any mind. Then a few weeks later, I figured out what she was referring to when I stumbled upon a New York Post page six column that came out on December 17, 2004. It read

SIMMONS RIPPED ON DRUG LAW:

"The man who founded the movement to get the Rockefeller Drug Law penalties repealed has blasted rap mogul Russell Simmons as a "nightmare" who "destroyed" the movement. Some of the penalties were merely reduced earlier this week dashing the dream of Anthony Papa, co-founder of Mothers of the New York Disappeared, who spent over a decade in state prisons after a Rockefeller Law conviction and launched the campaign to have the law repealed. Simmons, who has gotten a lot of publicity for campaigning against the tough laws, was present at a bill-signing ceremony Tuesday with Gov. Pataki, where he called the reform "a giant step forward." The laws, passed by Gov. Nelson Rockefeller in 1973 and 1974, meant that some low-level drug dealers went to jail for longer sentences than rapists or murderers.

Papa, now an artist and author of the recently published "15 to Life: How I Painted My Way to Freedom," says he was responsible for getting Simmons involved in the movement through Andrew Cuomo. "At first it was a dream come true," Papa told The Post's State Editor Fredric U. Dicker in an e-mail, "but it became our worst nightmare. Simmons the businessman's only concern was to cut a deal he did not care a hoot about human lives." Papa is seething that Simmons gave up the initial goal of total repeal in favor of "watered-down reform." He fumes, "Now people like Simmons are patting themselves on their backs along with the governor, [Sen. Majority Leader Joseph] Bruno and [Assembly Speaker Sheldon] Silver . . . I should have dogged him . . . but [I] figured he would help us. Instead, he destroyed the movement."

Simmons declined to hit back at Papa, saying that in his opinion, the reforms were a "good deal." "In my experience as a businessman, a good deal usually means everybody has to compromise," he says. "I'm sorry everybody's not happy. I'm glad that something was done. I'm not the reason the deal got made," Simmons states. "My name is not on the paper. But the governor did give me the pen he used, which is an honor . . . I respect and appreciate the hard work Anthony Papa did. I'm sorry he's upset with me."

I couldn't believe that my one paragraph email to NY Post state editor Fred Dicker had wound up in Page 6, the world's most premier gossip column. Six was the home to the rich, famous, and launched books and movies, sold magazines, and made and broke restaurants, reputations and sometimes marriages. It was notorious for breaking news of scandals. I also didn't know that Dicker was the undisputed king of Albany press. I met Fred through Randy who was a regular on his show and became its "official comedian". Fred has been described as a one-person media empire whose reach includes his column and an hour-long daily radio show with an influential audience. His column routinely generates a follow-up from the Associated Press Albany bureau and regularly drives news coverage. And it was said that his likes and dislikes can help make or break careers.

I was still hurting from the disappointing reform that was passed. I guess I was wrong to take it out on Russell. My friend Larry Goldfarb told me that it wasn't smart to pick a fight with Simmons. I knew he was right, Simmons was a powerful, rich and influential individual. I guess he had tried to do what he thought was the right thing to do. I took Larry's advice and I apologized to Russell in hope he would help us in the future to get real reform of the Rockefeller Drug Laws.

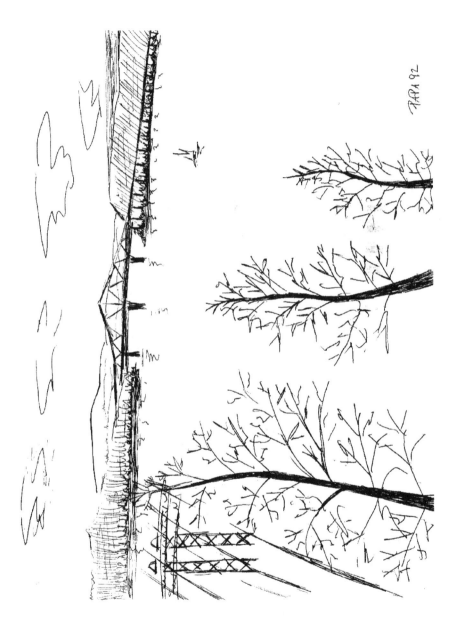

CHAPTER THIRTEEN

My Return to New York

In 2005, I returned to New York to start my life over once again from scratch. I was broke, and had no job. In many ways, I was worst off then when I came home from prison. I moved back home with my mother, and took the small room in the back of her apartment where my Uncle Frank had lived before he died. He was like a father to me, and had endured a lot of abuse by the system while I was in prison.

Every Saturday for the first three years of my incarceration, he visited me until he died of cancer. Almost every time he came to visit he was harassed by the prison guards. The most heart-wrenching experience he had was when a guard in the visiting area refused to let him in unless he showed him what the two-inch bulge was under his shirt. When he refused, the guard called additional security and forced him into a screening room. Six guards surrounded him, to see him lift his shirt, showing off the embarrassing protruding hernia he had developed. It was inoperable because of the cancer that had spread throughout his body.

I had been out of prison for eight years, but still had not resolved the most emotional issue I faced when I was released, which was re-establishing a relationship with my daughter Stephanie. I had not seen her for over two years and called her to tell her of my return. We agreed to meet. Stephanie was now 27 years old and had a life of her own. We talked of the past and how the time had flown by us. She shared her dreams with me and I told her mine. We both realized that we were tired of trying to avoid the relationship that eluded us. It would not be perfect but we agreed to maintain some sort of relationship on a regular basis.

My happiness in developing a relationship with my daughter was short lived. I received a phone call from Brazil and talked to my son Anthony Jr., who at 4 years old, in a painful voice, pleaded with me to come home. It was almost too much to handle, and I tried to deal with my sorrow by drinking heavily. I also started to hang out with people I should not have hung out with.

One of them was Sal, who I had helped with his drug case when I worked in the prison law library. Sal was back to his old ways and was flushed with cash. He offered me an opportunity to work for him. I knew it would be a big mistake if I did. My life was spinning out of control, and I knew that a major life catastrophe was not far away. I needed to find a job to keep me in check. I know that this would keep me walking on a straight and narrow road that would prevent me from returning to prison.

I started to reach out to people I had worked with it the past. One of them was Tony Newman who was the Director of Communications for the Drug Policy Alliance, a non-for-profit advocacy organization that was the largest group in the United States who advocated against the war on drugs. The organization envisioned new drug policies grounded in science, compassion, health and human rights. I had met Newman years before at the Puffin Room, an art space that held political happenings. It was the start of a great friendship both professionally and personally. Anita Martin the vice president of Legal Action Center (LAC) had invited me to the event. A few years later Anita invited me to another event, where I gave a very powerful speech that moved the audience.

One individual who was impressed was Hollywood filmmaker Doug Liman who was there to present the yearly Arthur Liman award for social justice. This was an award given in the name of his father Arthur Liman who chaired the Legal Action Center from its founding in 1972 until his death in 1997. In his honor, LAC launched the Arthur Liman Policy Institute which is the research arm of LAC which allowed them to expand their work in the fields of addiction, AIDS and criminal justice. Liman directed several big films such as Go, Swinger and The Bourne Identity. In his presentation, Doug gave a moving talk about his father, and promised to do a film about the war on drugs. During the event, Anita introduced me to Dough and half joking told him that I should be the subject of the film he wanted to make. I had told him I was writing a book about my life and wanted to send him a copy of my manuscript. He told me he would like to read it. Wow, I said. It would be a dream come true.

I approached Newman with the idea that he might help me in some way. We had stayed in touch through the years and worked on several projects concerning the repeal of the Rockefeller Drug Laws. I gave Newman a call and asked him if there were any openings at Drug Policy Alliance (DPA). Newman invited me over and we discussed the possibility of working there. He managed to convince Ethan Nadelmann the executive director and founder of DPA to give me a consulting job. I had learned a lot from Randy Credico, working with the Mothers of the New York Disappeared, in pitching a story out to the media. But soon after working with Newman, I knew I was going to learn much more. Newman was magic with the press. It was though he had this uncanny ability how to create media out of nothing. It was amazing to watch him work.

One of the first big stories I pitched came a few weeks after working at DPA. I received a call from Gregory Datch a NY Post reporter concerning the arrest of Julia Diaco an 18-year-old student at NYU that was busted for selling drugs. Diaco had made multiple sales of large quantities of cocaine and marijuana to undercover cops from her dorm room. But despite this, the rich and connected "Pot Princess" was sentenced in Manhattan Supreme Court to five years' probation upon completion of a drug rehab and education program for drug dealing. Datch wanted to know to know how I felt, since she was facing the same 15-to-life sentence I had gotten, but she did not get and instead got a slap on the wrist.

I told him that I knew that there were double standards for the rich and poor because New York's drug laws ensured that the privileged and connected receive leniency for the same offenses that send thousands of blacks and Latinos to prison. I told him of the high-profile case of Caroline Quartararo, a former spokeswoman on Rockefeller Drug Law reform for Governor George Pataki, who received a similar minor sentence after being arrested with crack cocaine. Quartararo was given treatment and a $250 fine. She was arrested for possessing three rocks of crack cocaine and pleaded guilty to seventh-degree criminal possession of a controlled substance. Then I told him of the other side of justice, and described how Ashley O'Donoghue a 23-year-old black man sold cocaine to two white students, who in turn, sought to resell the drugs on their Hamilton College campus.

The white students were caught and received probation and Ashley O'Donoghue was left to rot in prison, another casualty of the draconian Rockefeller Drug Laws. He was serving a sentence of seven to twenty-one years for a first-time nonviolent drug offense. Ashley was one of more than 4,000 people that were sitting in New York State prisons convicted of B-level Rockefeller Drug Law felony. I told the reporter that the cases of Julia Diaco and Caroline Quartararo proved that "if you were rich and privileged, you will likely receive compassion from the courts. While I supported the notion of compassion and access to treatment for people who use and abuse drugs, the reality was clear to me. People of color who got caught up in the criminal justice system generally receive neither. I explained that while drug use rates were similar between blacks and whites, approximately 92 percent of the people in prison on drug charges in New York were black and Latino. I saw it time and time again back in the law library in Sing Sing where I worked as a jailhouse lawyer. The prison was full of non-violent drug offenders of color.

I told Datch that our elected officials in Albany needed to take action to enact real reform of these laws, so that young men like Ashley O'Donoghue could receive the same compassion as those who are white, rich, and well connected or are employed by the governor. Datch thanked me and two days later his story on "the Pot Princess "came out, surprisingly, with most of the views I presented to him. After this I continued to push out a multitude of media stories relating to the issues that DPA has stood for. This led to a full-time position. I landed a job as a communications specialist in the media department, which allowed me to continue my activism and my quest to fight the laws that had imprisoned me. The job was a perfect fit because it permitted me to utilize my art to speak out for justice.

I realized that the position I had with the Drug Policy Alliance I could do a lot to help shape public opinion through the media. I already knew how powerful media could be when I worked with Credico. I also used the media to get my story out to the public and to draw interest in my story. This in turn enabled me to regain my freedom by getting executive clemency from Governor Pataki. While in prison every time I got a story published about myself, it brought me one-step closer to my freedom. I use to sit down behind by manual typewriter and pump out press releases about my art and how I was Pablo Picasso behind bars. It was one thing to call myself Picasso, and it did not mean much. But when Edward Lewine, a reporter from the NY Times picked it up and used it in a major profile of me, that meaningless hype turned it into a reality that became my ticket to freedom.

With the new job and a steady income, I decided it was time to go out and get my own place. I looked high and low for an apartment and found out quickly it was no easy task trying to get one. This was for several reasons including the fact I was an ex-felon. I found this out when I was honest in an application to rent an apartment. The co-op owner googled me and found out of my past and questioned me about it. I came clean. At that point, he denied my application. This was questionable, but I didn't even bother to argue with him, and continued to search for an apartment. It was hard to find a place and I wound up subleasing Randy's studio apartment for several months. Life was going well and I even got to see my son Anthony when he visited me from Brazil.

On the day, my wife and son were going back to Brazil Luciana asked me to go with her to pick up a gong at a music shop in NYC. She had begun studying with a gong master who was teaching her to heal people through sound. To save a few dollars on a cab ride to the apartment, I brought along a cart to carry the gong onto the subway. As I lifted, the gong to carry it down the subway stairs I accidentally unhooked the six-foot bungee cord that was doubled up around the box.

The force of the over stretched cord caused the hook to smash into the left eye of my glasses. I screamed as the lens exploded and shattered glass into my eye. Blood dripped down along my face as I rolled on the floor with pain. Luciana had thought I suffered a heart and ran to call for help. She found a cop who came and asked me what had happened. I refused medical attention and wanted to go home instead. Luciana got a friend to bring her and my son to the airport and I went to the emergency room. After a series of doctor visits, I discovered that my accident had increased my vision in my eye by 50%. The doctor described it as a medical miracle. I had actually given myself the equivalent of an eye operation.

In April of 2006, I saw that the drug war had reached the pinnacle of cruelty when Mitchell Lawrence, an 18-year-old Berkshire County teen, was sentenced to two years in jail for the sale of one joint worth of marijuana -- about a teaspoon. Lawrence was found guilty of distribution of marijuana, committing a drug violation within a drug-free school zone, and possession after he sold a 1.12-gram bag of marijuana to an undercover police officer for $20. This was the equivalent of a fat joint. While this outrageous case happened in a sleepy burg in Massachusetts, I found out that the case of Mitchell Lawrence was one of countless tales of drug war madness that took place on America's streets daily.

Detective Felix Aquirre, employed by the Drug Task Force, was assigned the duty of buying drugs from kids who hung out in a parking lot in Berkshire County in Massachusetts. Merchants had complained to police about the groups of kids that hung out there. Lawrence was there with his pipe and a few marijuana buds of pot in a plastic bag. He had no idea the parking lot was less than 1,000 feet from a preschool located in the basement of a church, nor did he know this parking lot was the site of a police sting operation.

The undercover cop approached Mitchell and asked him if he had some weed. Lawrence pulled out a small bag of marijuana. The cop offered him a twenty-dollar bill. Lawrence hesitated. The cop insisted. Lawrence, who had seen the cop hanging out with other kids, motioned the cop to follow him up the street where he intended to smoke with him. The cop waved the $20 in his face. Like a carrot dangling on a string, Mitchell, who was broke at the time, took the money. It was the only time Lawrence ever accepted money in exchange for marijuana. In the months that followed, the cop approached Lawrence again for marijuana. This time, however, Lawrence refused. Weeks later, a crew of undercover cops stormed Lawrence's home and placed him under arrest. On March 22, 2006, Lawrence was sentenced to two years in prison.

The disproportionate sentence of Lawrence was handed down one day before the release of a national report by the Justice Policy Institute (JPI): "Disparity by Design: How Drug-free Zone Laws Impact Racial Disparity and Fail to Protect Youth," which included research from Massachusetts, the state where Lawrence was arrested. The JPI study was commissioned by the Drug Policy Alliance, which found that drug-free zone laws do not serve their intended purpose of protecting youth from drug activity. The Massachusetts data on drug enforcement in three cities found that less than one percent of the drug-free zone cases actually involved sales to youth. Additionally, Massachusetts researchers found that non-whites were more likely to be charged with an offense that carries drug-free zone enhancement than whites engaged in similar conduct. Blacks and Hispanics account for just 20 percent of Massachusetts residents, but 80 percent of drug-free zone cases.

School zone laws had remained unchanged in Massachusetts because the legislature was promised that prosecutors were to use discretion, unfortunately that was not the case with Lawrence. Sadly, his was not the only arrest made at the same Great Barrington parking lot in the undercover drug operation in the summer of 2004. There was a total of 18 others but Lawrence was the only one to go to prison because he did not cooperate. Instead, he alleged that the undercover cop drank and smoked marijuana with other kids. This infuriated District Attorney Capeless, which led to Lawrence being charged under the safety zone laws to insure an increased penalty. When the other kids charged saw this they quickly took plea deals not wanting to face the same faith that Lawrence had received.

I started researching his case to find out what we could do to stop this madness. I discovered that District Attorney David F. Capeless was the man behind Berkshire County enforcement and entrapment. Capeless was a hard-nosed drug war zealot, who insisted that the drug-free zone laws were effective in combating drug use, even if it meant ruining a young people's life in the process. Lawrence was set to graduate from high school that spring. Instead, he watched his fellow classmates graduate from his prison cell. I realized that Mitchell Lawrence's case and drug free school zones nationally was an abuse of power from prosecutors through the application of mandatory minimums. These laws handcuff judges and force them to impose harsh sentences.

Lawrence's conviction inspired a group of concerned Berkshire County residents to seek Capeless' ouster in the forthcoming district attorney race. Defense attorney, Judith Knight answered the call to fill this role. Knight, a former assistant district attorney for Middlesex County said, "Lawrence's conviction was the tipping point" for her decision to run against Capeless in the upcoming Democratic primary election in September of 2006. Knight said that "a tough prosecutor is tough on crime and also has the ability to demonstrate compassion and insight when the case calls for it."

Knight, with her "Judy for Justice" campaign had hoped to follow in the footsteps of David Soares, who ran for district attorney and defeated Paul Clyne in Albany, New York in 2004. Soares ran a race primarily on the platform of Rockefeller Drug Law reform. He easily defeated the sitting district attorney who refused to change his views on the draconian drug law legislation of New York. But this did not happen in Berkshire County where Knight was easily defeated by Capeless. Many believe that her defeat was brought on by the fact that one of her clients who she defended in the Great Barrington parking lot undercover drug operation was arrested again for selling drugs. The DA's office had cunningly orchestrated the timely bust to occur the day before the election, which was covered by the media extensively. This sunk any chance that Knight had to win and mimic the victory David Soares achieved.

Albany County District Attorney David Soares was considered a hero by many for his bold stances and refreshing approaches to delivering justice. He first laid claim to this title in 2004 when he ran on a platform that advocated dramatic change in the draconian Rockefeller Drug laws that stood unchanged for 30 years. His victory over powerful incumbent Paul Clyne sent shock waves throughout the political landscape in New York's capital. Clyne was given a pink slip by voters for his vocal support of the Rockefeller Drug Laws and his staggering defeat triggered fear within the Republican Senate that they too might lose their jobs for not supporting Rockefeller reform.

Unlike many political figures that bob and weave themselves into office only to step away from the original platforms that brought them to victory, Soares has stuck to his guns and continues to speak out against inhumane and ineffective drug policies.

In 2006 while speaking at an international harm reduction conference in Vancouver, British Columbia, he told the audience that his advice to Canada is to "stay as far away from America's drug law policy as possible." His comments echoed the criticisms he made of New York's strict Rockefeller Drug Laws during his election campaign two years' prior by saying "the attempt to engage in cleaning the streets of Albany one $20 sale on the street at a time is a failed policy." He stuck by his view that more drug treatment, not more jail time, is the answer. But at the same time there are others like Dave Capeless who believes in a punitive approach to justice

We have two District Attorneys with opposing views on how to deal with the issue of treatment vs. incarceration for drug offenders. Who is correct? Recent studies have shown that treatment is the most humane and cost-effective approach to addiction. In November 2000, California passed Proposition 46, an initiative that allowed most people convicted of first and second-time nonviolent, simple drug possession to receive drug treatment instead of incarceration. More than 140,000 participants had entered the treatment program instead of imprisoning them resulting in the cost savings of approximately $1 billion. But sadly, to say even though the program was a success, because of economic reasons, the program was dismantled.

In a conversation with Soares, he told me that he desperately wanted to defer drug offenders to treatment rather than jail, but the powers-that-be in Albany had cut off his funding to do so. Without proper funding, increased numbers of people will be forced to compete for limited treatment slots. The cycle of addiction will continue, along with crime and recidivism. With the defeat of Paul Clyne, voters had effectively spoken out against the irrational method of trying to arrest your way out of the drug problem. With the election of Soares, the voters in Albany wanted more than outdated tough-on-crime zealots and chose Soares, who had chosen to be smart on crime.

On June 21, 2007, the New York State legislative session ended without any reform of the Rockefeller Drug Laws. To most people it did not mean much. But to Veronica Flournoy it meant her life. Veronica spent eight years in prison for a first time, nonviolent crime under New York's inhumane Rockefeller Drug Laws. Tragically, at the age of 39, Veronica died.

A spot discovered on her lung while in prison went untreated, which led to cancer that spread to her brain. She wound up in prison because she had a terrible drug addiction that compelled her to deliver drugs for her boyfriend to fuel her habit. The New York's district attorney's office pressured her to provide evidence against her boyfriend to help secure his conviction. Veronica was reluctant to cooperate out of fear for the safety of her family.

The system rewarded her refusal to cooperate by throwing the book at her and handing her a sentence of 8-years-to-life. She left behind her two-year-old daughter, Candace, and, while serving her sentence, she gave birth to her second daughter, Keyshana, who lived in the prison nursery until she was 13-months-old. Her elderly mother then cared for both children while Veronica did hard time at the Bedford Correctional Facility for women in upstate NY. While in prison, Veronica overcame her personal demons and received the treatment she needed to deal with her drug addiction.

Upon her release, Veronica reunited with her family and became a central figure in the Rockefeller reform movement. She worked hard to overturn the drug laws that had taken away her life as it had the many others that shared the "scarlet letter of addiction." Although she struggled with her life as a single parent and having to bear the stigmatizing label of "ex-addict" and "ex-felon," she became a true champion of those with substance abuse problems who were sentenced to prison instead of treatment.

Her two daughters who were aged 10 and 12, along with her 84-year-old mother had prayed for a miracle. Their lives were in shambles---

unable to support themselves, watching the life ebb away from a woman who was once so vibrant. Weeks before she died Veronica appeared on camera for a moving public service announcement calling on then Governor Elliot Spitzer to keep his word and deliver the reform he promised while campaigning for his governorship. Spitzer, who won his bid to become governor of New York, had learned to sidestep the issue of Rockefeller Drug reform while Governor of New York, in line with the legacy of his predecessor, George Pataki, who danced around the issue of Rocky reform for more than nine years. Sadly, Spitzer resigned his governorship in disgrace, leaving the Rockefeller Drug Laws the toughest in the nation.

Veronica's story reminded me of the horrors of drug addiction. It destroys lives. But far worse is to condemn those with drug addictions to imprisonment, while withholding the treatment they so desperately need. Our prisons are filled with tens of thousands of individuals with all kinds of drug addictions and psychological problems. Her case made me think if society should treat drug addiction as a criminal matter or a medical problem? For most people, treatment is much more effective than imprisonment for breaking their addictions, yet our prisons are full of drug addicted individuals.

Nonviolent drug offenders like Veronica should have been given an opportunity to receive treatment, not jail time, for their drug use. This would be a more effective not to mention much more affordable solution for the individual and the community. But instead of treatment Veronica was smacked with a stiff prison sentence and only three years out of prison at the age of 39 she was dead. I could not believe it. She had survived the horror of imprisonment only to die soon after leaving her two daughters with her 84-year-old mother.

With the death of Veronica, I was disappointed and compelled to try to do something. Despite several watered-down revisions of the Rockefeller Drug Laws which occurred in 2004/05 the draconian nature of the laws remained. Out of the 13,000 prisoners serving time under the Rockefeller laws only about 450 prisoners were freed from the retroactive revisions.

One of the opponents trying to stop the reforming the Rock Laws was NYC Special Narcotics Prosecutor Bridget Brennan. She single handling threw a wrench in the political machinery of Albany at the close of the 2007 session when she released a very damaging report about the release of Rockefeller Drug prisoners from the 2004 reforms. She proclaimed that kingpins and people convicted of high-level drug offenses were being released under the new Rockefeller Drug Law revisions. The report, titled "The Law of Unintended Consequences," was a lopsided review of the Drug Law Reform Act of 2004. The modest changes to the Rockefeller Drug Laws have allowed approximately 1,000 people convicted of A-1 and A-2 drug felonies to apply for resentencing. The controversial findings in the report bolstered Brennan's final conclusions which asked for a clarion call for a kingpin statute and the opposition to any additional reforms to the Rockefeller Drug Laws.

Critics quickly questioned the validity of the report, claiming that it contained skewed data and its creation was politically motivated. Our executive director Ethan Nadelmann quickly asked DPA staff to respond to her report. I decided to tackle it and wrote an op-ed that was published in Newsday. My piece was titled "The State Should Target the Real Drug Kingpins". I argued the case of Ashley O'Donoghue again and pointed out that Ashley was a low-level, nonviolent offender currently serving a 7-to-21-year sentence for the sale of 2 1/2 ounces of cocaine. In September 2003, the Oneida County district attorney claimed that the 20-year-old was a major drug kingpin and needed to face a life sentence under the Rockefeller Drug Laws. Reacting to a commonly used scare tactic, O'Donoghue agreed to a plea bargain. His A-1 felony, the highest possible felony, was reduced to a B felony.

Like magic, O'Donoghue was no longer a kingpin - that is, a drug dealer distributing extraordinarily large quantities. There were thousands of defendants just like O'Donoghue, whom prosecutors claim are kingpins one day and then, through plea negotiations, kingpins no more. I went through the same experience in 1984 when I was arrested for the sale of 4 ounces of cocaine. A Westchester assistant district attorney claimed I was a major kingpin.

But in the months that followed he offered me a plea bargain of three years to life, suddenly I was not a kingpin anymore. I argued that the report Brennan released was questionable in many aspects, but I agreed with Brennan on one point: New York needed a kingpin statute. Allowing prosecutors to define this term has meant that people like O'Donoghue and me were kingpins one day, but like magic, not the next day. New York needed a clear and reasonable kingpin statute that could be applied to real kingpins - bona fide major traffickers - not people convicted of low-level offenses.

The kingpin statute that Brennan called for was both unreasonable and incompatible with justice, because it was so broad. Brennan's report highlighted 84 drug cases handled by her office, with 65 applicants receiving judicial relief under the new law. Contrary to Brennan's tabloid like insinuation that the prison gates just opened up, each prisoner seeking resentencing had to go through a lengthy application process in order to see a judge for resentencing. At that point in time there were almost 4,000 B-level felons serving time in New York State for low-level, nonviolent drug offenses for small amounts of drugs. Many of the defendants had drug-addiction problems. These thousands of offenders are not classified as kingpins.

So why would Brennan actively oppose reforms to release them? It cost taxpayers millions of dollars to incarcerate these people when community-based treatment costs less and has proved more effective than incarceration in treating addiction. Brennan needed to be reminded that the governor, State Senate and Assembly leaders agreed reforms were necessary to equally balance the scales of justice in applying the law with the needs of protecting our communities. To cause a panic by releasing a questionable report was nothing more than additional punishment for those incarcerated and an underhanded political tactic to stop further needed reform.

If Brennan wanted a kingpin statute I argued, then let's fashion one for real kingpins, not for the low-level offenders. A number of officials went on record in support of Rockefeller reform. I named three important New York politicians that were elected into office. They were Governor Elliot Spitzer, Lt. Governor David Paterson and Attorney General Andrew Cuomo, who had all spoken out for reform in the past. But since they took high office, all three were surprisingly silent on the issue. I knew that before becoming NYS attorney general, Andrew

Cuomo threw a book release party for me at the Whitney Museum of American Art.

Attending the event were prominent individuals like Senator David Paterson, along with many other influential guests. Cuomo and Paterson spoke bravely about changing these draconian laws.

Governor Spitzer the then-attorney general of New York did not attend but wrote a letter instead. He said that my story was a "very personal and tragic story, like those of so many other nonviolent offenders languishing in our prisons on relatively minor drug offenses," and that it "illustrates the impact that our Rockefeller Drug Laws have had on a generation of New Yorkers. I applaud Mr. Papa's courage in speaking out and sharing his ordeal with the world."

I pointed out in the op-ed that I found it strange that the people who had supported Rockefeller reform in the past had now become so silent on the issue. My question was simple. I asked why do politicians who use political platforms to generate votes suddenly forget their past when elected to higher office. I addressed all three politicians. First I said in my view Governor Spitzer, does appear interested in correcting the criminal justice sector.

This was clearly seen by his success in removing exorbitant charges on collect calls made by prisoners to their families, and his attempt to downsize half-empty prisons. But his laudable efforts did not cue in on Rockefeller reform. Along with him was Attorney General Andrew Cuomo, who was actively involved in reforming the Rockefeller drug laws had not uttered a word about it. And to my dismay, Lt. Governor David Paterson who was arrested protesting the laws who represented a highly affected Harlem district as senator, has also steered away from the issue.

Only the week before the New York State Assembly had passed a bill trying to get further reform of the Rockefeller Drug laws. Cheri O'Donoghue had joined them at a press conference and talked about her son Ashley who was serving a 7 to 21 sentence for a first-time non-violent drug offense. She grieved for the son she had lost to these laws and asked why the Rockefeller Drug Laws had now not been a priority with so many politicians that had benefited from them in the past. I made the assertion that no one could answer her question and challenged Spitzer, Paterson and Cuomo to join the NYS Assembly and step up to the plate and advocate for meaningful reform.

I reminded them that they should remember their past intentions, especially when it affects the people who voted them into office.

I believed that the op-ed I wrote might be read by someone who might bring this issue to the attention of one of the three politicians I challenged. And to my surprise, it did! A week later, I received a call from the Lt. Governor David Paterson's office. It was his chief of staff telling me that Paterson was angry with me for writing the piece and saying that he was doing nothing to help change the laws to help individuals like Ashley, when in fact he was. I told him that if he was Ashley would not still be rotting in prison.

I knew I did not want to pick a fight with Paterson, after all he was an honorable man who always fought for Rockefeller reform in the past. But I explained that it seemed as though as soon as politicians went into higher office they changed their views about these Rock laws. I apologized and his spokesman quickly accepted my apology and told me that he would tell Paterson what I said.

A few days later I was surprised when I received a call from Cherie, Ashley's mother. She told me she had gotten a call from the Lt. Governor who he told her that he had placed a call to Brian Fisher the Commissioner of Corrections and asked him to place Ashley into a drug treatment program.

Upon completion of the program it would reduce the time Ashley would have to serve by 3 years. Cherie was happy beyond belief and thanked me for helping her son come home to her. After all, she had fought tooth and nail for years for his release. A few months later Ashley had returned home. I felt good about being able to help their family be reunited once again. It also showed me the power I wielded through my pen and the Huffington Post.

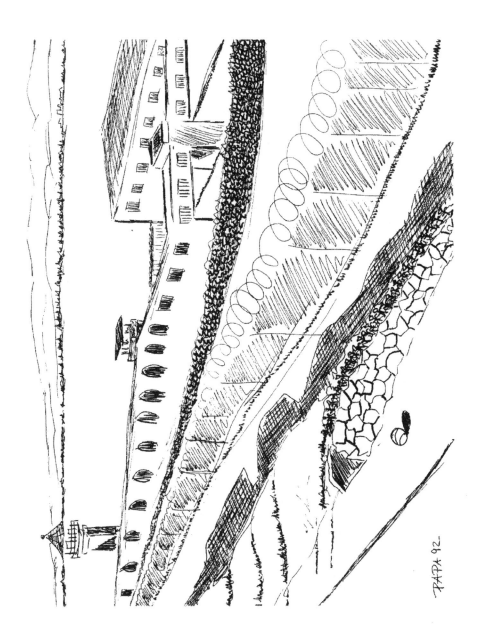

CHAPTER FOURTEEN

Russell Simmons and Lockdown USA

D id you ever have the opportunity to see something in your life, after the fact, many years later? Well this extraordinary happening occurred to me one day when it was least expected. While scanning the internet doing my daily research on the Rockefeller Drug Laws up popped a result that caught my eye. It was a promotional website about a new documentary that was being released about the Rockefeller Drug Laws titled "Lockdown USA." This was a documentary that was made by Michael Skolnik and Rebecca Chaiklin of Article 19 films which featured our group the Mothers of the New York Disappeared, its co-founder Randy Credico, Andrew Cuomo and Russell Simmons.

The filming took place several years' prior during the time when Russell became involved to repeal the drug laws of NYS thanks to Andrew Cuomo who brought him into the movement. I remembered all too well the highs and lows of what we all experienced during the creation of the Countdown to Fairness. This was the formation of a major coalition to repeal the draconian Rockefeller Drug Laws. Russell gave Governor Pataki a clear ultimatum. He demanded that he repeal the drug laws within 30 days or else he was going to organize 100,000 people in the streets of NYC to protest both the existing drug laws and Governor Pataki's failure to reform them in a positive way.

In theory, this was just the boost we needed to give energy to our movement. But it turned out to be a disaster for activists that had fought long and hard to do away with the horrible racist drug laws that had imprisoned hundreds of thousands of New Yorkers for many years. Much of the filming of "Lockdown USA" was done at Russell Simmons Fat Farms office on 37th and Broadway in the heart of the fashion industry of NYC. But I felt we got the short end of the stick when Russell literally jumped ship and left us hanging out to dry when he abandoned our repeal platform and decided to join forces with Governor George Pataki in pushing his watered-down Rockefeller Drug Law reform legislation which eventually passed in 2004. We were devastated by this and felt our movement was set back many years because of it.

Months after this happened I was standing on line in my Queens's neighborhood grocery store when I happened to bump into Russell Simmons. I was with my friend and fellow Rockefeller drug law activist Veronica Flournoy when Simmons approached me and went into a long explanation of why he left our side to join the governor in trying to reform the Rockefeller drug laws. He sounded sincere but no matter what he said to me I felt he could never justify what did. Bottom line he had left us all to join Pataki to save face because the governor did not change the Rockefeller Drug Laws. Despite what he had done to us, I decided to bury the hatchet and forgave Simmons. I told him I understood and shook his hand and embraced him in friendship.

But now, several years later, here I was reading the information about Lockdown USA on its website and I started to become enraged with anger when I felt that the film was just a ploy to boast Simmons involvement in the campaign to reform the drug laws. Lockdown USA was described as a documentary that was set on the front lines of the campaign to end the "War on Drugs" and to repeal the Rockefeller Drug Laws. The film had followed Wanda Best, whose husband Darryl was sentenced 15 years to life, as a first-time non-violent drug offender. It pointed out that when her husband was hauled off to prison for a crime he said he did not commit she was left to raise their five children on her own. The documentary interweaved the story of the Best family with a behind the scenes look at Hip Hop Impresario, Russell Simmons' colorful, unorthodox campaign to reform the Drug Laws. In 1973, New York State enacted the Rockefeller Drug Laws, which were the harshest drug control measures ever passed in any democratic nation. President Reagan declared the National "War on Drugs" in 1982 and cited The Rockefeller Laws as the model for new drug regulations. By 1983, 48 states had passed drug control measures based on the Rockefeller Drug Laws. These laws have resulted in the US prison population quadrupling and prisons becoming a thriving, profitable industry.

The narrative of the film went on to say that there were currently over two million people behind bars in America and one out of every 38 Americans is currently in prison or on parole and or probation. The United States spends over $100,000,000 dollars a week building new prisons. One of the central threads of the film was Darryl Best and his story was outlined. In the fall of 2001, Darryl Best was convicted of possession of cocaine. Darryl had been doing handy work at his uncle's house and signed for a Fed-Ex package that was addressed to a neighbor. The package contained a pound of cocaine. The District Attorney offered Darryl Best a one-year plea bargain, if he admitted guilt. But Darryl refused to take the plea, insisting on his innocence and claiming he wanted to set an example of integrity and honesty for his children. Darryl had contacted retired Supreme Court Justice Jerome Marks who had been a part of our organization and a leading activist fighting the Rockefeller Drug Laws. Judge Marks recommended an attorney for Darryl to represent him in his case. But things did not work out and Best went to trial and lost.

The Judge apologized as he realized that Darryl Best was going to be sentenced to 15 years to life, the minimum sentence they could give Darryl under the Rockefeller Drug Laws. The film showed the devastating impact of Darryl's incarceration had on his family and the noble fight his wife Wanda had launched, in her effort to bring him home to their family. In the spring of 2003, the Best family gained a glimmer of hope when Darryl was profiled in the Countdown to Fairness, which was helmed by Russell Simmons.

Lockdown USA followed Russell Simmons as he orchestrated a high-profile campaign, to raise awareness around the Rockefeller Drug Laws, with the intention of creating tremendous public pressure, forcing politicians to enact reform. Russell recruits high profile artists such as P Diddy, Jay-Z, 50 Cent, Mariah Carey and Tim Robbins to join the campaign and speak out on the issue. Simmons rallies tens of thousands of people and works throughout the night in heated behind the scenes negotiations with New York State Governor George Pataki and the State's top politicians.

The films website posed the question in a dramatic fashion asking if they would be able to make a deal. Lockdown USA captures the stranger than fiction, historic series of events as they have unfolded where the political establishment has been forced to reconcile with the burgeoning power of hip-hop.

When I finished reading the films description I immediately called Randy Credico and told him what I had thought. My first impression from reading its website was that the film was a slap in the face of all the activists that had worked so hard to reform these laws for years. This was because of the possibility that the film would glorify Simmons and support his role of turning against us and aiding Gov. Pataki. I then called Michael Skolnik and told him how we felt. Since Credico was a main character in the film he could cause a world of damage to it if he needed to. Skolnik knew Credico was a loose cannon and when I told him that if the film had been a vehicle to promote Simmons and his company, we were going to protest the film with our group the Mothers of the New York Disappeared. Michael wanted no part of us. He knew what we were capable of and had witnessed the power of the collection of families that were part of our organization when we protested against politicians in Albany New York. In the past the press had a field day painting a picture of injustice that made politicians cringe in their pants. Skolnik assured us that the film was not what I thought it was.

Michael waved the white flag and wanted peace. He suggested that we view the film and make a judgment for ourselves. We agreed and a screening was set up at the Drug Policy Alliance's (DPA) office in NYC where I worked. A small crew of staff members including its media director Tony Newman was invited to the viewing. Both Michael and Rebbeca gave small presentations before the film started to lay out their intentions why they had created the film. When the documentary was being shown, it was very hard for me to watch it because of the bad taste that was left in my mouth by our failure to repeal of the Rockefeller Drug Laws. When I watched the film, I was surprised to see that true to Michael's word, the film did not glorify Simmons. In fact, the film showed how Russell fell flat on his face in trying to change the Rockefeller Drug Laws.

One part of the documentary totally blew my mind. It offered me a look into part of my past life that I had never seen before. A meeting was set up with Gov. Pataki at his NYC office located at 40th and 3rd Avenue. When we left Russell's office to go there, Ben Chavis told us there was no room in Simmons SVU. Chavis was Simmon's right had man and the president of his Hip Hop Action Network, an advocacy organization that did tremendous work in the field of civil rights. He said that people including DPA's Deborah Small were going to ride along with Simmons. Small had somehow managed to become Simmons advisor in his dealings with Rockefeller reform. She was also the State director of Drug Policy Alliance and had recently had a fall out with Credico. This was because of her influencing Simmons to give up his hope of repeal of the Rockefeller drug laws and instead talking him to support reform. Her thought was that the NYS legislature would never consider repeal of these laws and that a compromise of reform was more plausible. But our view, along with Andrew Cuomo, was to stick to our guns and demand repeal so we would get a better deal when negotiating.

The camera zoomed in on both Simmons and Small as they rode to the governor's office. A conversation developed where Smalls suddenly became emotional and told Russell that Credico and I could not be allowed to attend the meeting because it would be a disaster. Simmons listened for a moment than blurted out "then fuck them they are not attending". When the car arrived Chavis approached us and told us he had bad news and told us that the governor's office had called and told them that they did not have any room for us to attend the meeting. The camera zoomed in on us and showed Credico and me looking at him in disbelief. Not being able to meet with Pataki and tell him our position totally blew our minds.

Now years later there I was soaking in what I had seen. I sat in dismay and became furious as I watched, almost ripping the cover off the sides of the chair I was sitting in, as I tightly gripped it. The film had revealed the truth of why we were not permitted to attend the meeting. It was Small that convinced Simmons not to let us attend the meeting. But it was several years later and now it was part of my job at DPA to find ways of trying to get additional reform of the Rockefeller Drug Laws. I thought the film was a good way of getting some important media on the issue. So, we told Michael we would help him to promote the film and use it as a vehicle for outreach to create public awareness about the drug war in New York State.

We were invited to help with the press for the release of the film and attended a meeting. But all those plans discussed about using the Best family as a center point of the press soon fell apart when Darryl Best left his wife and 5 daughters. Darryl had fallen prey to the typical post prison blues that effect most individuals that return to society after being exposed to the psychological damage of imprisonment. It was a shame but it was also the reality of the consequences of imprisonment. Despite this the documentary went on to become a big success and it aided in the eventual reforms of the Rockefeller Drug Laws that followed.

RaPa 92

CHAPTER FIFTEEN

Addiction and Celebrities

Working at my job every day I saw stories splashed across news that exposed the realities of drug use in America. From celebrities to politicians to athletes and ordinary people, the war on drugs loomed large. But I found that the public especially loved stories about celebs with substance abuse problems. When conservative commentator Rush Limbaugh had a clash with the law concerning his addiction to prescription painkillers he became a national symbol for drug addiction. It reminded me of the fact that drug addiction did not discriminate, but unfortunately our drug policies did. Rush was investigated for illegally obtaining thousands of addictive prescription painkillers. But instead of going to prison criminal charges were dropped against him in Florida when he worked out a plea agreement.

This included a $30,000 penalty and continued drug treatment. Limbaugh contended that his addiction was a by-product of taking painkillers for chronic pain from a back injury. But Rush's addiction brought out a good point. Many people with diseases ranging from back pain to cancer have chosen to treat their pain with a natural alternative, marijuana. What was the distinguishing difference? One drug is demonized, while the other was not.

A few weeks before, Limbaugh got arrested he had weighed in on the Food and Drug Administration's (FDA) announcement that there were no "sound scientific studies" supporting the medicinal use of marijuana. His diatribe was characteristically callous and harsh toward sick and dying people who use medical marijuana as Limbaugh blathered "the FDA says there's no -- zilch, zero, nada -- shred of medicinal value to the evil weed marijuana. This is going to be a setback to the long-haired, maggot-infested, dope-smoking crowd."

This distain for medical marijuana patients was not the first-time Rush showed a lack of compassion to people who use drugs or suffer from addiction. Limbaugh was also the man who scoffed at the idea that African Americans were disproportionately arrested on drug charges, and suggested that the solution was to arrest more white people. Interestingly enough, Mr. Limbaugh sang a different tune when he was the white person who could have easily ended up behind bars if he was not the famous radio personality that he was. But in the end, I supported Rush as I did many celebrities that followed who had brushes with the law because of their drug addictions.

In 2008 Tatum O'Neal, the Oscar-winning actress, took a plea deal on July 2 stemming from her June 1 arrest while supposedly trying to score some crack cocaine in New York City's Lower East Side. She was initially charged with possession of a controlled substance and faced a year in prison if convicted. The court allowed her to plead out to a disorderly conduct charge and ordered her to attend two half-day drug treatment sessions. She followed the court's orders and they eventually dismissed the cocaine possession charges.

O'Neal had been open about her history of heroin addiction as outlined in her memoir, *A Paper Life*. When she was arrested by undercover officers, they searched her and found two bags of cocaine along with an unused crack pipe. She had initially told police that she was doing research for an acting role. Then she changed her story and told them that the death of her 16-year-old dog nearly triggered her into relapse. Some say O'Neal was treated with a slap on the wrist. Others say she did not deserve to do any jail time because of her addiction.

This begs a critical question that we as a society need to address and one that I constantly asked. Should we treat drug addiction as a criminal matter or a medical problem? For most people, treatment is a much more effective approach than imprisonment for successfully breaking their addictions, yet our prisons are full of individuals whose only crime is their drug addiction.

According to Justice Department statistics, the U.S. holds a firm lead in maintaining the most prisoners of any country in the world. In 2006, the Justice Department recorded the largest increase since 2000 in the number of people in prisons and jails. Criminal justice experts attributed the exploding U.S. prison population to harsh sentencing laws and record numbers of drug law violators entering the system, many of whom have substance abuse problems. Nonviolent drug offenders like Tatum O'Neal should have been given an opportunity to receive treatment, not jail time, for their drug use.

This would be a more effective (not to mention much more affordable) solution for both the individual and the community. Prosecutors in many states such as New York, where they have leeway to recommend a defendant to treatment instead of incarceration, more than likely will not do it. This is because it would not be considered a "win" for them. In effect, the system does not reward prosecutors for doing the compassionate thing. In my view, prosecutors live and die by their rates of convictions, so why would they want to be compassionate if it did not help with their careers?

At that time, I thought that O'Neal could have been considered a role model to millions of young people all over the world. I thought that her experiences with addiction and the realities of the drug war would have encouraged her to join our movement to reform U.S. drug policy. If she decided to take up the cause of treatment, instead of imprisonment, she could help change laws across the country.

After all, if treatment instead of jail is good enough for her as she struggles with her addiction, surely it is good enough for the tens of thousands of others just like her who struggle with their substance abuse problems every day. But to my great sadness, she did not join our movement.

Paris Hilton had similar taste of the sting of the war on drugs when she pled guilty in 2010 in Las Vega, to two misdemeanors. One charge was for possessing a small amount of cocaine and the other for obstructing an officer. In return, she received one year's probation. Under the plea agreement, Paris avoided doing jail time by agreeing to pay a $2,000 fine, and to perform 200 hours of community service, and to complete a drug treatment program. The judge who sentenced Hilton told her that "Any new arrests terminate your criminal probation and you will serve a one-year sentence."

Hilton had two previous brushes with the law the most serious in 2007, when she was arrested for driving under the influence (DUI) which led to her doing 23 days at the Century Regional Detention Facility. Like tens of millions of Americans, Paris Hilton wanted to use drugs, either to get in touch with reality or to escape from it. The question I asked was did she have the right to put substances in her body, if she did not hurt others? Or, did she deserve to go to jail, for doing so? Every year millions of other Americans are arrested for minor drug law violations - but most of them do not get the same breaks that Hilton, O'Neal and Rush had received.

Sometimes it takes a traumatic experience to awaken the hidden self. But Hilton's twenty-three days in jail and her multiple arrests for drug use have not seemed to give her the wakeup call she needed. But it did give her a taste of life in the gulag. In that short time, I gather she felt the reality of what it's like to lose your life as you know it. Sitting in a small cell can provoke profound existential questioning - I'm sure Hilton saw the light, even if just for a moment. There is something mystical about spending time in a cage. Since there is nowhere to go, you pace the perimeter of your cell. Back and forth or around in circles, all the while reliving the crime you committed that brought you there.

When it gets bad, you start reading the Bible and praying to the Lord for forgiveness. From published accounts, that's exactly what Paris did. But the problem Paris faced as an ex-con is one that all ex-cons experience, and one that can lead them down the road to recidivism. When you are released, you want to forget the prison experience. You do your best to block it out. In her case, all those feelings she built up inside her brought on by her longing for her lost freedom when she was in jail.

How do I know? When I completed my twelve-year stint at Sing Sing, the first day I got out I almost completely forgot all the feelings I experienced while I was there. I forgot about how my existence was reduced to daily routines and calculations. I forgot about measuring time in reference to the day at hand and the functions associated with it - the head counts and bells that the prison used to maintain security and order. This was a problem and many of those who feel the harrowing experience of imprisonment readily want to forget about it.

Paris had felt the sting of the government's zero tolerance policy on drug use that incarcerates hundreds of thousands of Americans. But I wondered how long she would remember it. I recall her on the Larry King Show she was asked if she was planning to help others. Paris was humbled by her 23-day stay in jail and told King "That's something I was actually thinking a lot about in jail. I feel like being in the spotlight, I have a platform where I can raise awareness for so many great causes, and just do so much with this, instead of, you know, superficial things like going out. I want to help raise money for kids, breast cancer and multiple sclerosis." Soon after that Hilton was rejected from entering Japan because of her drug conviction forcing her to cancel her tour.

I thought that somehow she would join our movement and become a spokesman for our upcoming battle with the legislature in trying to get additional reforms of the law. But I was dead wrong. I reached out to her and got no response. People told me I was crazy to think I could get a high-profile celebrity to join our movement. Maybe I was, but I knew that someday a celeb who had felt the pain of being imprisoned for putting a substance in their body would help change the system.

No sooner than I wished for someone to fill that role Actress Lindsay Lohan returned to jail in September of 2010 for failing a drug test. This was her third time she had been locked up for violating the terms of her probation stemming from her 2007 conviction for DUI and drug charges. There is no doubt that she has a problematic relationship with alcohol and other drugs - but what she needed was access to an effective drug treatment program, not a "skid bid," to help her with her drug problems. In my experience, I witnessed hundreds of drug addicted people cycle in and out. Like Lohan, many were given "skid bids," slang for a short sentence, usually measured in months instead of years and meant to help them with their drug problems.

But it's well established that incarcerating people who use drugs does far more harm than good. It does nothing to treat addiction, it's much more expensive than real treatment, and it's an affront to human rights and civil liberties. Our drug policies fail to account for the fact that drug use is a health issue and that relapse is an expected part of the recovery process. Lohan was just one of hundreds of thousands of people in the United States who will spend the night locked in a cage for their drug problems. She has admitted that she has a problem. In recent posts on her Twitter account she wrote, "Substance abuse is a disease, which unfortunately doesn't go away overnight," and "I am working hard to overcome it and am taking positive steps." Taking responsibility for one's actions is a powerful step in the right direction.

But unfortunately, our government and the powers that be continue to lock up people with drug addictions instead of giving them treatment. I think that most fail to realize is that relapse is an expected part of recovery. Treatment is valid for fighting the demons of addiction and an effective tool in overcoming the government's use of incarceration and punitive measures in response to low-level, nonviolent drug law offenses stemming from drug addiction.

Maybe it was wrong of me. I was just about to give up hoping for a high-profile celeb with a substance abuse problem to join us. I almost had given up when suddenly out of the blue, that someone appeared.

CHAPTER SIXTEEN

Cameron Douglas

One of the biggest celebrity drug bust stories of all time came about when Cameron Douglas the son of academy award winning actor Michael Douglas got arrested by a multi-task force law enforcement team headed by the Drug Enforcement Agency (DEA). The DEA had existed for more than 40 years but Congress has rarely scrutinized the agency, its actions, or its $2 billion budget. Little attention has been given to its role in fueling mass incarceration, racial disparities, the surveillance state, and other drug war problems. The failure to exercise oversight has led to questionable enforcement practices, numerous scandals and human rights abuses, and open defiance of laws requiring decisions be based on scientific evidence.

The DEA had been watching Cameron for 3 years and had built a watertight case against him for drug dealing, which included large amounts of meth and cocaine through the mail via fedex. This compelled Douglas to seek a plea agreement for his cooperation against his suppliers. What really got my interest in his case was why did the DEA watch him for three years? I figured that they waited a long time in order to build a very solid case against him because he was the son of a rich and famous movie star. The impact of arresting him for selling drugs would be a media goldmine for the government in their ability to send their message of zero tolerance drug policy to the population of America.

After researching the facts of the case I found that Cameron Douglas was not the drug kingpin the DEA painted him to be. Instead I found out that he was just a troubled 32-year-old hooked on drugs since he was 13 years old. It was at this point I decided to defend Cameron and show that he was a prime example of the abuse DEA has been involved in. Douglas was facing a stiff 10-year mandatory sentence under federal guidelines. I thought it was absolutely absurd to lock him up for that much time when it was plain to see he was a drug addict who needed treatment not incarceration.

I began to write a series of articles supporting him on my Huffington Post blog. The first piece was titled "Michael Douglas' Son Should Not Go to Prison." Life imitating art always intrigues me I declared. Michael Douglas who starred in *Traffic*, the Academy-Award-winning film about the drug war in America, now faced a real-life situation like the role he played. In the film Michael Douglas played the United States Drug Czar whose daughter becomes addicted to heroin. Throughout the film, he struggled with his daughter's drug addiction and the futility of the drug war.

In life Cameron Douglas, got arrested by the DEA (Drug Enforcement Agency) in a sting operation for possession of methamphetamines with the intent distribute in New York City. It was not the first brush with the law for Cameron who had several arrests for cocaine possession and a 1996 bust for drunk driving. Reports also pointed out the good possibility that he had a severe drug problem. The role of drugs and drug addiction loom large in our society. The question I pose is should Cameron Douglas be put in prison or should he be able to seek drug treatment instead? Treatment is a valid vehicle for fighting the demons of addiction, and an effective alternative to the government's use of incarceration and punitive measures in response to low-level, nonviolent drug law offenses stemming from addiction.

According to Justice Department statistics, the U.S. holds a firm lead in maintaining the most prisoners of any country in the world -- now at 2.3 million and rising. There are an estimated 500,000 drug offenders in prison. Additionally, hundreds of thousands are incarcerated for drug-related violations of parole and probation, as well as for other crimes related to drug addiction. Criminal justice experts attribute the exploding U.S. prison population to harsh sentencing laws and record numbers of drug law offenders entering the system, many of whom have substance abuse problems.

Again, I asked the question, should we treat drug addiction as a criminal matter or a medical problem? For most people, treatment is much more effective way to overcome addiction, yet our prisons are full of drug-addicted individuals. Nonviolent drug offenders should be given an opportunity to receive treatment, not jail time, for their drug use. This would be a more effective and much more affordable solution for the individual and the community. Addiction affects tens of millions of people around the world. For most, it fills a void in their lives and becomes a crippling crutch. How best to treat addiction is a serious question we need to explore. Rich or poor, young or old, addiction has no boundaries - but the drug war does. Our 30-plus-year war on drugs has stifled the open debate society should be having about addiction and how best to deal with it.

I have always advocated the fact that we should give Cameron Douglas the drug treatment he needs instead of imprisonment. Why do I say this? I too faced a similar situation. Instead of treatment, I received a 15 year to life sentence under the Rockefeller Drug Laws of New York State. I was granted clemency by Governor George Pataki in 1997 after serving 12 years in prison for a first-time non-violent drug sale. It was a waste of valuable tax dollars and human life to send me to prison for all those years. Instead of demonizing addicted individuals and sending them to prison, we need an alternative approach. Let's shift the focus from criminalization in drug policy and support a public health model. Not sending Cameron to prison would be a good example of taking a step in that direction. It's time to treat addiction for what it is, a medical problem, not a criminal one.

Soon after the piece was published, I was conducted by email from a girl who described herself as Cameron Douglas's friend. She told me she had read my article on Cameron and sent it to his mother Diandra, who was divorced from Michael Douglas. At that point I got Cameron's contact information from her and sent a letter to Cameron along with a copy of my book "15 to Life." In my letter, I told Cameron to hang in there and to keep his faith. Several weeks later, I got a response from him.

I knew he was going through hell and was getting deeper into the trap of the prison labyrinth. His downward spin had been a continuous disaster with one bad drama after another. He had been under house arrest and was staying at his mother's upper eastside apartment in Manhattan. Because of his bad drug addiction, he pulled one of the dumbest stunts I ever heard of. Cameron called up his longtime girlfriend Kelly Sott and asked her to bring over his gym bag and continuously emphasized to make sure his blue electric toothbrush was in it. The private security guard that listened in on his conversation became suspicious. When the bag arrived, he immediately searched the blue electric toothbrush and found it contained 20 bags of heroin. His girlfriend was arrested and sentenced to 8 months in jail and Cameron's bail was revoked. He was sent to Metropolitan Correction Center (MCC), a Federal Bureau of Prisons holding facility located at 100 Center Street in Manhattan. The facility was designed to house federal prisoners of all security levels that were to appear before the U.S. District Court for the Southern District of N.Y. Some notable prisoners that stayed there were John Gotti and Bernard Madoff. Cameron was represented by two high-powered teams of lawyers who managed to maintain his cooperation agreement, which shaved five years off of his sentence. One team was led by Nicholas M. Defeis and the other was the law firm of Lankler Siffert & Wohl LLP. His sentencing date was set for April 20th 2010

I was interested in seeing what the judge would say about his case so I went to his sentencing and brought along Tony Newman my friend and colleague. As we stood in line to enter the courtroom a young woman in front of me caught my attention. I recognized her face from my Facebook account. I asked her if we were friends on Facebook. She said that we were and her name was Jen Gatlien. I immediately remembered her.

She was an ex-girlfriend of Cameron and a filmmaker. Jen was the daughter of night club king Peter Gatlien who owned several New York nightclubs. He was once dubbed as the "King of New York Clubs" who owned The Limelight, Palladium, Club USA, and the Tunnel. Jen had told me that her father had been deported to his native country of Canada which was the result of the government's persecution of him, which evolved from a federal investigation into the sales of party drugs like Ecstasy in his clubs. She recently produced a film about her father titled "The Limelight" and another titled "Holy Rollers" which was about a young man from an Orthodox Jewish Community that becomes an Ecstasy dealer. So, she told me she was very aware of the situation with the war on drugs. It had affected her life tremendously.

We entered the packed courtroom and took our seats. In the front row sat Michael Douglas and Cameron's mother Diandra. Both parents looked extremely nervous and who could blame them, their son was about to face the United States of America's zero tolerance drug policy through the voice of a sentencing judge. Alongside of them were attorneys and a bunch of reporters all waiting for Cameron to make his appearance. It seemed as though the packed courtroom was sitting on the edge of their seats waiting for the moment of truth to happen.

Finally, U.S. District Judge Richard Berman entered the courtroom and he began his rant about what he was about to do. I had heard this legal rhetoric before during my criminal trial. He was laying out the facts that would justify the sentence he was about to impose on Cameron.

After about 20 minutes Cameron was escorted into the courtroom and stood at a table before the judge. He looked healthy and fit, dressed in a neat suit. When it was time, Cameron stood at his table and addressed the judge. He was somber as he told Berman that he was sober for the first time in his adult life and was grateful for the chance to get clean. He went on to apologize to his family and loved ones for putting them through what he described as a living nightmare. Cameron told the judge that he wanted to try and become a role model to his younger siblings and told the court that he believed that things would be different in the future because he had the support of his family.

Although Cameron had faced a 10-year sentence, the judge gave him a break for his cooperation against his suppliers and sentenced Cameron to 5 years in prison. At this point, I thought that Cameron would have learned his lesson and settle in to do his time. He had everything going for him, including being sent to pretty comfortable minimum-security camp. But I was wrong. A few months later Cameron was busted with drugs while he was in prison and sentenced to an additional four and a half years. What blew my mind was the way he relapsed. While in MCC, his female lawyer had fallen hard for Cameron and he convinced her to smuggle in 36 Xanax pills in her bra for him

In my Huffington Post syndicated blog, I reported about it in a November 2011 opinion piece: New Charge for Cameron Douglas: Judge Shocked That Drugs Are Available in Prison

I went on to report that when you thought it could not get worse for Cameron Douglas, the son of movie star, Michael Douglas -- it does. It was just reported that Cameron, who is serving a five-year sentence for drug dealing, now has pleaded guilty to drug possession while in prison. He took a plea bargain and will be sentenced to an additional year to 18 months in prison. The judge in his case, U.S. District Judge Richard Berman, was puzzled by the lack of security in the prisons. The Associated Press reported that the judge assumed that prison facilities are safe and well-managed when he sends someone to prison. He was under the assumption "that these types of things don't go on." With all due respect, to the judge, I say that he is clueless. It's a well-known fact that drugs are easily obtainable in prisons. You might wonder how I know this.

I served a 15 to life sentence for a non-violent drug offense under the Rockefeller Drug Laws of New York State. When I went to Sing Sing Correctional Facility in Ossining, NY, I was shocked to find the availability of almost any type of drug you wanted. It was a simple process. If you had the cash, you could get the stash. There was even a prostitution drug ring run by female officers there. In my book *15 to Life* I discuss this in detail in a section titled "Swing Swing."

Some drugs were hidden in packages sent from the outside. Peanut butter, for example, was excellent for smuggling drugs into the prison. The peanut butter would be melted down in a microwave and scooped out to make room for the drugs.

It would then be replaced and the jar would be heat-sealed in the microwave. Some people would actually have the container professionally shrink-wrapped before mailing it to the prison to give it a store-bought look. Prisoners' visitors also brought drugs into the prison. They'd transport them in a body cavity. I once knew a guy who smuggled drugs in his baby's diaper -- extracted them in the visiting room bathroom, and then passed them on to a prison mule, who'd clear security easily. Corrupt guards and civilians who worked in the prison also brought in drugs. Drug dealing was a lucrative way to supplement their low-paying state salaries, and since they weren't subject to intrusive searches like prisoners, they could smuggle in much greater quantities. They didn't have to rely on body cavities to conceal drugs. They'd simply bring them in their handbags or pockets. For the right price, you could virtually get any type of drug you wanted. Word of mouth usually advertised who had what. The price of drugs varied, but the rule of thumb was four times the drug's street value. A ten-dollar bag of heroin on the street would cost forty dollars or the cash equivalent in cigarettes since currency was not allowed in prison. If you didn't have smuggled-in cash or store-bought smokes, you could make payments through "send-outs," essentially street -to-street transactions.

If you got hooked on drugs, you could count on paying with more than currency or cigarettes. Some guys got in so deep they sold their bodies to get a fix. Whether or not you used drugs on the outside, it was easy to get hooked on the inside. It was said that if you didn't have a habit when you came to Sing Sing, you could easily leave with one. Sing Sing was not special and reflects the reality of drugs and use of drugs in prisons. In Breaking the Taboo, a film by Brazilian film maker, Fernando Grostein Andrade, the failure of the war on drugs on a global scale is documented. And one of the main points throughout the film is the availability of drugs in prisons across the world. I was honored by giving the closing line of the film in which I say, "if you can't control drug use in a maximum-security prison, how can you control drug use in a free society".

So, the Honorable Judge Berman, I ask you to please go easy on Cameron Douglas, who has admitted that he is addicted to drugs, when you sentence him for his additional crime. Cameron did what many drug-addicted prisoners do when they are imprisoned. They seek to get high to escape the living hell they are in, even if it means breaking the law.

Cameron's lawyers went into damage control mode and tried their best to prevent the judge from sentencing Cameron to more time. But they went up against a judge that had had it with Cameron's shenanigans. The judge threw the book at Cameron and sentenced him to an additional four and a half years in prison.

Judge Richard Berman, who had to be one of the most clueless justices in the federal system, whacked Cameron with additional time for what is essentially Cameron's very bad drug habit. According to Talk Left, an on-line news site the judge in his legal reasoning said: "I don't believe that I have had another case ever of a defendant who has so recklessly, and flagrantly, and wantonly and criminally acted in as destructive and manipulative a fashion."

I heard what the judge thought but I guess he did not know what drug relapse was about. My immediate response was what good was it to sentence an admitted drug addict to additional time in prison, which is costing the taxpayer a ton of dough to make a point? We know Cameron had a bad drug habit that clouded his mind. It's apparent after all the blundering and idiotic bad moves he has made. I have written about this many times in The Huffington Post. But in reality, it is an additional four and a half years -- two and a half more than the government sought to punish Cameron for his crime of addiction. Was it really worth it? Substance abuse is a disease, which unfortunately doesn't go away overnight. I know that Douglas pissed off the judge but Berman should realize that our drug policies fail to account for the fact that drug use is a health issue and that relapse is an expected part of the recovery process.

In my experience doing a 12-year sentence for a nonviolent drug law violation, I witnessed hundreds of drug addicted people cycle in and out of the prison I was in. It's well established that incarcerating people who use drugs does far more harm than good. It does nothing to treat addiction, it's much more expensive than real treatment, and it's an affront to human rights and civil liberties. Unfortunately, our government continues to lock up people with drug addictions instead of giving them treatment.

I am saddened that Cameron has to learn the hard way about his addiction. I feel sorry for him and his family and pray that he survives his prison experience. Prison is a horrible place and until he accepts responsibility for his actions, Douglas will forever be a prisoner to his drug addiction.

Soon after an amicus brief was filed by the Drug Policy Alliance on behalf of a wide array of New York State's and the nation's leading medical and substance abuse treatment authorities on Thursday, May 3, 2012, a New York federal appeals court challenging what may be the longest-ever federal prison sentence imposed for the simple possession of drugs for personal use behind bars. The unprecedented, nearly five-year prison sentence for simple drug possession was meted out last year to Cameron Douglas, son of actor Michael Douglas.

As reported by Jesse McKinley of *The New York Times*, Cameron Douglas who began abusing drugs at age 13 and who then got deeply hooked on heroin for many years, pled guilty in 2010 to participating in a drug distribution ring. He was sentenced to 60 months' imprisonment for his conduct and remanded to federal prison where, despite his long-time problem with drug addiction, he was not given any drug treatment. He was caught with very small amounts of opioids for personal use, including a single dose of a medication used to treat heroin dependence that he had obtained without a prescription.

Prison officials placed him in solitary confinement for 23 hours a day for 11 months and denied him social visits with family and friends. But the federal district court which imposed Cameron's original 60-month sentence wasn't satisfied with these punishments, and nearly doubled his sentence for his drug relapse by adding an additional 54 months to Cameron's term.

Cameron's attorneys appealed his new (54-month) sentence, noting that it was significantly longer than any sentence imposed in modern legal history for simple drug possession behind bars, and arguing that the judges wrongly departed from the federal Sentencing Guidelines in imposing this excessive prison term. Notably, a wide array of New York State's and the nation's leading medical and substance abuse treatment authorities are supporting Mr. Douglas' cause.

The New York and California Societies of Addiction Medicine -- representing the two most prominent organizations of addiction specialists in the country -- and a host of other medical, public health and human rights organizations, along with prominent individual physicians and substance abuse researchers, filed a friend-of-the-court in support of Cameron's appeal. In their brief, the medical experts contend that Mr. Douglas' drug relapse behind bars is not surprising, particularly given the fact that he, like so many other inmates suffering from addiction in American prisons and jails, are not provided any meaningful drug treatment during their incarceration. The health experts claim that to sentence Mr. Douglas to an additional 54 months for his drug relapse -- particularly in the absence of treatment -- is not only counterproductive to Mr. Douglas' health and goals for recovery, but is, inhumane. They argue that such a sentence is futile both as a means of deterring drug use and obedience with the law, and that Mr. Douglas' medical conditions deserve adequate treatment, not incarceration sanctions.

"Tacking on more prison time for a person who is addicted to drugs because they relapse behind bars goes against fundamental principles of medicine, inflicts unnecessary suffering and undermines both safety and health," notes the brief's author, Daniel Abrahamson, director of legal affairs for the Drug Policy Alliance. "Such a response only fuels the vicious cycle we see daily across the country of drug-dependent persons being imprisoned while sick, coming out sicker, and then returning to jail even quicker -- at huge expense to everyone." The experts note the lack of adequate drug treatment in the nation's prisons and jails, particularly for opioid-dependent persons, and urge corrections officials to remedy this situation as a critical step to breaking the cycle of addiction that affects the great majority of persons incarcerated in the U.S.

On April 15, the Second Circuit Court of Appeals denied Cameron Douglas's appeal that challenged his additional 54-month sentence for possessing drugs while imprisoned. The federal appeals court found that the federal trial court had not abused its discretion in sentencing Mr. Douglas to the increased prison time. The 34-year-old Douglas is now scheduled for release in 2018. Soon after, I invited Cameron's girlfriend Kelly Sott to stop by DPA's midtown office.

It was here that we had a conversation that led to Cameron to write an article about how he felt about what had happened to him. On June

11, 2013, his opinion piece "Words behind Walls" was published in the Huffington Post.

Cameron wrote: Well let me start by saying that I appreciate the opportunity to share some of my thoughts and feelings with you. I hope maybe in some way, this gives you a little window into my reality and more importantly, into my heart. So, here I sit at my little table in the belly of the beast, writing to you. I have spent close to two of my four years of incarceration in solitary confinement. If this seems like a long time, it is magnified in light of the fact that my time spent in the box is largely due to two dirty urines -- one of which was false, which is a story for another time. For the other, I was also given an additional 4.5 years on top of my initial five-year sentence, as if 11 straight months in segregation, locked down 23 hours a day, was not enough.

The bigger picture is much more disturbing, however. There are half a million other people in the U.S. who, like me, will go to sleep behind bars tonight because of nothing more than a drug law violation. Our prisons are filled with non-violent drug offenders who are losing much of what is relevant in life. This outdated system pays little, if any, concern to the disease of addiction, and instead punishes it more harshly than many violent crimes. And even more exasperating is that many of the people responsible for this tragedy disregard documented medical research and the reality of our country's unsustainable prison overpopulation.

Why? I'm sure I'll be terrified by the answer. However, I humbly propose we start seeking the truth. I'm not saying that I didn't deserve to be punished, or that I'm worthy of special treatment. I made mistakes and I'll gladly and openly admit my faults. However, I seem to be trapped in a vicious cycle of relapse and repeat, as most addicts are. Unfortunately, whereas the effective remedy for relapse should be treatment, the penal system's "answer" is to lock the door and throw away the key. Somehow, with the astronomical rate of recidivism, largely due to drug violations, no one seems to comprehend that tossing individuals desperate for skills to cope with addiction behind bars, no matter for how long a period of time, does absolutely nothing but temporarily deter them from succumbing to their weakness. Instead of focusing on how many individuals this county can keep imprisoned, why can we not focus on how many individuals we can keep from coming back?

As for now, I can only hope that the educated, just, and decent men and women who hold positions of influence will find the courage to fight for change because they understand what is inherently right. In doing so, they will start gaining the support necessary to begin breaking these malignant molds that are such a detriment to our society and culture as a whole. I guess that's enough about that from me for now. Thank you for bearing with me, and I apologize if I come across as ranting.

I've had more than my fair share of time to ponder the issue, and only mean to stimulate some thought on the topic. Nevertheless, I feel thoroughly blessed. I have a beautiful and loving family who have faithfully supported me every step of the way, believing in me and refusing to give up in the face of one bleak adversity after the next. However, through these obstacles and carrying with me this love, I have managed to build a strong faith, and I feel in the deepest recesses of my heart that there is a beautiful purpose hidden along this painful journey.

And no matter what my surroundings or conditions, I am determined to find within myself the design for which I was born, and by doing so, fulfill my humble part in this extraordinary existence. Maybe one day, my family, my future children, and whomever I have the privilege of coming to know, will be able to regard me as a man who endeavored to leave this planet just a little better than the way I found it. At the bottom of his op-ed he placed his bio which read:

Cameron Morrell Douglas was born in 1978 into an American dynasty, 3rd generation of the legendary Douglas acting family. Accomplished DJ and budding actor, Douglas starred alongside father, Michael, and grandparents, Kirk and Diana, in the 2003 film 'It Runs In the Family,' and played the lead role in National Lampoon's 'Adam and Eve.' In 2009, Douglas was arrested by the DEA for large-scale narcotics distribution, and received a 5 year sentence. In 2011, Douglas was brought back before the judge, and was given an additional 4.5 years- the longest-ever sentence imposed for obtaining a small amount of drugs in prison for personal use. Although the sentence was challenged due to its extreme harshness, the appeal was lost. Douglas has vowed to bring attention to the mistreatment of non-violent drug offenders and plans to found a non-profit to help the nation's troubled youth. Douglas' expected release date is in 2018.

In September of 2013 I sat in front of my television and watched Michael Douglas receive an Emmy award for Outstanding Lead Actor in his role as Liberace in Behind the Candelabra. He shocked the world and me when he used his Emmy winning speech to grieve over the actions of the U.S. prison system for not allowing him to visit Cameron because of his son's use of drugs while imprisoned. The Bureau of Prisons punished Cameron by not allowing his father Michael or other family members to visit him for two years. When I heard this I could not believe it.

I immediately went into action and created a petition on change.org. It challenged the punishment that prevented Michael from seeing his son, who was thrown into solitary and denied phone calls and visits and many other privileges. My petition asked Attorney General Eric Holder and Warden John Caraway to allow Michael to visit his son. I went on to say that every father should be able to see his imprisoned son. I found it incomprehensible that this was being done when Michael Douglas was also suffering from cancer at the time. Soon the petition started to take off getting tens of thousands of signatures putting pressure on prison officials by getting extensive media coverage.

Radar Online a major on line gossip magazine reported it quoting me saying that "At first, Michael blamed his son for the mess he got into, but now, he is questioning the Bureau of Prisons and asking why he is being prevented from visiting his son for two years. Prison does not end at the prison wall, it severely affects the family members and loved ones of those who are incarcerated. Michael Douglas is being punished for his son's drug addiction." Everything was working until I was told to take down the petition by Michael Douglas attorneys. I did and then the shit hit the fan. Little did I know that Cameron's mother Diandra had written an email to many of her famous and rich friends asking them to sign the petition. These friends included Charlie Rose, Yoko Ono, Calvin Klein and Bo Derek. The N.Y. Post got hold of the message and published an article which quoted her "We have not seen our son for over a year, and the government is telling us we cannot see our son for TWO YEARS!" please sign!

Since the petition was no longer up everyone wondered why it was taken down. I started to receive dozens of calls from journalists like NBC's Kate Snow and emails from major news sources around the country all wanting an answer. I totally freaked out and could not answer anyone because of privacy issues. My good intentions to help Cameron and Michael Douglas almost got me fired when a tremendous amount of negative press followed speculating why the petition was removed. After this I stopped all communications with the press and did not answer the phone for weeks until the bad press stopped. My pain was somewhat relieved when some months later I was very happy to hear that Michael Douglas had been granted a special visit with his son. It seemed that the petition had worked after all.

Sometime later I received an email from Cameron via his ex-girlfriend Kelly Sott telling me *"You tell him I am more than grateful for all of his devoted support... It means more to me than I know how to express over an email, however I very much look forward to the opportunity of doing so in person. He is a man whose strength and voice I admire greatly... As far as I'm concerned he's done nothing but a great help and I am eternally grateful for it"*.

On August 2, 2016 I reported in the Huffington Post that Cameron Douglas was set free after serving 7 years. Well, almost free I said. He obtained an early released to a federal half-way house in Brooklyn. So in reality he had one foot in prison and the other foot out of prison. I contacted him via our Facebook accounts. From what he told me he seemed to be doing well, working and adjusting to life and ready to write about his prison experience and resume his acting career. I wish him luck and hope he does not forget what he said about using his prison experience to fight the war on drugs.

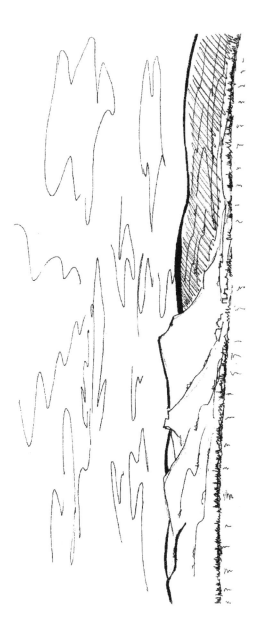

PAPA 92

CHAPTER SEVENTEEN

Preppie Killer Robert Chambers Drug Sale gets him More Time than the Murder he Committed

In 2007 Governor Spitzer created the NYS Commission of Sentencing Reform to make a comprehensive review of New York's sentencing structure, practices, and the use of alternatives to incarceration. The 11-member Commission was chaired by Denise E. O'Donnell, Assistant Secretary to the Governor for Criminal Justice and the Commissioner of the Division of Criminal Justice Services. A series of meetings were to be conducted where the sentencing experts were to provide an in-depth review of New York's sentencing structure and practices.

One of the issues they were to study was the Rockefeller Drug Laws. The panel was to hear from testimony from a wide range of speakers including politicians, activists and treatment providers. Meetings were to be held at three locations which were in NYC, Albany and Buffalo. Gabriel Sayegh our State director for DPA who was running the New York project for reform asked me if I would testify at the hearing.

I thought about it but had mixed feelings going in front of a panel of legislatures and other officials and telling my story. I remember doing this when I first came out of prison going up to Albany to meet politicians face to face and begging them to help change the laws. I remember as clear as a bell going to a meeting with assembly members who listened to a group of us. One by one we gave passionate reasons why the laws should be changed. As I was telling my story Joe Lentol, a Democratic Assemblyman out of Brooklyn, interrupted me. He said, "I hear you, but if I try to change the laws I would look soft on crime and my constituents would not vote for me and I would lose my job. I realized at that point I was wasting my time and decided to try and do something different that would make a difference. It was then I realized that I would need to change public opinion in order for any politician to go out on the limb to support change. I then co-founded the Mothers of the NY Disappeared. We went on to generate a tremendous amount of publicity through creating human interest stories.

I knew I needed to generate some press, our way, in order to positively influence those sitting on the Commission. So I began to search for a hook to use in my messaging, and to my surprise, I looked no further than the front page of the NY Post when I saw the strangest pick for me to use. A photo of the infamous Robert Chambers adorned its cover. Chambers had served 15 years in prison for the notorious murder of Jennifer Levin in 1986. He had met the 18-year-old girl at a local pub and later that night in nearby central park Levin was found dead. Robert claimed that he accidentally strangled Levin during rough sex. While out on bail a video of Chambers appeared on the internet that showed him strangling a toy doll. This angered New Yorkers and Chambers became hated by the general public. Despite his horrific crime, Chambers was allowed to plead guilty to first-degree manslaughter and was sentenced to five to 15 years.

Now, 21 years later, Chambers had been arrested for selling cocaine to undercover officers and was facing life in prison under the Rockefeller Drug Laws. I could not fathom such a thought that he received more time for selling drugs than the brutal murder he committed. When I started traveling around the office and telling people of my thoughts the feedback I got was not great. I often raised eyebrows when I wrote a story because I usually took a path no one else dared to, or wanted to, for that matter. As the case unfolded, it was apparent that Chambers, along with his girlfriend Shawn Kovell, who was also arrested, were both heavily addicted to drugs. They were described as "crack heads" by detectives who searched their disheveled upper east side apartment. Despite significant evidence against him, Chambers has pleaded not guilty to drug charges that could have landed him sentences of 15 to 30 years on each count.

I had no sympathy for him as I recalled the gruesome details of his 1986 case. It ended the life of an 18-year-old girl and caused tremendous grief for her family. But Chambers also had a history of drug addiction. While in prison, he served additional time for smuggling and selling drugs. A year after his release in 2003, he was arrested again while driving with a suspended license and officers found drug residue in his car. He pled guilty and served 100 days on a misdemeanor charge.

I wanted to make it clear that I was not advocating for Chambers despite the fact that he had a severe drug addiction. But I wanted to point out the that the most outrageous fact of this case was that Chambers faced more time now for a drug offense under the Rockefeller Drug Laws, than he did for taking Levin's life. There was something very wrong with this equation. I thought about the thousands of nonviolent Rockefeller offenders serving longer sentences than people who commit rape or murder. Many of them first time nonviolent offenders, who had made mistakes in their lives who were sitting in prison despite two minor reforms made by the legislature in 2004 and 2005.

The first of the hearings was set to be heard in New York City, the second in Buffalo and the third in Albany New York. I wanted to send the commissioners a strong message and I knew that it would be better received by them, if it was through a newspaper opinion piece, where tens of thousands of people would also be reading my thoughts. It would be much stronger than me just testifying in front of them. I started pitching around the story around and finally hit pay dirt when the New York Observer, a somewhat conservative newspaper, agreed to run my op-ed titled "Isn't it Strange". The op-ed appeared a day before the hearing in NYC. Two days later, I got an email from one of the commissioners, Paul Shechtman who was a powerful attorney and the former director of criminal justice for Gov. George Pataki. He had read the piece and told me to keep up the good work.

I knew I needed to keep up the press presence in order to put our issue out in front street, so the commission would have to study it. I renamed the op-ed, make several changes, and submitted it to the Buffalo News, where it was published again. I repeated this, and also got the piece published in the Albany Times Union! The op-ed was published in three regional papers that got the attention of hundreds of thousands of viewers, including the commissioners. But despite my success in publishing my opinion piece, the commission released their preliminary report and failed to address the issue of Rockefeller Drug Law reform. Denise O'Donnell, state commissioner of criminal justice services and chairwoman of the Commission on Sentencing Reform, said the issue would be addressed in the final report that was due in March of 2008.

My response to this was published in several on line news sources including AlterNet, Counterpunch and the Huffington Post. I said that despite what O'Donnell said the evidence was already in. The issue did not need any more studies, and instead, needed the political will and action to change the laws. I told the commission that they must consider the families of those incarcerated, those rotting away in prison, and the precious tax dollars being wasted on its archaic sentencing structure. There were hundreds of nonviolent Rockefeller offenders in prison serving longer sentences than those of convicted murderers for what was essentially a moral crime. Something was fundamentally wrong with a system that advocates serving more time for a nonviolent drug offense, then for a hideous crime, committed by a sociopath like Robert Chambers.

Eventually Chambers agreed to a plea deal that landed him in prison for 19 years. That's four more years than the 15 he served for the brutal 1986 Central Park murder of Jennifer Levin. So outraged was Jennifer's father, Steven Levin, that he publicly denounced the plea deal saying, "he gets 19 years for dealing coke to drug addicts and 15 for strangling my daughter -- that's pretty unjust." In addition, many New Yorkers would agree.

My point was that Chambers was a drug addict. His habit had dated back many years before he entered prison. But instead of his dependence on illegal drugs ending once he entered the prison system, his drug habit actually got worse. You might wonder how someone could possibly catch, or maintain, a drug habit while serving time in the maximum-security prisons where Chambers was housed. I can tell you first-hand, since I served 12 years of a 15-to-life sentence for a nonviolent drug conviction in New York State, at about the same time Chambers was incarcerated. Drugs were, and still are, readily available in prison. I have repeatedly said that If you didn't have a drug habit going into prison, you surely could leave with one because the availability of drugs behind the wall.

My view was that Chambers was a product of an inept NYS correctional system. It's no mistake or anomaly. If incarceration were truly rehabilitative in nature, then it would have some therapeutic value to those who cycle through the system. Instead, much the same way drug prohibition fails to keep drugs off our city streets, it fails to keep drugs out of the jails and prison cells. Seemingly, by design, drug abusers are taken into the New York prison system where they continue to use drugs but fail to receive any kind of quality substance abuse treatment.

Upon his release, Chambers continued the behaviors he knew best. He got high. He got back together with his girlfriend, Shawn Kovel, and they both spiraled down the path of drug addiction. When Chambers and his girlfriend were arrested for selling cocaine to undercover police officers, he faced top felony counts that could have landed him in prison for life. The New York District Attorney Bob Morgenthau vowed that Chambers would spend the rest of his life prison.

Soon after, his girlfriend, Shawn, was allowed to enter rehab on the condition that, if she completed the program, she would not be going to jail at all. The question I asked is why did the New York DA's office decline to offer Chambers the same consideration? They both seemed culpable of the same crime. They both were drug addicts caught selling drugs to other drug addicts.

In an op-ed by the *New York Post*, Randy Credico wrote a stinging opinion piece suggesting that the reason Chambers had been treated, as a kingpin, is that the entire case was a cheap publicity gimmick by the New York City DA's office. Chambers was a small-time dealer who sold drugs to feed his addiction. When the police found out about him through an informant, they sent in an undercover cop to make several small buys from Chambers. After several attempts, they finally convinced Chambers to get them a few ounces of cocaine -- just enough to trigger a felony charge. Since Chambers appeared to be a severe addict, his connection would not trust him with the drugs. The supplier agreed to deliver the goods but on the condition, he waits in another room during the transaction with the undercover cops. The transaction was completed and the supplier got away, he was never arrested. Credico asked a good question, where was he? It seemed that his supplier got away with murder.

The supervising prosecutor, Dan Rather Jr., also was involved in another high-profile drug case a few years back, the case of Julia "pot princess" Diaco, the NYU drug distributor whose widespread operation was way up the ladder from the lowly dime bag dealing that supported Chambers' habit. But Diaco came from a wealthy family, unlike the destitute Chambers. She was sent to rehab, with the charges dropped.

Randy Credico told me that the NYC District Attorney's office left nothing to chance. It had a top prosecution team put in place and they waited for the right moment to get the right judge in the Chambers case. The case was mysteriously sent over to Judge Edward McLaughlin who, according to Credico, is super pro-prosecution. He spent years as an assistant district attorney to Morgenthau. Once they got the case to McLaughlin's courtroom, the District Attorney had moved the ball into the end zone. Chambers joined the thousands of other poor, low-level addicts, mostly black and Latino, serving impossibly long prison terms for minor drug infractions under the Rockefeller Drug Laws.

Credico also raised a good point when he told me "Let's be honest, "Robert Chambers isn't going to prison for his drug offenses. Rather, he's going to prison for the death of Jennifer Levin again." Whatever the reason, the Chambers case put a much-needed spotlight on the Rockefeller Drug Laws and its draconian sentencing.

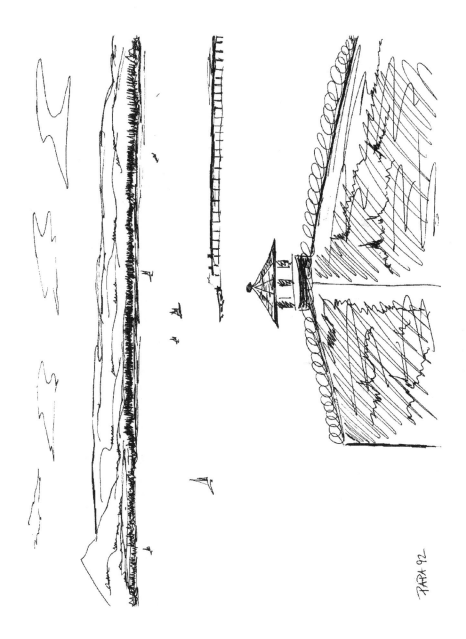

PAPA 92

CHAPTER EIGHTEEN

Governor Paterson Gets Historic Drug Reform

I had known Gov. David Paterson for many years through my work as an activist. When David was a Senator from Harlem whose district was heavily affected by the Rockefeller Drug Laws he had become a staunch opponent of these laws. Paterson worked hand and hand with us to fight for reform and even went to the point of getting arrested with us in 2003 in front of then Governor George Patak's NYC office. He spoke at several events I had, including a book reading at the Hue Man book store in Harlem and my book part at the Whitney Museum of American Art.

We were happy when Gov. Elliot Spitzer appointed him Lt. Governor in 2007. The following year David Peterson assumed the office of governor of NYS when Gov. Elliot Spitzer had to resign in the wake of a prostitution scandal. The tough on crime former attorney general, turned governor, got caught with his pants down and socks on, when Ashley Dupree, the escort he had sex with blew the whistle on him.

On April 24 2009, after years of struggling to achieve meaningful reform I attended an historic bill-signing ceremony that put another nail in the coffin to halt the 36-year reign of injustice promulgated by the Rockefeller Drug Laws of New York State. Time stood still for me as I embraced governor and thanked him on behalf of the tens and thousands of people that were affected by the laws, and all the people that fought so hard for many years to reform them. The ceremony took place in Corona, Queens, at the Elmcor Community Center. Governor David Paterson was joined by legislative and community leaders to pay tribute to long-time Rockefeller reform champion Assemblyman Jeffrion Aubry, who was a drug treatment counselor at Elmcor before he entered the political arena

It was surreal watching Gov. Paterson sign the document that would put into place the meaningful reforms that activists like me had sought for many years. Paterson stood tall behind a podium and spoke: "This is a proud day for me and so many of my colleagues who have fought for so long to overhaul the drug laws and restore judicial discretion in narcotics cases," he said. "For years, thousands of New Yorkers have spoken out against the Rockefeller Drug Laws" When Paterson ended his speech I ran to the podium and embraced the governor. His security private guards quickly surrounded me not knowing if I was a threat or not. But they backed off when they heard me thank him on behalf of the tens and thousands of people that were affected by the laws and all the people that fought so hard for many years to reform them.

The bill enacted broad modifications to the long-failed Rockefeller Drug Laws, including restoring judicial discretion in most drug cases, expanding alternatives to incarceration, and investing millions in treatment. Activists pointed out that after nearly 36 years of ineffective mandatory minimums, mass incarceration, institutional racism and billions in wasted taxpayer dollars, these critical reforms were long overdue and essential for making a better New York. Gov. Paterson has helped to move our state in new direction on drug policy, one based on public health and safety, in fairness and justice.

This shows what is possible when people come together and work for change. While advocates applauded the changes to the law, they also pointed out that reforms should have gone even further. For instance, some mandatory minimum sentences for drug offenses remain intact, and harsh penalties for low-level drug offenses remain on the books.

To see this day arrive was without a doubt, a total vindication for me. Nothing in the world could have prepared me for life in the gulag. It was a living nightmare. Not only did I lose my family, I lost my life, as I knew it. When I arrived at the prison to serve my 15 to life sentence I was surrounded with a sea of faces of men who had lost all faith in their lives. It was the lowest point in my life. The 12 years I spent at Sing Sing taught me well about life. Through my deprivation, I found meaning in my life and it guided me to become an activist, fighting the laws that took my freedom away. Upon my release, I made trips to Albany to speak with legislators. Most of them had a dual view of reforming the laws. Their public view was that the Rockefeller Drug Laws were working fine. Behind closed doors, they agreed the laws needed to be reformed. But they were afraid of publicly speaking out against them because it would cause their political deaths.

My idea then was to try and change the way politicians thought about New York's drug laws by changing their constituents' views. I took that concept and, in 1998, I co-founded Mothers of the New York Disappeared modeled after their Argentinean counterparts. This advocacy group was comprised mostly of family members of those imprisoned by the Rockefeller Drug Laws. We formed a street movement that generated tremendous press by utilizing the human element of the issue. It was a long row to hoe, but we managed to shift public opinion and exert public pressure on the politicians. In 2004-05, the first reform changes were passed.

These new changes in the laws did not come easy because of the NYS legislature's reluctance to change the long-standing political quagmire that was created in 1973 under the leadership of then Governor Nelson Rockefeller. At that time, New York State passed the toughest drug laws in the nation. Their enactment had been considered the answer to solving the so-called drug epidemic. But the reality was far different. The harsh sentencing guidelines with their mandatory minimums did nothing more than fuel the prison industrial complex giving relief for economically depressed rural upstate communities by incarcerating low level non-violent drug offenders.

This led to the building of thirty-eight prisons since 1982, at a cost of over a billion dollars annually, to operate them in Republican senate districts. The Rockefeller Drug laws became embedded in the political climate of these upstate rural districts becoming a cash cow for them

Joining these politicians were prosecutors who became staunch opponents of any Rockefeller reform legislation. They used the Rockefeller Drug Laws as a powerful prosecutorial tool whose use was claimed to shield society from the harms associated with drugs and addiction. But in reality, the only solution these laws offered was based on a massive incarceration scheme that led to incarcerating hundreds of thousands of low-level, non-violent drug offenders to prison instead of treatment. Of these, over 90 percent were black and Latino. The Rockefeller Drug Laws had evolved to become a racist entity that was a complete failure in balancing the scales of justice with the needs of protecting our communities.

But we battled for years with staunch opponents of reforming these laws. Some had stood firm and others had flipped flopped on the issue, when by circumstance, they could use the issue of Rockefeller reform as a platform for their own political agendas. In September of 2009 Judge Leslie Crocker Snyder, decided to run for the position of New York City District Attorney, due to the fact that D.A. Robert Morgenthau was retiring. He had held office for 24 years. Crocker was a "hang em' high" judge who was infamous for handing out stiff drug sentences under the Rockefeller Drug Laws. She wrote a book, 25 to Life that documented her career as a tough prosecutor and judge. But remarkably Snyder now supported Rockefeller Drug Law reform. I almost fell off my chair when I heard this.

I met Snyder years ago when I was asked to be a guest on "Full Nelson," a talk show on Fox hosted by Rob Nelson. When I found out that she was also on the show I contacted Randy Credico, who co-founded the Mothers of the New York Disappeared with me. Our group advocated for those who had fallen through the cracks of the Rockefeller Drug Laws. Many of us were deemed kingpins by individuals like Judge Snyder. But in reality, many of us were not. One individual who Snyder sentenced was Jose Garcia, who at 69 years old died in his prison cell in upstate New York. As a graduate of New York Theological Seminary, I was chosen to perform the eulogy in a special prayer we conducted in front of Governor Pataki's NYC office. Hundreds of people attended along with Jose's elderly wife Hilda. We all prayed that the Rockefeller Drug Laws would be reformed in the name of Jose Garcia.

I made a plan to put Judge Snyder in the hot seat and thought it would be a rare opportunity to confront her for her actions. I contacted the producer and asked him for three guest tickets to the show. I called Randy and asked him to bring two family members of loved ones who were sentenced by Judge Snyder to sit in the audience. Doreen Lamarca's brother, Mike Lamarca, was sentenced to 25 years to life. Evelyn Sanchez's son, Junior Gumbs, was sentenced to a 33 to life term under the Rockefeller Drug Laws.

Snyder and I got into a heated debate on the show. Attempting to quell our differences, Rob Nelson turned to the audience for questions. Randy Credico raised his hand and furiously waved. He was chosen. My plan was working until Credico burst into a heated rant against Snyder, asking her why she had sentenced Doreen and Evelyn's loved ones to such an extraordinary amount of time behind bars. Ms. Sanchez, who was dying of cancer and had spent her life savings to obtain legal representation for her son Jr. Gumbs, began to cry. Snyder turned red and was flabbergasted by the event. After the show she complained to producers that she was set up. Because of this, the show never aired.

A few years later, I did a pilot reality show about prison. One of the guests was Judge Leslie Crocker Snyder. She was rather cocky when she began bragging about how criminals called her "The Princess of Darkness." I remember asking her to explain her position on the Rockefeller Drug Laws. She said she supported 90 percent of them. At that time over 90 percent of those incarcerated were black and Latino. This alarmed me. I thought, "How could she support a law that was obviously racist?" It told me something about her.

But because Snyder was running for office in a place where a majority of New Yorkers supported Rockefeller reform, she sounded nothing like the old "Princess of Darkness." Did I think Snyder really supported drug law reform? No, I did not. She knew that she needed the black and Latino vote. And she knew that public opinion had shifted, as the wastefulness and ineffectiveness of harsh sentences for drug law violations has been brought to light over the past decade. I guess running for a political office has a way of changing a person's thinking. So, because of this I decided to run a campaign against her and wrote about why she should not become NYC's next District Attorney. I even started a Facebook campaign which featured a video by Rockefeller drug law survivor Terrance Stevens who had spent 10 years in prison sentenced under the drug laws. What was poignant about his case was that he had his time in a wheel chair paralyzed with muscular dystrophy, eventually securing clemency by Gov. Pataki.

On Sep. 15, Cy Vance Jr. overwhelmingly beat Leslie Crocker Snyder in the race to be Manhattan's next district attorney. It seemed like Snyder's past had followed her. Snyder, who built her career as a ruthless prosecutor and judge, was beaten so badly that the *Village Voice* quoted her on election night saying that she was retiring from politics and going to China. In my view, Snyder lost because of her over-reliance on a misguided tough-on-crime approach, and because of her inability to balance her decisions with common sense and compassion. In the past Snyder portrayed herself as a John Wayne type of crusader of justice who kicked butt and took no names. Yes, I knew she had stated in the media that she had only aimed the barrels of her gun at the bad apples of society. But the main problem I had, along with a majority of New Yorkers, was she could not tell the difference between apples and oranges.

In her run for Manhattan District Attorney Snyder completely revamped her image and attempted to portray herself as a progressive thinker. She suddenly flipped her position on issues like the Rockefeller Drug Laws and the death penalty. Not long before she ran for DA she was such a strong supporter of the death penalty that she said she would insert the needle herself to deliver the death sentence. She also suddenly claimed to be a leader in the epic struggle to reform the Rockefeller Drug Laws. Her record as a judge told a different story, sentencing low-level offenders to tremendous amounts of time for drug convictions.

The office of District Attorney demanded a competent leader that possessed a balanced view of justice predicated on the concept of being tough on crime, but also being smart on crime. The voters of Manhattan spoke out and elected Cy Vance Jr. as their district attorney. When appointed to office Vance he said he would try new approaches to cut crime and I wished him luck. The message I gave to Vance is that if he adopts a balanced approach to justice that incorporates compassion, he will go a long way. And as for Judge Snyder, I bided her farewell and I wished her ride on a slow boat to China was a good one.

In August of 2010, another staunch opponent of Rockefeller Drug Law reform bit the dust. Senator Dale Volker (R. 59th District) announced his retirement after 35 years. For many years, Volker was one of our toughest opponents. He swore up and down if the Rock laws were ever reformed, the floodgates of hell would open. I challenged him about the influence of the many prisons he had in his district about 13 years ago on CNBC's Charles Grodin Show. Volker became enraged when I told him the reason he supported the Rockefeller Drug Laws was because of the many non-violent prisoners he housed in the half dozen prisons that were part of his district, which in turn fed his community and allowed him to stay in power.

It was suspected that Volker retired because legislation was signed into law by Governor Paterson that would bar legislative districts from counting imprisoned individuals in state prisons as part of their population. Without the many prisoners in his Volker's district, it would be deemed unconstitutional thus in theory eliminating his job.

New York became the second state, following Maryland, to end the practice. For years, New York activists had called for the dismantling of prison-based gerrymandering (PBG) that allowed mostly rural counties to inflate their population numbers. This resulted in financial rewards for those communities that utilized it. Brent Staples of the *NY Times* colorfully described PBG when he once said, "There are many ways to hijack political power. One of them is to draw state or city legislative districts around large prisons -- and pretend that the inmates are legitimate constituents." The new change could dramatically change the state's political dynamics. PBG was an unfair practice that increased the populations of rural upstate districts with prisoners who were mostly from urban areas.

According to Peter Wagner of the Prison Policy Initiative, an organization that pioneered the challenge of PBG, when legislative districts were to be redrawn in 2011, 26,000 prisoners would be counted as part of their home communities in the five boroughs of NYC, instead of the prisons they were housed in. Although the state practiced PBG for many years, nothing could be done because of the powerful politics associated with incarceration -- fueled by the war on drugs. If you connected the dots, you would see that PBG was tied into the prison industrial complex, money raised from the local, state and federal levels.

But the tight grip of the instilled corrupt political process of PBG was broken when a powerful coalition was created headed by Senator Eric T. Schneiderman (now Attorney General of NYS). He became lead sponsor of the bill that challenged PBG and eventually became law. Schneiderman said that "Equal representation under the law benefits everyone. The practice of counting people where they are incarcerated undermines the fundamental principle of 'one person, one vote' -- it's undemocratic and reflects a broken system. This legislation is as simple as it is fair: it requires that legislative districts at every level of government contain an equal numbers of residents." According to research done by the Prison Policy Initiative in 2002 seven New York State Senate districts depend on prison-based gerrymandering to maintain their existence.

This included Senator Volker. Through perseverance and determination, we did not give up the fight to achieve meaningful reform and that year we achieved it. Now, it's time to embrace the changes and set free those who have been imprisoned under harsh and unjust mandatory sentencing, allowing those who are eligible for judicial relief to be reunited with their families and start productive lives as citizens of New York.

PAPA 92

CHAPTER NINETEEN

My Return to Sing Sing Prison

At 7am in the morning I received a call from my sister Angela who lived in Florida. She had received a call from my mother's Bronx neighbor who said Lucy had collapsed and could not get up off the floor. I quickly left my Queens apartment and jumped on a train to travel to my mom's South Bronx apartment. My mind wondered as I stood on the crowded subway car. I thought about my childhood and how my mother struggled to raised me as a single parent.

We were poor and lived in the ghetto of the South Bronx where my mother worked as a meat wrapper in the local supermarket. Lucy had been a good mother to me and now as I thought about it I felt guilty that this had happened to her. If she wasn't alone this would never had happened. She had begged me not to leave to go on my own when I got out of prison. But I had to go in order to get my life back on track. Now, the guilt was getting to me. What a fucked-up son I have been. All of a sudden, many dormant thoughts started to emerge. I started to think that I didn't give her the love she deserved.

I always wanted to buy her a house so she could live in comfort, but I did not come through. My mother had been stuck in the same ghetto neighborhood for the last 40 years living on social security and barely had enough money to pay her $214/month rent-controlled apartment. I helped her as much as I could and gave her money every month to supplement her income. I shook my head in shame as I got out of the train and headed for her apartment. She lived alone in her three-room apartment for years.

When I got to the apartment building, the stench of urine hit my nostrils as I skipped up the stairs passing the littered, full vestibule. I banged on Lucy's door and waited for an answer. A minute or two passed by as I yelled for her. "Mom - Mom, are you all right?", I asked. No answer. I firmly pressed my right ear to the door to listen for a sound. I freaked out when I heard a faint voice calling for help. I put my ear to the door and heard my mother cry, "Help me, help me". I immediately banged on the next door where Toni, one of my mother's closest friends, lived.

Several minutes passed as I heard the tumble of several locks turning in order to open the door. Toni appeared and handed me a key without saying a word. The painful look on her face told it all. At the same time, I inserted the key my mom's caretaker appeared. "I came as fast as I could" Arleen said. She was Lucy's angel taking care of my mom and being there for her when she was in need. We opened the door and I was shocked to see Lucy on the floor, in a semiconscious state.

We both picked up my mom and, as we lifted her to her chair, her eyes rolled back and at the same time a pile of blood splattered down her leg and onto the floor. Panic hit the both of us. Arleen cried out, "Oh my God, call the ambulance". I did and minutes later the NYC fire department arrived. Two medics examined my mother and told us that her blood pressure was dangerously low.

As we traveled to the hospital, the female medic told us we were lucky to have found her in time. She asked me if she had displayed any symptoms of illness recently. A week before I remembered she wasn't feeling well when I went over to her apartment on a Sunday to get a painting of mine from her bedroom closet where I kept my artwork. I thought it was strange she would not even get up from the couch where she was laying. I rubbed my head and thought I should have done something then but I didn't. Now, here she was, close to death and I felt so guilty.

The emergency room of Lincoln Hospital was full of patients. It looked like a war zone. The South Bronx neighborhood was notorious for murders and was a hub for crime. The doctors surrounded my mother as they examined her and asked her questions. After twenty minutes, a doctor approached me and told me that my mother was bleeding internally. She was being transferred to another part of the hospital for additional examinations. I followed them to the sixth floor and a nurse instructed me to sit in the waiting room. My heart beat rapidly as I nervously waited for a doctor to tell me the diagnosis.

A half hour passed and the nurse called me to come to the examination room. A doctor with a heavy Nigerian accent introduced himself. "Your mother has a bleeding ulcer," he said. We need to immediately operate to stop the bleeding. I shook my head in disbelief and asked if she would be all right. "I can't be sure. It depends on a lot of factors", he responded. I inhaled deeply and raised my shoulders, and I slumped in grief. Another nurse came by with bunch of forms to fill out. I signed them and my mom was transferred to another floor where she was operated on.

My sister Angela called me as I waited for the operation to be performed. "Oh My God", she cried as I told her what had happened. Several hours passed when finally, a German doctor approached me. He had performed the surgery. "Your mother is very lucky to be alive, he said. She had a hole in her stomach the size of a silver dollar. "Let's pray for the best", he said. My mother was then transferred to the recovery ward so I waited for several hours until I found out she would recover. I left the hospital exhausted and headed home for some well-needed sleep.

The next day when I returned, I found out she had been transferred to the ICU unit where she was under careful watch. My sister Angela had arrived from Florida with her son Vinnie. I needed my sister to be with my mom because she was better than me to handle sickness. Angela had her experience with it because she suffered from HIV for 25 years. We use to call it "the monster" back at Sing Sing where I saw a huge number of prisoner's wilt away and die from medical complications.

As I walked into ICU ward, I was stopped at the reception desk by the head nurse. "I'm here to see my mother Lucy Pretto," I said. She smiled and had a nurse escort me down the hall to a room where my mom was resting. From a distance, she looked fine. But when I got closer, I saw a tube protruding from her mouth that was hooked up to a machine. It made me sick to look at her in that condition. My mother had always been a strong person. She had a tenacity and stubbornness unmatched by anyone I knew. She would defend me to the death.

When I was imprisoned, she appeared at an art exhibit I had at New York Theological Seminary. A reporter from the NY Times approached her and asked a biased question about me. My good friend and mentor, Fielding Dawson, told me my mother was like a "pit bull" defending her pup. It was a perfect description of how she was. But now, here she was lying helpless as a baby in the hospital bed, hooked up to a machine that made me want to cry.

After two weeks, my mother convinced her doctors she was ready to go home. A nurse on the ward had advised me she should go to a rehabilitative section of the hospital for a few weeks until she was stronger. Lucy refused to stay and one of her doctors told me we could not force her to stay. We arranged for her release. When they rolled in the wheelchair, my mother struggled to stand up. This should have told me she was not ready to return. When the ambulance drivers had to carry her along with her wheelchair up the stairs, I knew she was still very sick. That night was a nightmare and I was helpless to give her the care she needed. She was so weak she could not swallow her medication. I called my sister who had returned to Florida and told her to get on the soonest plane back to New York. When Angela arrived, I called another ambulance and checked my mother into Montefiore hospital where her primary doctor had a practice. Several days later when she was ready to be transferred to a rehabilitation hospital, complications set in and suddenly she could not breathe. A team of doctors examined her and found a lump in her throat. She was diagnosed with an incurable form of thyroid cancer. It spread so fast the doctors could not believe it. Soon after this my mother died.

At her funeral, she lay in her coffin as I held her hand, I remembered back to the day when I was released. I had sworn to her that I would never return to Sing Sing. But over a decade later, I was ready to return to the maximum-security prison. However, this time I was not there to serve time for committing a new crime. Instead, I was there on a tour of the prison with my producer and screenwriter, doing research for a film about my life story.

When the idea of going back to that hellhole was suggested by my producer, I panicked. A chill ran up and down my spine. Terrible memories flooded my mind. I did not want to go back to the gulag that kept me captive for the most productive years of my life. This was the place that almost took away my humanity. After a few days, the initial fear of returning to Sing Sing disappeared. I realized how important it was in order for the screenwriter, Mike Jones, to truthfully capture my story on film. I agreed to go, and arranged the tour through the Commissioner of Corrections. The night before the scheduled tour, I could not sleep. I called a friend who had done time with me at Sing Sing. "Rich" I said, "Do you think Big Don is still there?" Don was the ultimate gangster who ran wild at Sing Sing. Rich told me that Don had been transferred from Sing Sing years ago. I was relieved.

The next day I met Brian and Mike in midtown Manhattan and we drove up to Sing Sing. During the hour plus drive to the prison, I tried to focus on the positive aspects of the tour, and how it would help Mike tell the story. But dark thoughts entered my mind, causing me to invent dramatic scenarios that would put my life in danger. After all, Sing Sing had become a living nightmare to me, and a place where I saw firsthand the strongest of men, become broken by its absolute paternal authority.

We were an hour early for our planned tour and decided to go to the Joseph G. Caputo Community Center where they had life-sized exhibits of Sing Sing. This included authentic cells filled with prison artifacts and even a replica of the electric chair that had electrocuted hundreds of men and women. I knew of the Center from my days in prison, where Flo who ran the hobby shop, exhibited our art there. Once a year they staged a show and artists from Sing Sing participated in it. The art displayed were paintings, ceramics and objects from the wood shop. Also, included were beautiful handmade boats and leather goods, handbags and wallets. Our driver pulled in the driveway of the center and all of a sudden, a group of men surrounded the car. We freaked out not knowing that we had stumbled upon a pick-up area for migrant workers who met there for day labor jobs from residents of the town. Mike explained that we were there to visit the Center, and as he was talking, another car pulled in, inviting a half a dozen men to work for the day.

We exited the car and soon found out the Center was not open. Mike and I stood there while Brian walked to the other side of the building. A few minutes later Brian appeared in the Center and opened the door for us. He told us he had found a side door that was not locked and walked in. Technically, he had broken in the place and we entered illegally. I was paranoid as we walked around and passed a glass display case, which contained dozens of weapons that were confiscated from the prison. They were shanks (knives) of all sizes. One shank reminded me of the six-inch blade that was planted under the mattress of my bed in my cell. I discovered it when I was resting in my bed and felt a lump through the cheap bedding. Someone had hidden it there and I automatically thought that I was being set up. Several busts were made by a rogue crew of guards, who by all accounts, had the same shank planted in other prisoner's cells.

Once busted, facing hard time in solitary confinement, the prisoner was compelled to tell the guards anything they knew about illegal activity in the prison. I quickly took the shank and placed it under my jacket, and when the cell doors were opened for the run for chow, I disposed of the blade in a trash can on the gallery. Looking at the knives at the Center brought back a light-headed feeling that was reminisced of my life back at the prison. Brian on the other hand was having a ball sitting in the cell and making believe he was locked up doing a prison bid. We walked around until it was time to go to the prison for our tour.

When we arrived at the prison, my eyes focused on the guard towers that surround the facility. I painted those huge fearful towers many times as a prisoner along with the thousands of miles of razor wire that encompassed its exterior. As I entered the main gate, my body tensed up. The years of emotional turmoil caused by living at the prison for twelve years appeared once again. I began to feel dizzy and nauseous. I wasn't sure I could go through with it. Brian and Mike looked at me and asked if I was all right. I took some deep breaths and retained my composure.

The entry room of the prison was manned by two correctional officers. The female officer asked us to sign in and she picked up the phone to announce our arrival. She issued us visitor badge and a few minutes later, the tour guide appeared. He was a tall heavyset old timer that had worked at the prison for twenty-six years. I recognized him from my days at the prison. I couldn't believe he was still there. I guess you can say he was doing a life sentence, like the many men who were imprisoned there.

He was very friendly and assured us he would give us a good tour of the prison. The Deputy of Security arrived for a briefing with us. He asked us where, exactly, we wanted to go. It was as though we were given the green light to go anywhere in the prison. The tour was set up with the Commissioner of Corrections, Brian Fisher. I had met him months earlier at an event that was held for the historic signing of the 2009 Rockefeller Drug Laws reforms. Governor Paterson and a host of government officials appeared at a drug rehabilitation center in Queens New York for the event. When I got to the event, I saw Assemblyman Jeff Aubry who was being acknowledged for his work in helping pass the legislation. Jeff had been a drug counselor at the Center for years before getting involved in politics. We embraced each other and smiled. I asked Aubry if he had seen Commissioner Fisher lately. "He's here" he replied. I asked him if he could bring me to him. When I met Fisher he recognized me.

We met when he was the warden of Sing Sing prison years before at an event held by "Rehabilitation through the Arts". This was an organization that taught acting in the gulags of New York State. Brian Fisher was a patron of the arts and was very much into using art as a rehabilitative tool. "You remember me, I said. "Of course you are Picasso", he responded as he chuckled.

I pulled out a copy of an article and handed it to him. It was a piece by Variety titled "Producers Lock up Prison Memoir". It detailed how my book had been optioned and the screenplay was being written by Variety alumni Mike Jones. "I want to go back to Sing Sing", I said to him as I carefully read the piece. He looked at me intensely as I told him my plan. "So, you want to go back to your cell? he asked. Yea, we want Mike, who is writing the screenplay, to really feel the vibe of the prison so he could write the next "Shawshank Redemption". (This was my favorite all time prison movie starring Tim Robbins and Morgan

Freeman.) He laughed as we exchanged small talk. "Ok" he said. Have your people call my people and I will arrange it.

Now, here I was at Sing Sing, a little startled, being able to tell the Deputy of Security where I wanted to go. It was as if I had carte blanche. The Deputy agreed to most everything I asked as he outlined the parameters of our tour. He explained we could not go up into the tiers of the prison housing units because it would be too dangerous. Sing Sing's blocks that housed prisoners were units of cells, stacked upon each other, three tiers high. When you passed through the entrance, you were entering a very dangerous maximum-security prison. When he said this, the three of us looked at each other with a touch of fear. I thought about the daily stabbings by the predators that roamed the prison when I was there.

The old timer knew the gulag inside out and made sure we saw it through his eyes. During the three-hour tour, I saw more of the prison than during my twelve years of imprisonment. The scenes of systematic dehumanization were almost too much to handle. We arrived at A-block, a housing unit that held about seven hundred men. It reminded me of a giant airplane hangar with three floors of cages stacked upon one another. It was known as the biggest cellblock in the United States. It had a notorious history, which included prisoners being tossed over the top railing to fall to their deaths. The block was out of control and resembled the Wild West, when outlaws ruled the land. Prisoners constantly were fighting and generally, it contained an atmosphere of mass confusion throughout its structure.

When I looked into the cells, it brought me back in time. One of the most vivid memories of my stay at Sing Sing was a night where I was on the verge of deep depression. Thoughts of suicide lay fresh in my mind after seeing a prisoner down the tier hang himself ending the agony of his imprisonment. I had tried suicide once back in county jail and now the same suicidal thoughts were invading my mind. When I first experienced this, I went to the prison shrink. He gave me some medication that put me in a stupor and immobilized me. Luckily, a friend told me to stop taking the medication or I would become a victim of the prison. The administration liked to control its prison population through medicating them. Instead of the medication, I found music to be a soothing vehicle to control my depression and to snap me out of my misery. It was past 9 pm, lights were out and it was quiet time.

The rules of the prison forbid lights being on and radios played. It created an eerie silence that added to the mood I was in. I pulled out my FM radio from my stash draw in a secret compartment that was hidden in my desk. The moon light shining in from the oversized windows of the block were my only source of light. Most of them were broken and full of holes created by prisoners throwing objects through them in an attempt to get fresh air to circulate the putrid stench of the housing block. I walked to the front of my cell and stuck my mirror out to see if the night guard was making his rounds. After seeing the coast was clear, I went over to my desk and pried open my secret containment space, which contained my contraband FM radio. The container was a one-inch crawl space that was hollowed in the desk draw. It became a perfect fit for my makeshift FM radio.

If you got caught with a radio, you would go to solitary confinement. This was because the administration said we could make the radios into instruments that could monitor the guard's radio frequency on their two-way radios. The music box contained two parts that was held together with rubber bands and paper clips with a tiny speaker. It had no casing. I bought it for a carton of cigs from an old timer.

The radio had probably been around for many years. It was a ritual to get the radio to work and 50% of the time it didn't work. I could not get any stations because the reception was horrible in the cell. In order to remedy that problem, I used a copper wire unwrapped from a coil that was originally from a magnet from an electronic device that I bought. I snaked the wire across the cell and out over the metal cage that surrounded the tier. In the near dark, I played with the wires and tapped the circuit board in hope I would get it to work. Nothing was easy in prison and every move you made had to be calculated.

A single error could escalate into a major life-threatening catastrophe if you were not careful. I got caught up in trying to fix my radio and almost forgot about the night guard who was making his rounds. He was known as Tom the peeping guard who liked to catch guys in compromising situations like jerking off. He was a pervert. Tom tried to sneak up on me but I heard his keys brush up against the metal cell bars. He shined his flashlight in my face and then onto my bed. By that time, I already covered the radio with a towel.

Tom looked into my eyes and smiled and he went on his business to catch somebody in the act. I continued to play with the radio all the while thinking of the dead guy down the tier that hung himself in his cell. I kept saying to myself maybe that it was the easy way out instead of doing my 15-year sentence. As the thought of suicide grew in my mind and my depression began to rise, I snapped out of it when suddenly sounds from the radio began. It was ironic that the song played was Bobby McFerrin's "Don't Worry, Be Happy." The soothing music took the place of static and in the dark and silent night, I was lifted from the thought of killing myself.

Walking through the prison opened up memories of deep wounds that I realized had never healed. I started hyperventilating and felt weak. The prison with its nightmarish grip had grabbed me once again. Brian saw that something was wrong and asked "Hey Tony" you OK? We could end it now he said. Mike nodded and agreed. I stopped for a moment and leaned against the wall to catch my breath. "I'm OK, we need to see the school building. We walked down the tunnel from A block passed the five-building gate and outside to the long stairway to the school building.

When we got there, I was shocked to see that the prison administration had installed two metal detectors which were walk throughs and telephone booth sized. Apparently, security was heightened because of the recent assaults and violence that had escalated at the prison. Originally, we had arranged to meet Dennis Manwaring there. He was the special subject supervisor at the prison when I was there, and still worked at the prison. Dennis was instrumental in getting me to show my work at the Whitney Museum of American Art. He was a good guy one of the few who treated prisoners with dignity. But by the time we got there, Dennis had left and the school was empty. It was count time. This was when all the prisoners returned to their housing units to be counted and the information went on to the watch commander where he would submit the information to headquarters in Albany, NY.

They did this four times a day, seven days a week in all 63 prisons in the state of New York for security reasons. As we walked the halls, it felt strange to see the classrooms. They had not changed at all. I passed one of the rooms where I attended Bronx Community College. I remembered my teachers and there was one in particular I would never forget His name was Sam Schwartz. Sam was a real character. He was a hip middle age yippee type of guy who wore a ponytail who taught a health course for Bronx community college. In the classroom, he taught like no other type of teacher. The first two classes with Sam were cool. But by the third class, everything had changed for the worst.

When entering the classroom, we noticed that his happy demeanor was gone. In its place was a stern and angry look. He waited for the class of about 35 students to sit in their seats. Everyone was carrying on and having a good time. "OK", he said, "Settle down. Everyone take out a blank sheet of paper and put the rest of your belongings in front of your seats. We are having a test which will be worth one third of your final grade".

The entire class freaked. The atmosphere turned into pure tension. Prisoners started to look nervously at each other. One big black guy named Carl, who was convicted of a double homicide, spoke out and said in a loud mean voice "You didn't tell us last week we were having a test today; this shit isn't fair." Sam stared the convict down and yelled at the guy, "This is my class and I run the show. If you don't like this, you can leave the class now". Sam even pointed at the door showing Carl the way out. Carl's eyes rolled back and he turned purple as he bit his bottom lip.

The killer did not say a word. Sam addressed the class and told them that he wanted a 300-word essay on what the first two classes were about. The room became silent and you could hear a pin drop. "You have 30 minutes," he said. As the student prisoners wrote, the temperature of the room elevated, and you could feel the heat. Sweat poured from some of their foreheads as they quietly wrote their essays. After a few minutes passed, Sam, who was sitting at his desk looked up and suddenly yelled, "OK stop! And put your pens down and pay good attention to what I am going to tell you". The entire class stared Sam down.

Many of them wanted to do him bodily harm. Sam put on the biggest grin I ever saw, raised his arms and told the class "You have now experienced a natural cocaine high." He smiled widely and went on to tell us about alternatives to using drugs through music, meditation and other means. Everyone started to laugh and a slow applause broke out into a big roar. Carl, the murderer, could not believe what had happened and told Sam he was out of his fucking mind.

But the school building was not a place full of constant laughs. It was a dangerous place because if its location. The rule of thumb was that if you lived in one of the several housing units you were confined to that area with limited movement to other parts of the prison. The school was opened to anyone who had signed up for the available educational programs there. Because of this, it was a hub of criminal activity. It was a point of entry to the other popular places where prisoners could congregate and meet like the hobby shop and the law library.

Drug dealing was rampant in the prison, especially in these areas where prisoners could meet one another with little suspicion. Most of the time guards turned their eyes away preferring to pass their time quietly rather than enforcing dangerous rules. This was especially true for the experienced guards. Almost always, they left the policing policies to the new guards who were rookies.

Now here during the tour minus the prisoners, the school building was virtually empty and looked harmless. We traveled to the basement where I taught an art class. To my surprise when we entered the area, the officer on duty was sleeping on his post. When he lifted his head to see who had awoken him I recognized the guard. He was the same guard who had worked at the school when three prisoners had escaped from its second-floor window.

They had managed to bribe a civilian to get a pair of wire cutters they used to cut through the fence that blocked off the prison from the railroad tracks that cut through the heart of the prison. After climbing down a ladder made of hundreds of pairs of shoelace strings, the prisoners ran onto the tracks and escaped. The prison went on a lockdown for three days until they were all captured. It was during this time that I created a body of art that captured the experience of imprisonment.

Brian and Mike looked at me intensely as I told them of the tale of the escape. Jones took notes as I answered their questions. We left the school building soon after and were returning to Gate 18 where the tour had originated. As I passed five building, a voice yelled out "Hey Rambo". This was the nickname some convicts gave me when I was doing time years ago. I got that name when my Uncle Frank had gotten me several posters of Sylvester Stallone when he starred as a war veteran named "Rambo."

I turned towards the voice and saw it was Chino, a guy who I worked with as a clerk in the law library with me 15 years ago. Chino was still in prison doing a 25 year to life sentence for murdering a drug dealer who sold him a fake $10.00 dollar bag of dope. A smile came to my face as I walked towards him to say hello. But in a flash, the tour guard blocked my path and sternly told me "Remember, no talking to prisoners".

I stooped down low and quickly spun around turning my back to the prisoner. I felt like a snake thinking how Chino must have felt by my giving my back to him. I didn't look back as I walked out of the housing area. The prison did not change at all since I had lived there. It was a place that dehumanized individuals and knew how to punish prisoners to the fullest extent of the law both physically and spiritually.

As we walked passed a row of cells I saw several more men I had known when I left the prison twelve years prior. One guy in particular I knew had a bad substance abuse problem that constantly landed him in and out of trouble with the law. He visited me at my job a few years back and told me he was doing good peddling goods as a street vendor in NYC. No doubt, he either had a new charge or was there because of a parole violation. He saw me and raised his hands up high as he shook his head in what seemed to be an acknowledgement that he had fucked up. It was at that point that I thought about how these prisoners kept coming back to prison. I knew through my activism that the rates of recidivism were sky high.

When we left A-block I nodded my head, disgusted at the state of being, and swore to the producer and screenwriter that I would do something to stop the rampart recidivism that existed. When we returned to Post 18 to check out, I handed my identity card I wore doing the tour to a female guard. I must have blanked out and mistakenly heard the guard give me an order to search me.

I stood there planting my feet firmly on the ground as I tensed up staring at her. I went through the motions of a body search placing my hands behind my head. I opened my mouth and lifted my tongue up and down to let her see that I did not have contraband. She raised her eyes and asked me what I was doing. I quickly regained my composure and apologized for my actions. As I walked out of the prison, I knew that despite all my years of freedom, the prison and all of its coping mechanisms that I used for survival had not left.

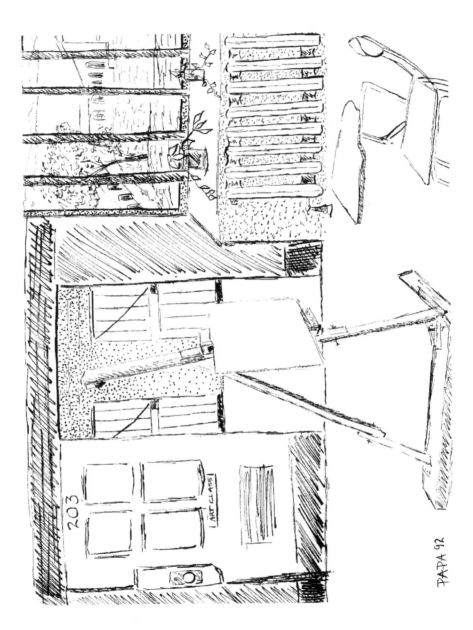

203

ART CLASS

PAPA 92

CHAPTER TWENTY

Judge Jerome Marks, a Hero's Hero

My trip to revisit Sing Sing was a costly one. I began having nightly dreams of being back in prison. A repetitive and frightening dream I had was of a correction officer entering my 6x9 cell and conducting a search. This time I had recognized the face of the guard who began his terrorizing hunt for contraband. It was Officer Vega, the guard who used to be the officer in charge of 7 Building.

He ruled the housing block with an iron fist and inflicted psychological terror upon those prisoners who had the fortune to live in honor block. Vega was famous for his sneak attacks waiting for the least unsuspecting moment to make his rounds so he could find you doing something that was against the institutional rules. He would walk quietly pass the cells and rush into the doorway to catch you out there. Prisoners were scared to death of getting caught because if they were issued a misbehavior report it would lead to getting kicked out of the honor block and being thrown back into the general population.

Life in honor block was like living in heaven compared to living in the hellholes of other housing blocks at Sing Sing. It took years to get into honor block and the trick was to stay clean and have no tickets for misbehavior. I remember I was living in A-block, and was on the waiting list for over two years, when I was called to move. Early in the morning, the guard on patrol banged on my cell door with his stick and yelled "Hey P-685 pack up your shit, you are on the move." My first thought filled me with panic. I hated moving from one cell to another. It was a hassle to pack everything you owned and shove them into your state issued potato sacks. Make it quick the guard muttered, "You're going to honor block." I was relieved to hear this. I had heard that living there was a luxury compared to the mass confusion of A-block. When I got there, the rumors I had heard were true.

Sitting in my assigned cell, I waited in silence for the prisoners to return from programming. From my experience in other housing areas, this was the time that began the roar of prisoners screaming and radios blasting. But when the bell rang signaling prisoners to lock in for the afternoon count the noise and carrying on was not there. Instead it remained quiet.

At times now in the realm of quietness I think about my past and it brings about a rage of what had happened to me. But the rage created a purpose in my life. I had vowed to get the Rockefeller laws reformed and find vindication in seeing them changed. Along the way, I met a lot of heroes that helped me to reform the laws. But once in-a-while, you get to meet a hero's hero. This was Judge Jerome Marks. Jerry was a former New York Supreme Court Justice, and he was a hero's hero. On March 9, 2011, he died at age 95. Judge Marks had a long and distinguished career as a New York elected official and jurist.

He served as state representative for six years beginning in 1963, and later as a Supreme Court Justice until he retired in 1992. In his retirement, Marks devoted his life to change New York's draconian Rockefeller drug laws and helped secure clemency for prisoners rotting away in prison for their roles in minor drug crimes. I met Jerry in 1998 when he spoke about the Rockefeller Drug Laws at Judson Memorial Church in the west village in NYC. We became good friends and were close. So close, the Judge even performed my marriage ceremony to Luciana in his apartment in 2004. Marks became a tireless activist who helped Rock Law offenders receive their freedom. Both as a friend and a mentor, Judge Marks influenced me to follow his path to become a freedom fighter and to fight for justice for the marginalized and disenfranchised. In 1999, New York Times columnist Bob Herbert wrote a beautiful piece titled "Angela's Champion":

One of the cases that caught Justice Marks's attention in The New York Law Journal was that of Angela Thompson, who was arrested in 1988 at age 17 for selling two ounces of cocaine to an undercover cop. She had no previous record and was acting at the direction of her uncle and legal guardian, who was a drug dealer. Nevertheless, under the strict terms of the Rockefeller drug laws, Ms. Thompson was sentenced to 15 years to life in prison. When Judge Marks read about the case he knew it was a case of injustice and immediately began the process of successfully launching a campaign to acquire executive clemency for Angela from former New York Gov. George Pataki

His close friends called him "The Judge." He had a quick wit, even in his late years. He was also a poet and from time to time, especially in front of an audience; use to love to recite his often politically laced poetry. Political comedian, Randy Credico, who recently ran against Sen. Charles Schumer, and I were honored to have dinner with the Judge every Friday night for years. We often discussed the concept of justice over a martini, and he schooled us well. Credico, in remembering The Judge, told me, "Judge Marks used his power to save rather than destroy lives and was the embodiment of the word justice. He was a servant and not the master of concept of justice. Unlike the men and women who wear robes who hypocritically pass judgment of the poor, the disaffected and the hopeless in the current base, corrupt and Kafkaesque world of criminal justice. Judge Marks served God's natural law rather than man's artificial law."

Terrance Stevens' case was another that Judge Marks took on. The Judge helped Stevens, who at the time of his arrest was paralyzed from muscular dystrophy, secure clemency from Gov. Pataki. But being confined to a wheelchair did not stop the State of New York from sentencing him to 15 years to life. The judge in Stevens' case did not want to sentence him under the mandatory provisions of the law but he had no choice. While serving his sentence at Green Haven Correctional Facility in Stormville New York, an article appeared in the NY Times detailing Stevens's plight. Judge Marks wrote him and a friendship developed, leading Marks to champion his cause. Judge Jerry Marks had a great impact, not only on the people he helped but also the hundreds of lives that were saved through the Rockefeller reforms he advocated for.

The Judge knew that my life as a street activist and freedom fighter was not a pretty one. I worked long hours with little or no pay and not much job satisfaction and most of the time you did not see immediate changes in what you may be advocating for. I use to talk to him about this. But Jerry told me something I will never forget. He told me that the greatest satisfaction he got in life was helping those who were subjected to injustice. I took this to heart and realized that Jerry had impacted my life through his advocacy for those less fortunate. I began to follow his path and began to search for people to help. I did not need to search that hard because I knew of many cases of injustice. One in particular was that of Anthony Williams whose mother Queen Nazimova Varick was an original Mother of the New York Disappeared.

In 1992, Anthony Williams, now known as Amir Varick Amma, was sentenced to 25 years to life for a non-violent drug offense under the Rockefeller Drug Laws. Amir was convicted of two felonies, the worst of which was the sale of 2 ounces of cocaine in Albany County. Amir was badly assaulted by the police when he refused to give up his accomplices. His refusal to cooperate guided Judge Keegan to sentence him to twelve and a half years to life on each charge, meaning he had to serve 25 years. Most judges would have incorporated the two charges together, resulting in a twelve-and-a-half-year sentence. But Keegan was a "hang em high" judge, part of a tightly knit crew of upstate judges that dished out extraordinary sentences for drug offenders.

Amir challenged his conviction, but lost every legal challenge he pursued. On the outside, Amir's greatest supporter was his mother Queen Nazimova Varick. Over the years, she fought tooth and nail to get her son out of prison. She joined our group the Mothers of the NY Disappeared, and became an outspoken advocate of reforming the draconian Rockefeller Drug Laws. She did this despite the fact that she was suffering from several ailments, including cancer, but she never gave up hope that her son would return home to her.

In 2004, the NYS legislature passed some incremental Rockefeller reforms that would help individuals like her son Amir who were sentenced to extraordinary amounts of time. Amir filed an application only to be denied. The judge could not even address his motion because he had been busted for smoking marijuana in prison. For this they gave Amir 60 days in solitary confinement and took away his merit time, rendering him ineligible for judicial relief under the new reforms of 2004.

Activists quickly rallied together to seek justice for Amir, but to no avail. Amir then filed for executive clemency, but his application was denied. Amir did not give up hope and in 2009, under the new Rockefeller reforms that were championed by Gov. Paterson, Amir was finally granted his freedom. On March 23, 2010, after 19 years in prison Amir was released. He came by my office and I hugged him. I shared a laugh with him when he showed me a check he had received, issued by the prison from their parole release funds in the amount of eighty-three cents. What the hell he was supposed to do with that check, I asked. When I telephoned Albany County District attorney David Soares and asked him his opinion of Amir's case, he described it as a travesty of justice. That single joint Amir smoked cost him an additional 5 years in prison and taxpayers roughly $250,000.

Was it worth keeping him in prison and punishing him for an additional five years after serving fourteen years for a first-time non-violent crime? It made me think of how many other Amir's were wasting away in our prison system, contributing to the mass incarceration of Americans in the United States.

EPILOGUE

The road following imprisonment is not an easy one. As you have read, I know because I have walked it. When I was released over 18 years ago from the living nightmare of imprisonment, I found that returning to the real world was both frightening and unbelievably difficult. Freedom smacked me in the face swiftly, and it was quite overpowering. As the gate of the prison opened and I walked out a free man, I should have been the happiest person alive but I wasn't. My cautious first steps out of Sing Sing prison were scary. My main concern was the question that every prisoner facing release thinks about, "Will I be able to survive life on the outside?"

I prepared myself the best I could by taking advantage of all the rehabilitative programs that existed at the time. But even though I thought I was well prepared, I struggled when released into the world. Today, it's hard to imagine how those coming home from prison can deal with freedom now that most of the rehabilitative programs are gone, leaving them less prepared than ever to return to society.

Recently HBO's John Oliver exposed the reality of re-entry and pointed out that leaving prison can be just as bad as being in it. He said that America has set up prisoners to fail when re-entering the real world. I hate to say it, but Oliver is correct. Thanks to long-sought sentencing reforms, a growing number of people now under confinement are being released into the community before completing their prison terms. Each year 700,000 prisoners are released, which is four times the number twenty years ago. Sadly, two-thirds of those released will return to prison because of a new crime or parole violation within three years.

Millions of individuals have been sent to prison under the incarceration boom of the 1980's and 90s that was largely the result of draconian drug sentencing laws. The "tough-on-crime" era coincided with massive cuts to prison programs. Formerly incarcerated people reentering society will face a daunting array of problems preventing them from successfully reintegrating. These include not being able to find employment or secure housing, dealing with substance abuse, mental health problems, and difficulties in re-establishing and developing relationships.

On top of this, they also must face counterproductive and debilitating legal and practical barriers, including state and federal laws that hinder their ability to qualify for a job or get a higher education. As a result, communities have been struggling to handle the extraordinary increase in the flow of people from prison cells into society. At the policy level, lawmakers are now forced into questioning the draconian policies of the past and are calling for solutions to ensure that released prisoners can become productive members of society. One of them, Senator Jim Webb, a 2015 presidential candidate and leading proponent of prison reform, has said, "America's criminal justice system has deteriorated to the point that it is a national disgrace. With five percent of the world's population, our country houses twenty-five percent of the world's prison population.

Calling America "a nation of second chances," President Barack Obama has shown his commitment to fixing a broken criminal justice system by granting commutations to 872 individuals that were sentenced to out-dated and unduly harsh sentencing laws as of October of 2016. This included many individuals who were serving life sentences. The commutation of these prison sentences given to non-violent drug offenders represents in what the White House hopes will be just one prong of a broader push by to overhaul the criminal justice system, making it fairer while saving the government money.

To date, the President has granted commutations to more prisoners than the past 11 presidents combined. He committed to continuing to grant additional commutations and pardons throughout the remainder of his presidency. By granting those men and women their freedom, President Obama displayed his administration's attempt to reduce mass incarceration and roll back mandatory minimum sentencing laws. The clemencies granted were the result of recent improvements in the commutation process by the Justice Department which included a fast-tracking program that implemented a stream lining of the application process to prisoners that were eligible under newly set criteria. Obama, sensing the difficulty of the transition from prison to the free world, has sent those granted clemency a pep talk letter which outlined a plan for a successful transition.

In the letter, the president told them they had demonstrated the potential to turn their lives around and it was up to them to make the most of the opportunity. He also pointed out that it would not be easy, and they would encounter many who would doubt people with criminal records could change, but he believed in their ability to prove the doubters wrong.

In writing this letter President Obama might have been trying to give those granted clemencies the much-needed personal support to overcome the legal barriers that exist for those who face freedom that is swift and often paralyzing, which leads in many cases, to the road to recidivism. Post prison life, the other side of freedom, is a life, which in many ways is even more dramatic and at times arguably harder than life behind bars. If being back on the outside weren't so shocking, trying and dramatic, then certainly the majority of those released wouldn't find themselves being back behind bars in three years. This would be from either being rearrested for a new crime or from a minor technical parole violation. As someone who was sentenced to life in prison for a first-time nonviolent drug crime, I know how important second chances are. In 1997, after serving 12 years I was granted executive clemency by New York Governor George Pataki.

Without a doubt, how these prisoners re-enter and adapt to society will have an important role in determining the future granting of clemency by executives that wield the power to do so. I truly hope that those individuals, who were granted their freedom by President Obama, set a good example upon their release and become productive tax paying citizens.

Recidivism among ex-convicts is a major problem plaguing our nation. Due to the economic crisis, there is now a major call for decarceration in the United States. National headlines are reporting that many states are reducing their current prison populations as a way to deal with the economic downturn. Some states are even compelled to do so. Now with bipartisan support many politicians are calling for reforming the U.S. prison system. To do so all we need is to follow the lead of countries that have successfully changed the way they deal with the drug war and the treatment of prisoners.

We could look at the ways Portugal and Norway have solved similar problems. In Portugal, they decriminalized drugs in response to a growing drug and public health crisis. About fifteen years ago, the government of Portugal shifted their entire approach to drug use away from arrest and punishment and towards public health. Instead of being treated strictly as a criminal problem drug use and its policies were treated as a public health issue and addressed by public health officials and doctors. Because of this crime was reduced dramatically.

Out of a population of 5 million people, Norway has a prison population of 4,000. If compared to America's 2.3. million prison population out of its total population of 318 million, we can see it's quite a difference.

Norway's 20 % recidivism rate is one of the lowest in the world compared to the United States, which has one of the highest at almost 70 percent according to the Bureau of Justice Statistics. Most Norway prisoners fail to return to prison because their country relies on a concept called restorative justice, which aims to repair harm caused by crime rather than punish people. Prisoners are treated like human beings and live in a humane environment. Their prisons have no bars on their windows and cells have been replaced with rooms that contain their own showers. In sum, their system focuses on rehabilitating prisoners in a human environment instead of just warehousing in cells and treating them like animals.

The current decarceration of America is beyond anything that we have ever seen. Hundreds of thousands of unprepared prisoners are returning to a society who is unprepared to accept them. It is up to our political leaders to find solutions that will aid with the release of prisoners and create therapeutic solutions to the problems associated with re-entry from the point of views of both released individuals, and the communities that they will be entering. If not, the road to recidivism will continue to fuel the mass incarceration of Americans.

Locking people up for nonviolent drug crimes has become the way of life in the United States. Because of this, our prisons have become tremendously overcrowded and our criminal justice system is broken. To remedy this, former Attorney General Eric Holder initiated a number of proposals to end mass incarceration, including the revamping of harsh sentencing guidelines and the rollback of mandatory minimums. Even President Obama has offered to help fix the broken system by using his pardon powers to help free nonviolent drug war prisoners who have fallen into the cracks of the criminal justice system.

When thinking about ways of helping those prisoners that have been subjected to bad drug laws, I thought the best way to help them is to bring attention to their cases through the media. As a drug war activist, I've seen that to be successful in the avocation of an issue, you have to keep pushing it out to the public so it becomes a repetitive theme, akin to a moving poem or a haunting melody. With this in mind I decided to create a program that would give prisoners the ability to tell their stories to the world. The more stories presented that showed the failure of these laws, the better the chance that positive reforms can occur.

So in January of 2013, the Drug Policy Alliance took out ads in the *Prison Legal News*, a monthly American magazine and online periodical that reaches a vast population of prisoners. The ads asked prisoners to give us information that would be entered in a database for possible use. Soon after, I started to receive hundreds of letters from prisoners poignantly telling their tales of how they have had fallen victim to the drug war. The more stories we can hear of those subjected to draconian sentencing laws, the better chance we have to fix this broken system. You can help contribute to this project, too. If you know of someone who is imprisoned for a drug crime, please contact us at:

Drug War Stories
c/o Drug Policy Alliance
131 West 33rd Street, 15th floor,
NY, NY 10001 or tpapa@drugpolicy.org

Information to include in your correspondence:
- Name of the incarcerated individual
- Current prison he/she is in
- Kind of drug involved
- Length of sentence
- Weapon involved (yes or no)
- Contact information for person on behalf of imprisoned individual (email / phone number)

Their stories, and those of countless others, must be heard.

About Anthony Papa

S ince his release in 1997, Anthony Papa has become an articulate and sought-after advocate on drug law reform and criminal justice issues. At this moment, he is in the middle of the issue of re-entry appearing in national stories about prisoners being released early. National media outlets such as CNN, N.P.R. and journalists writing stories for major magazines and newspapers such as *Time* and *The New York Times* continue to turn to Papa, not only for his informed analysis but also for his personal commentary on issues in the news.

Mr. Papa has a syndicated blog on the *Huffington Post* and his stinging editorial pieces have appeared in news sources across the country, resulting in a strong following for his commentary. Some of the newspapers his writing has appeared in include the *New York Times*, *USA Today*, *Newsday*, *Albany Times Union* (NY), *Buffalo News*, *Amsterdam News*, *The Villager* (NY), *The Post-Standard* (NY), *Springfield News-Leader* (Missouri), *Westside Gazette* (Florida), *The New York Sun*, *Detroit News*, *Daily Challenge* (Brooklyn, NY), *The Tallahassee Democrat* (Florida), *Seattle Post-Intelligencer*, *Jackson Advocate* (Mississippi), *Tennessee Tribune*, *New York Beacon*, and many more. In addition to his work in print journalism, Papa has appeared in or on numerous broadcast outlets including CNN, N.P.R., C-SPAN, Court TV, NY-1, Regional Network News (RNN), Democracy Now, and Air America. Stories about Papa have been written in dozens of regional papers across America such as *The New York Times*,

The Washington Post, Variety, New York Daily News, New York Post, The Village Voice, Albany-Times Union, New York Resident Magazine and *The Nation,* among others. In April 2009, historic reform of the Rockefeller Drug Laws was made and Mr. Papa was in the middle of it all, appearing in different media news sources, most notably the *New York Times.* Mr. Papa has also maintained a significant presence on the web appearing in numerous web magazines such as *Counterpunch, AlterNet, and the Huffington Post.*

Anthony Papa is also a gifted painter and installation artist whose work has been widely exhibited at top venues like the Whitney Museum of American Art, and leading contemporary galleries such as Chem & Read Gallery in New York. His art has been featured as cover pieces for books and periodicals including, *In These Times, Colorlines, Art Times, The Humanist* and *High Times. New York Times* art critic Roberta Smith praised his seminal self-portrait "15 Years to Life" as an "ode to art as a mystical, transgressive act that is frightening and liberating, releasing uncontrollable emotions of all kinds."

Donatella Lorch of *The New York Times* has said his "reality is a canvas of rage and sorrow." *The Amsterdam News* exclaimed, Anthony Papa's self-portrait *'15 Years to Life'* is as unsettling as 'The Scream,' the masterpiece by Edward Munch." The Associated Press noted, "His paintings have brought him distinction both inside and outside prison walls." Recently he showed his art installation "The Drug War" on Governors Island in an exhibit *August of 2015,* which received tremendous media coverage including the NY Times, NY Post, DNA Info, EFE wire service and Getty Images along with Art Net.

Mr. Papa is also a motivational speaker who has delivered his multimedia presentation in a multitude of different venues. He was invited to be the keynote speaker for numerous and diverse audiences, from Harvard University to the John Jay College of Criminal Justice, to churches and schools that work with troubled youth, to the League of Women's Voters, to the Bar Association of the City of New York, and the Lower East Side Girls Club.

Papa has also tried to bring his story to the big screen. In 2004 he sold his life rights and *"15 to Life"* was optioned to become a feature film.

His two producers Brian Swibel, and Barrett Stuart tried and but for various reasons they could not get the job done. Papa's life rights were then reverted back to him. Several very successful directors have been interested in his story like Doug Liman and Derek Cianfrance. Because of his great skill of persistence Papa has no doubt that his story will one day reach the big screen!

Additional Books Anthony Papa has written

15 to Life: How I Painted My Way to Freedom (Feral House 2004)
6 x 9 / 208 Pages / Hardcover / Illustrated / ISBN: 1-932595-06-6

"Anthony Papa has written a riveting account of how he courageously painted his way to freedom from prison after unnecessarily serving twelve years. His story puts a human face on the nearly one million nonviolent drug offenders confined in prisons throughout the country."

— Susan Sarandon, actor/activist

"Papa's story gives me the chills. He's been through so much you won't believe it 'till you read it."

— Jack Black, Actor

"A powerful memoir of one man's struggle for freedom, *15 to Life* tells in vivid prose the story of Anthony Papa, a painter and a casualty of the War on Drugs. This journey of a soul shows the power of art to transcend the violence of prison, and all that is possible when the human spirit refuses to be contained. Papa's account should be required reading for New York lawmakers and all Americans who care about civil liberties."

— Sister Helen Prejean (Dead Man Walking)

"Anthony Papa's *15 to Life* tells of a heroic escape from a brutal system by a man who refused to give up. A thrilling, unforgettable read!"

— Tim Robbins, Actor

"Anthony Papa's *15 To Life* is a must-read for the hip-hop community. Over 94% of the 18,000 people locked up under New York's Drug Laws, the harshest drug laws in the country, are black or Hispanic. Like Papa, I am trying to end these racist laws. We need your voice. You can start by reading this book"

— Russell Simmons, Chairman Of Hip-Hop Summit Action Network

"Papa is a true American hero whose ingenuity and never say die attiude conquered frightful adversity "

— Jason Flom, President Atlantic/Lava Records

"Anthony Papa's 15 TO LIFE is a gripping account of justice gone wrong and an inspiring story of personal triumph. It is a scathing indictment of the antiquated Rockefeller drug laws that have imprisoned thousands of nonviolent offenders and wasted billions of dollars of taxpayer money."

— Andrew Cuomo, Former US HUD Secretary

"The Rockefeller Drug Laws must change and Papa's "15 To Life" is a good reason why!"

— Frank Serpico, Legionary Former NYC Police Officer

"15 To Life" is an unbelievable story about one man's journey through a living hell and how he survived and now is fighting to change the most racist drug laws in America. Read this book - learn something!

— Al "Grandpa Munster" Lewis, Actor/Activist

Made in the USA
Charleston, SC
05 December 2016